CAROLINA BASKETBALL

Carolina

·····A CENTURY OF EXCELLENCE·····

Basketball

Adam Lucas

With the assistance of

Matt Bowers, Lauren Brownlow, Jeffrey Camarati, *and* Steve Kirschner

Foreword by Dean Smith *and afterword by* Roy Williams

UNIVERSITY OF NORTH CAROLINA PRESS   CHAPEL HILL

PUBLISHED IN ASSOCIATION WITH THE UNC–CHAPEL HILL DEPARTMENT OF ATHLETICS

All rights reserved. Designed and set by Kimberly Bryant in Merlo, DIN, and Myriad types. Manufactured in the United States of America. The paper in this book meets the guidelines for permanence and durability of the Committee on Production Guidelines for Book Longevity of the Council on Library Resources. The University of North Carolina Press has been a member of the Green Press Initiative since 2003.

Library of Congress Cataloging-in-Publication Data
Lucas, Adam, 1977–
Carolina basketball : a century of excellence / Adam Lucas ; with the assistance of Matt Bowers . . . [et. al.] ; foreword by Dean Smith and afterword by Roy Williams.
   p. cm.
ISBN 978-0-8078-3410-7 (cloth : alk. paper)
1. University of North Carolina at Chapel Hill—Basketball—History. 2. North Carolina Tar Heels (Basketball team)—History. 3. Basketball—North Carolina—Chapel Hill—History. I. Bowers, Matt. II. Title.
GV885.43.U54L825 2010
796.323´6309756565—dc22   2010018369

cloth   14 13 12 11 10   5 4 3 2 1

For Stephanie,

McKay, and Asher,

who taught me that

a game of basketball

in our driveway can

be even more fun

than a game in front

of 70,000 fans.

CONTENTS

FOREWORD

I've always believed that college basketball is about the players, so to me, 100 years of Carolina Basketball should celebrate the young men who have worked so hard to represent the University of North Carolina. Without them, we wouldn't need coaches like me. When I look back at the history of Carolina Basketball, I think first about the players.

The way I think about them might surprise you. Our players have given me so many memorable experiences. It's those interactions on and off the court—even more than the wins or the championships—which I have treasured.

Yes, it was exciting to win the 1982 national championship. But winning that one game against Georgetown didn't make me a better coach or a better person. What did enrich my life was watching Jimmy Black display all the attributes of a true captain, a freshman named Michael Jordan come of age, Matt Doherty compete on every possession, and the stellar play of James Worthy and Sam Perkins. Being six points better than Michigan in 1993 shouldn't say anything remarkable about me. But how could I not have enjoyed watching George Lynch's extraordinary play and leadership, Derrick Phelps's tenacity, Donald Williams's making shot after shot, and Eric Montross's inside dominance? I mention these players not to single them out from all of the other great players and memories, but to emphasize that to me, those experiences would have had the same tremendous value whether we had won or lost our final game.

The essence of basketball is a team concept, the blending of many personalities and talents through shared experiences. That's what attracts all of us who spend

our lives with this beautiful game. We want to be part of a cohesive team, we like watching it progress throughout a season, and, of course, we like to compete together. If you take one single player, assistant coach, office staff member, or other team personnel away from any of my 36 years as the head coach at North Carolina, my experience would be changed for the worse. When I wrote my first book, *A Coach's Life*, I wanted to call it *Just Call Me Lucky!* I still think that would have been an appropriate title, because it was my good fortune to have been involved with so many quality individuals.

It surprised me sometimes to realize the important role that Carolina Basketball played in the lives of our fans. On a regular basis, I reminded our players that no matter how they might be treated on campus, and no matter how many people watched on television, there were always billions of people elsewhere in the world who had no idea we were playing or cared about the outcome of our basketball game.

But thousands of you did care, and still do. Now, I'm one of you. I watch on television, cheering for every player, yet fretting over every possession. Being a fan is in some aspects more challenging than being on the sidelines. I believe it would have been tougher to spend 36 years as a fan than 36 years as the head coach.

One thing we have in common, though: we experienced the same thrills from a wonderfully gifted group of players. In the following pages, I hope you enjoy looking back and remembering all that they were able to accomplish—both on and, more important, off the court. Please remember to thank them for the memories!

—DEAN SMITH

IMAGES OF 100 YEARS

Photo courtesy of UNC Athletic Communications

(opposite) *Photo by Sally Sather*

Photo by Hugh Morton
(Courtesy North Carolina Collection,
UNC–Chapel Hill)

Photo by Sally Sather

(opposite)
Photo by Hugh Morton (Courtesy North Carolina Collection, UNC–Chapel Hill)

Photo courtesy of UNC Athletic Communications

*Photo by Allen Dean Steele/*Daily Tar Heel *1982*

Photo by Bob Donnan

Photo by Jim Bounds

(opposite)

Photo by Bob Donnan

Photo by Hugh Morton (Courtesy North Carolina
Collection, UNC–Chapel Hill)

(opposite)
Photo courtesy of UNC Athletic Communications

Photo by *Jeffrey A. Camarati*

Photos by Jeffrey A. Camarati

Photo by Jeffrey A. Camarati

1 : A NEW GAME
ARRIVES ON CAMPUS

Amid advertisements for the Ithaca Gun Company and $1.50 year-long subscriptions ("payable in advance or during first term"), agitation for change could be found on the pages of the University of North Carolina student newspaper, the *Tar Heel*, in the fall of 1910. "Why not some basketball?" the editors asked. "Out of 700 healthy young Americans, we ought to be able to get a bunch of fairly respectable players[;] anyway it would help relieve some of that January and February monotony."

It was less than 20 years after Dr. James Naismith had developed the basic rules of basketball and nailed peach baskets to the side of a 10-foot elevated track in the gymnasium of the YMCA Training School in Springfield, Massachusetts. Naismith was simply looking for a way to entertain his students during the frigid New England winters; his diaries reveal that basketball's creator was concerned about the game's viability.

"I busied myself arranging the apparatus all the time watching the boys as they arrived to observe their attitude that day," Naismith wrote. "I felt like this was a crucial moment in my life as it meant success or failure of my attempt to hold the interest of the class and devise a new game." One of the first students to arrive was a southerner, Frank Mahan. Mahan looked up at the baskets and reviewed the rules. Naismith recorded the first player's response as follows: "Huh. Another new game."

Despite Mahan's lukewarm reaction, basketball caught on. Since most of the early players were accustomed to football, Naismith initially spent a considerable amount of time reminding his pupils that it was illegal to tackle the player with the ball. The backboard was created because students enjoyed standing on the track behind the basket and knocking away good shots taken by the opposing team. Today, the backboard is used by shooters as an offensive advantage, but it was created as a defensive measure against overzealous fans.

A team size of five players per side had become standard by 1898. In 1906 one of Naismith's less-patient cohorts had the idea of cutting the bottom out of the peach baskets to eliminate the need to climb a ladder to retrieve the ball after every successful field goal. The YMCA helped spread the game's popularity in the early years, and colleges soon adopted the new sport. The first intercollegiate five-on-five game was played on February 9, 1895, as the University of Minnesota's School of Agriculture defeated Hamline in a high-scoring 9–3 shootout. By 1901 prominent colleges like the University of Chicago, Columbia, Dartmouth, Yale, and the Naval Academy were sponsoring men's basketball teams.

Carolina's border rival, the University of Tennessee, had fielded a basketball team during the 1908–09 school year and issued a challenge during the fall of 1910 for a game against UNC. Basketball programs were also beginning at in-state rivals Trinity (eventually Duke), Davidson, Wake Forest, and North Carolina A&M (eventually NC State).

In Chapel Hill, however, the school supported two primary varsity sports: football in the fall and baseball in the spring. Football was by far the preferred sport, but head coach A. E. Brides's squad was coming off a disappointing 3–6 record that included a 7–0 loss to Virginia, the team's fiercest rival. Southern Railway had offered a $3 round-trip special for the 7.5-hour one-way trip to Richmond for that game; hundreds of fans signed up. The mere departure of the football team for their season finale was cause for a page-one banner headline in the *Tar Heel*.

But the final play from scrimmage marked the beginning of a barren time on the Carolina sports calendar, and many believed that basketball could fill the void. The game had been an intramural activity since 1900 and seemed ready to be elevated to varsity status. "With the football season a thing of the past, and with baseball several months in the distance, what better time could be found for arousing interest in basketball and for placing the game permanently among our sports?" the *Tar Heel* asked on November 30, 1910. "It has such a place in nearly all institutions like ours. Judging from the college papers, it is a popular game wherever instituted. Many times has basketball been discussed as a game we ought to have; more than once attempts have been made to establish it; resolutions have been written setting forth the desirability of the game; but, so far, the basketball team has not become a reality." There was a note of envy in their plea. Ivy League colleges were closely watched and often emulated. If Yale and Dartmouth students were playing basketball, then shouldn't Carolina students play it too?

In order to establish the game as a varsity sport, the school needed two key components: players and a head coach. Players, it seemed, wouldn't be a problem. This wasn't the scholarship era. Filling a team would be a matter of placing an ad in the campus paper and waiting for prospective applicants to arrive. Very few, if any, would have legitimate basketball training, which meant that the role of the head coach would be even more important. He wouldn't simply be guiding his team; he would also be explaining the game to most of his players.

Nat Cartmell was a renowned sprinter who'd won a pair of silver medals in the 1904 Summer Olympics and gold and bronze medals in the 1908 edition of the Games. He was brought to Chapel Hill in 1909 to coach the track team but somehow earned the title of men's basketball coach the next year; there were no funds to hire a full-time basketball coach, so Cartmell's admitted lack of knowledge about the game was an insignificant issue.

By early December, equipment had been ordered and tryouts were scheduled. Popular undergraduate Marvin Ritch was the student ringleader, and he rallied a respectable crowd of interested students for the team's first practice, held from 7:00 to 9:00 P.M. in Bynum Gym. After months of pushing for a basketball team, the *Tar Heel* was dubious when its writers got their first glimpse of the new product.

About twenty-five men showed up the first night and went through the preliminary practice of passing the ball and taking shots at the baskets. This has been about all they have done so far. The goal shooting, however, has not been very good, owing to the slick floor, the bad lights and the extreme liveness of the backboards. These backboards are a great deal liver than any the men have been accustomed to; in fact they are so live that it takes a perfect shot to make a basket. But this is probably a good thing, since it will make the men throw much more accurately than would otherwise be the case.

The team had a heavy Charlotte influence, as a group of former high school teammates were eager to make the transition to college basketball. A partial list of surnames of students who tried out during the first week includes: Smith, Duls, Hanes, Gordon, Floyd, Applewhite, McKnight, White, Long, Ritch, Voils, Tillett, Carrington, Halliburton, Huske, Robertson, Horton, Ranson, Holmes, Parrish, Jones, Jeffries, Patterson, Flume, Stewart, Solomon, Leigh, and Blacock. The monogram winners from the university's first basketball team would be George Carrington, Ferdinand Duls, John Floyd, Henry Long, Roy McKnight, Marvin Ritch, Junius Smith, William Tillett, and William Wakeley.

While Cartmell was trying to assemble a team from the interested students, he also had to put together a schedule. Most potential foes had already set their 1910–11 slates, but there were enough local opponents to form an abbreviated eleven-game schedule. Seven of the eleven games were at home, one of the road games was at Wake Forest, and three other road games were played in Virginia. "The Virginia game is the big noise of the schedule as far as the Hill is concerned. As usual we are ready to do anything that is fair and square to beat the Old Dominion representative," the *Tar Heel* noted.

The program held its first intercollegiate contest on January 27, 1911, with Virginia Christian as the visiting opponent. Attendance was recorded as an encouraging 200 fans, although some were surely there out of sheer curiosity. Practice had gone well—other than a brief hiatus when an unknown thief stole the team's basketball, requiring the squad to place a classified ad in the *Tar Heel* asking for the ball's expedient return. By the time Virginia Chris-

Carolina won its first game, beating Virginia Christian on January 27, 1911. (Photo courtesy of UNC Athletic Communications)

tian arrived, the ball had been returned. Carolina's youthful starting lineup consisted of three freshmen and two sophomores. Ritch, the squad's captain, gave a pregame speech that was a harbinger of the Carolina Way: "He told the boys that if one forward threw 10 goals and the other only two then that would be six goals apiece—and the same with regard to the other positions. 'So play for the team and forget yourself.'"

The halftime speech was less eloquent, as Cartmell reportedly "cussed good and artistically" after an uninspired first-half effort produced a narrow 13–11 halftime lead. It must have worked, as Carolina posted a high-octane 29 points in the final 20 minutes of play on the way to a 42–21 victory. The win shared space on page one of the next edition of the *Tar Heel* with a story noting that "the best football coach in the South," Branch Bocock, had been hired from Virginia Tech to serve as Carolina's new coach. (Bocock stayed exactly one season, posting a 6–1–1 mark before returning to Virginia Tech.)

The paper was not particularly impressed with the basketball results: "The visitors put up a good game and fought with more spirit than did our team. Their handling of the ball and passing were much better than ours. In fact, they had us beat to a frazzle in passing, but Carolina's weight and reach told in the final score. After the game the visitors spoke well of our bunch, saying that the Carolina quintet was a remarkably strong one to have had only three weeks of practice together, and that it ought to develop into a good team before the end of the season."

After five straight home wins, the program's first defeat came in its first road game, a 38–16 loss at Wake Forest. The next game was the much-awaited challenge match in Chapel Hill with Tennessee, a team in contention for the Southern Intercollegiate Athletic Association championship. Players from both teams noted the challenge of playing on a slick playing surface caused by a dance held in the gym a few days earlier, but Carolina players stayed upright long enough to claim a 40–21 win.

Cartmell's job description included much more than just giving colorful halftime speeches. He occasionally had to serve as a referee, and in a March 1 loss to Virginia, he refereed both the basketball game and a halftime boxing exhibition that featured two members of a university boxing class going at each other for three rounds. His fame in track and field also kept him busy, as amateur sprinter and longtime rival Lawson Robertson challenged him to a race. In 1905 Cartmell had defeated Robertson in the 100 meters; Robertson won a rematch in Philadelphia in the 1908 Olympic trials, but Cartmell won the decisive race in the 1908 Olympic semifinals. Now, Robertson wanted yet another rematch, this time offering to race for a prize of 200 British pounds or $1,000.

"If Robertson is anxious to run me I will sign articles with him for a race of any distance from 150 to 500 yards, for as much money as he cares to get together. The race can be run on any fair cinder track," said Cartmell. The race never happened, but it might have made for an engaging halftime show.

The success of the basketball team meant that creative halftime entertainment wasn't a necessity. A hefty 50-cent admission was charged for the home game against Virginia. The rowdy crowd saw an 18–15 Carolina defeat, but the game illustrated one of the problems of the early era of basketball: the teams often played by different rules. Virginia used intercollegiate rules, which permitted dribbling. Until that point in the season, Carolina had played by YMCA rules, which did not allow dribbling. Carolina players resorted to tackling to stop the unfamiliar dribbling tactics, and the game officials—Cartmell and the Virginia head coach each took on refereeing responsibilities for a half—were kept busy mediating a handful of scuffles, including an incident when Ritch bit the Virginia center's shoulder. "Time and time again Virginia would race down the floor dribbling, and in shooting distance of the goal a Carolina player would go after him almost in the manner of a football tackle and stop him with the score missed by a grazed basket," the *Tar Heel* reported.

The positions were the same—each team had a center, two forwards, and two guards—but games during that first season were not high scoring. Carolina exceeded 42 points just once—a 60-point explosion against the Durham YMCA. The 7–4 record would ultimately prove to be Cartmell's best in four seasons as a head coach, a referee, and a sprinter emeritus. Despite the strong Charlotte core, much of the inaugural team scattered shortly after the season-ending 33–31 defeat at Virginia Christian. Even the captain, Ritch, transferred to Georgetown. With just seven players on the roster, the 1912 team struggled to a 4–5 finish. Despite this disappointing record, the program's second season contained an early highlight, as over 2,000 people attended the game against Virginia Tech—then known as Virginia A&M—on February 16, 1912. "The A&M contest proved conclusively that basketball has come into its own in this state," declared the *Alumni Review*. Indeed, by 1913 the varsity schedule included eight games against in-state competition, including the first-ever game against NC State (a 26–18 road defeat).

Cartmell retired as a sprinter in 1912 to devote his full attention to his faculty and coaching duties at Carolina. The coach posted a winning record in his fourth season, but he was soon forced out after a gambling probe. Because of Cartmell's great popularity, his departure almost halted the program. Under new coach Charles Doak, the former baseball coach, just six players tried out for the 1915 team. They struggled to a 6–10 record, including dropping five of six at the end of the season. But they very nearly achieved something arguably more

impressive than an undefeated season: the program almost broke even for the first time. The final ledger showed that the basketball program lost just $62.38. Losses for the players might have been more substantial, however, since they were required to buy their own shoes and launder their own uniforms.

Although it was probably tempting to skimp on the laundry fees, players often benefited from looking sharp on the court. To bolster attendance, dances were sometimes held immediately after basketball games. At Wake Forest in 1916, females attended the game in full evening attire. Each lady stood on a balcony and threw a red carnation with her name attached; the recipient was her partner for that evening. Even the visiting Carolina players were included in the dance, which followed a 27–22 Wake win.

With the position tied to faculty status, the basketball head-coaching job was a revolving door in the program's first decade. Doak was replaced after just two seasons by Howell Peacock, a former Georgia star and future doctor. Peacock oversaw the program through World War I. The war crippled intercollegiate athletics across the nation, and Chapel Hill was certainly not spared. Almost every member of the football team saw action overseas, and the basketball team was similarly depleted. There was a brief moratorium on teams traveling outside the town in which their college was located, and the Carolina program played a limited schedule of nine games in 1917 and twelve games in 1918.

War veteran Fred Boye assumed the head-coaching position for the 1919–20 season. It was the perfect time for the explosion of the basketball program, as the postwar period saw an American public hungry for the distraction of sports. The Intercollegiate Athletic Association had been formed in 1905; it would eventually become the National Collegiate Athletic Association (NCAA), which promoted athletics as a legitimate enterprise of an institution of higher learning. Meanwhile, men returning from the war had spent much of their down time playing baseball, football, and even basketball. They wanted to enjoy the same sports back home. Even the usually stodgy *New York Times* noticed the explosion of sports in the United States: "The nation released from years of gloom and suppression is expressing the reaction by plunging into sport." Physical education in the nation's schools was turning from the standard gymnastics of the 1890s and early 1900s to a greater emphasis on sports and games.

In Chapel Hill, that reaction took the form of boisterous crowds for basketball. Football was still king, of course, with every game doubling as a joint sporting event–social occasion and attended by the vast majority of students. But basketball was gaining in both popularity and fan fervor. For a 1921 game against Virginia, the gym was packed by 6:45 for an 8:00 P.M. tip-off. Late-arriving students watched while hanging from punching bags or from gallery supports. The "January and February monotony" lamented by the student paper in 1910 had officially been conquered.

(opposite)
Bynum Gym, UNC's first basketball home, was named for William P. Bynum, grandson of N.C. Supreme Court judge William P. Bynum. (Photo courtesy of the Yackey Yack)

2 : WHITE PHANTOMS HAUNT THE SOUTHERN CONFERENCE

A s basketball emerged as a popular addition to the college-athletics landscape, Carolina was undergoing a series of changes in conference affiliation. The first conference was founded in 1894 by Vanderbilt professor William Dudley, who sought to standardize player eligibility rules and host an annual track meet and basketball tournament. Somewhat surprisingly, considering the power wielded by football, there were no plans to name an official football champion. The league Dudley created, the Southern Intercollegiate Athletic Association (SIAA), began with seven charter members, including North Carolina. Six more schools joined the following year, almost immediately making the league unsettlingly large. The SIAA also showed very little discretion in admitting new members, which resulted in powerhouses like Carolina, Alabama, and Tennessee sharing a league with Gordon Military Academy and Dahlonega (now North Georgia).

One of the biggest debates of the era concerned the eligibility of freshman athletes. In general, larger schools opposed making freshmen eligible, while smaller schools favored it. The reasoning was much the same as it is today: big schools didn't want their newest stars transferring to smaller schools to get immediate playing time, while smaller schools thought offering their freshmen playing time was the only way to field competitive teams. Freshman ineligibility was known as the one-year rule, and it caused nearly constant bickering between schools. Carolina and NC State eventually went so far as to suspend formal athletic relations with each other over State's reluctance to adhere to the one-year rule. State, along with some other schools, preferred a five-month rule that only required a freshman to be enrolled for five months before he was eligible to play.

In 1915 some of the larger members of the SIAA—including Carolina—formed the similarly (and somewhat confusingly) named Southern Intercollegiate Conference and declared that all members would abide by the one-year rule. However, despite the new conference, the schools did not withdraw from the SIAA or conduct any formal events. The SIAA continued to hold annual votes on the one-year rule, but members never reached a consensus. In December 1920 the Southern Conference was expanded to 14 members, and plans were made for the first year of legitimate operations during the 1921–22 season. Carolina again was a charter member, joined by Alabama, Auburn, Clemson, Georgia Tech, Georgia, Kentucky, Mississippi State, Tennessee, Maryland, NC State, Virginia, Virginia Tech and Washington & Lee. All the charter members also retained their membership in the SIAA.

Before the first year of the Southern Conference's official operation was even halfway over, the league again announced expansion intentions, this time with a target membership of 16 schools. But narrowing the field of expansion candidates to two schools proved to be difficult, and the league instead added six, picking up Florida, Louisiana State, Mississippi, South Carolina, Tulane, and Vanderbilt. After the 1922 season, SIAA resignations began en masse, and only Vanderbilt retained dual membership. With many of the prominent southern universities in the fold, the Southern Conference quickly became one of the nation's top college athletic associations. It was thought to have the strictest regulations in the country: a one-year rule for initial eligibility, a no-transfer rule, and a three-year rule that limited an individual's participation in a sport to just three seasons. More important for the future of basketball on the Carolina campus, the league also decided to hold a postseason basketball tournament.

Basketball in Chapel Hill was thriving on the court, but the sport remained unsettled in terms of its administration. While Fred Boye continued to be listed as head coach through the 1923 campaign, in reality the 1922 and 1923 teams did not have an official head coach. Baseball and football coach Bob Fetzer often accompanied the team on road trips, but he was unsure of his basketball acumen and usually chose to sit in the stands rather than on the team bench.

The lack of coaching didn't inhibit the results on the court, however, as Carolina established basketball dominance within the state and beyond. There had been a noticeable local push to make the game faster. Traditionally, northern and southern styles of play had stark differences: the North was the home of slick passes and fancy dribbling, while the South's game was slower and more structured. On-campus reaction to the movement to a faster game was mixed. On December 13, 1921, the more traditional *Tar Heel* wrote:

There has been considerable agitation among collegiate circles during the past two or three years to make the Southern game of basketball like the Northern game, namely, purely a passing game, fouling for personal contact. Saturday night's exhibition was a demonstration that such a procedure would be a rank failure if brought on too suddenly

Durham native Cartwright Carmichael was UNC's first All-America in 1923. (Photo courtesy of UNC Athletic Communications)

in the South. The element of roughness in the game lends, if anything, more interest to the game, and if it is made entirely a passing game, as Coach Steiner would have had it, it would have been even worse than it was from a spectator's standpoint, and it was about as bad as it could have been.

The arrival of Cartwright Carmichael in 1922 gave Carolina the talent to play multiple styles, as he joined brother Billy on the 1922 squad that went 15–6 and claimed the first-ever Southern Conference tournament title. Because of the size of the Southern Conference, the league tournament was a grueling event that required four straight wins to claim the championship. Behind the athletic Cartwright Carmichael, who would eventually become UNC's first All-America in any sport, Carolina played an up-tempo brand of basketball that had resulted in some impressive wins during the regular season, including a 49–19 blowout of NC State and a 44–28 drubbing of South Carolina. Sportswriters for the *Atlanta Journal* were captivated by UNC's unusual style of play—breaking 40 points in a game was still a novelty, and Carolina did it six times during the 1922 season. In an article dated March 4, 1925, they described how the Carolina players "swept through and around the men from New Orleans, passing the ball so swiftly that their play was hard to follow." They lauded the team from Chapel Hill for moving like "shadows and ghosts," coining the nickname "White Phantoms" because of their white jerseys (with a navy interlocking "NC" on the front). It was a moniker that would stick for a quarter of a century.

The *Tar Heel* noted that the first-ever postseason championship sparked a wild campus celebration: "News reached the University village of the brilliant finish . . . and a drizzling, bitter rain failed to prevent a great celebration by the students, who pranced about the campus with guns, pistols and old time Carolina spirit. A bonfire was built and burned in spite of the downpour, while the word went round that the Tar Heel five had captured none other than the championship of the South."

The 1923 team was even better, rolling to a 15–1 overall record. Carolina cruised through the regular season undefeated, its closest game being a one-point win at Duke. They rolled into Atlanta as the league's top seed, defeated Mississippi College in the first game, and then lost a 34–32 stunner to the University of Mississippi in the second game. The loss ended the season; it also marked the end of the squad playing without an official coach. "If Carolina continues to lead the South in this branch of athletics," the *Tar Heel* declared, "a capable coach will have to be employed, regardless of the ability and experience of the varsity players."

Norman Shepard came to Chapel Hill with the intention of attending law school and perhaps doing some coaching on the side. He'd spent three years in the army—including 18 months in France as an artilleryman during World War I—and played some minor-league baseball upon returning to America. Now he wanted to continue his education, and he was willing to coach the basketball team in his spare time. "I hadn't intended to stay in coaching," Shepard said upon accepting the job—not exactly comforting words for a team that had just spent two seasons essentially coaching themselves.

Shepard's meager enthusiasm for returning to coaching was doubtless enhanced a bit by the formidable team he inherited at Carolina. In addition to Carmichael, the 1924 squad also included Jack Cobb, who became known as "Mr. Basketball" on campus. At 6-foot-2, Cobb was tall for the era, but he was not a true post man. Instead, he was the forerunner of today's wing players who are equally comfortable shooting, rebounding, and passing. In an age of specialization, his versatility was unique. Cobb, a Durham native, was a creative scorer who averaged 15 points per game in an era when the entire team averaged approximately 35 points per game.

Both Cobb and Carmichael made first-team All-America in 1924, leading a Carolina team that regularly bludgeoned opponents. Again, the closest regular-season victory was over Duke, this time a three-point win in Durham in which high-scoring Carolina was limited to just 23 points. That was one of just five games during the 22-game regular season that was decided by single digits, setting the stage for a second straight top seed in the Southern Conference tournament.

Jack Cobb, known as "Mr. Basketball," won National Player of the Year honors in 1926. (Photo courtesy of UNC Athletic Communications)

The event was once again held in Atlanta, and this time it ran concurrently with a Bible conference for Baptist ministers. A handful of ministers snuck over to the Atlanta Auditorium for the four-day event. Spotted by the ever-watchful Atlanta press crew, the next day's paper noted, "We have decided to withhold their names and not give them away to their flocks back home."

The good reverends saw quite a display from the White Phantoms. Carolina won easily over Kentucky and Vanderbilt; they then defeated Mississippi State, 33–23, to reach the conference finals. The opponent was Alabama, a team that had brought only eight players on the trip. Foul problems in a low-scoring game quickly reduced Alabama to just four eligible players; Carmichael intervened and allowed a fifth player to stay on the court. The

The 1924 Tar Heels went undefeated and were later named national champions by the Helms Foundation. (Photo courtesy of UNC Athletic Communications)

extra man didn't help, as Alabama's offense couldn't keep up with the fast-paced Phantoms, and Carolina won the Southern Conference tournament for the second time with a 26–18 victory. One member of the Atlanta press corps argued that Carolina's entire roster should be named All-Conference.

Back on campus, students and fans had gathered at Gooch's, a popular coffee shop that also had a Western Union service.

Long before time for the wire a crowd of students began gathering around Gooch's, each sure of the victory, but tense with excitement while awaiting the final score. When the news finally came several hundred students started a stampede for the Old Well straining their lungs with old fashioned "War-Hoops." . . . Yells were given for each member of the team, one for the whole team, one for Alabama and one for the Scrubs.

After singing "Hark the Sound" they snake danced through the Quadrangle where more yells were given. . . . [School president] Dr. [Harry Woodburn] Chase made a five-minute talk between yells and cheers. . . . It was one of the greatest days in the history of athletics for Carolina, he said, and hoped for many another like it.

Someone shouted "On to Durham!" The crowd took a vote, then they walked for 2 1/2 hours, singing and chanting through the streets of Durham, "keeping four abreast and almost perfect step." The mob visited Cobb's home, where the standout player's father was awoken by the 300 exuberant voices. He was happy to see the crowd and had already heard the good news. They then went to Carmichael's house, and his father came out dressed in a bathrobe. "In his Carolina days he told them, it took three days to walk to Durham. He had been staying up nights to get the news from Atlanta, and expressed himself as being well pleased at the results." The crowd then went to the courthouse, where someone read the article about them coming to Durham from the *Morning Herald*, which was already out. Then everyone dashed into the cafés: "Bewildered waiters rushed frantically to get through the numerous orders. Finally the students took the situation in hand and waited on themselves." Many in the group then fell asleep in hotel lobbies or on street corners or sought a ride home.

It was, perhaps, the earliest known forerunner of a good Franklin Street storming.

THE LESS-IMMEDIATE AFTERMATH of the 26–0 1924 season was mixed. Despite the Southern Conference tournament drawing sellout crowds of 5,000 fans to almost every session, some creative accounting resulted in Carolina taking a $100 loss for the weekend.

The financial loss was compounded by yet another head-coaching loss, as Shepard departed after just one season. He had enjoyed his time in Chapel Hill. "It was a polished little village and really was a garden spot," he said. "It was like one big family. Everybody who went there loved it." But he had never intended to make the town his permanent home. Seeking to escape coaching, he took a job as a tobacco manager for Liggett and Myers in China. The coaching profession always seemed to find him, however, even on the other side of the globe. Shepard played for and coached the Chinese basketball team in the Far East Olympics; after returning to the United States, he spent three more decades in coaching at Guilford, Davidson, and Harvard before finally retiring in 1968.

Not for the last time, Carolina turned to a member of the family to fill the head-coaching vacancy. Monk McDonald, a three-year letterman from 1921 to 1923, was named head coach for the 1924–25 season, and he oversaw the extension of the school-best winning streak to 34 games before losing 23–22 in a road game at Harvard. McDonald continued the team's dominance of the Southern Conference, as Carolina did not lose a regular-season conference game for nearly five years. The White Phantoms claimed another Southern Conference tournament title in 1925 and made it three straight under new head coach Harlan Sanborn

Members of four Southern Conference championship teams from the 1920s celebrated a reunion at the Morehead Building on February 1, 1952. Jack Cobb (back row, fourth from left) and Cartwright Carmichael (back row, sixth from left) were among the attendees. (Photo courtesy of UNC Athletic Communications)

in 1926. Jack Cobb would leave Chapel Hill after that season as the reigning National Player of the Year and UNC's first three-time All-America.

There was no official national postseason tournament in 1924. Seeking to establish some sort of recognized national title, Bill Schroeder and Paul Helms formed the Helms Foundation in 1936 in Los Angeles. They put together a panel of experts to select national championship teams all the way back to 1901.

There were two primary contenders from 1924: the undefeated White Phantoms and the Butler team, coached by Hall of Famer Harlan Page, that won the Amateur Athletic Union (AAU) national championship in Kansas City. That tournament was a collection of mostly recreation-league and YMCA teams rather than a collegiate event. Cook Paint Company won the tournament in 1928 and 1929, just before Henry Clothiers began a three-year run as champion in 1930. To win the 1924 event, Butler defeated Kansas St. Teachers and the Kansas City Athletic Club. The Helms Foundation factored in this somewhat dubious Butler competition—plus the Bulldogs' 11–7 overall record—and awarded the 1924 national championship to North Carolina.

3 : WINNING GAMES, FIGHTING BATTLES

The unbeaten season solidified the North Carolina basketball program as a regional juggernaut during the mid-to-late 1920s. Playing most of its home games in the spartan Old Tin Can, Carolina lost just six games in Chapel Hill in the 1920s. The program similarly dominated the Southern Conference: Carolina lost only nine conference regular-season games in the decade while winning four tournament titles. Today, that type of success implies stability—a long-term plan and a "program" that operates under the same guiding principles for an extended period of time. What made Carolina's dominance even more remarkable was that there was very little year-to-year continuity. Head coach Norman Shepard was replaced after one year by Monk McDonald. McDonald stayed one year and was replaced by Harlan Sanborn—who also stayed only a year before being replaced by James Ashmore. Although Ashmore was Carolina's head coach for five seasons, he was perhaps less successful than any of the one-year coaches before him.

In reality, the team's head coach seemed to have little impact on its win-loss record. In an era when coaches almost always had other jobs on campus, having talented players was much more important than any particular in-game expertise. That did not mean that college basketball was devoid of ingenuity. Sanborn had arrived as a respected prep-school coach. In an effort to build a bridge to the past, he announced plans for a Board of Strategy composed of former player Billy Devin and current seniors Billy Dodderer and Jack Cobb. Their job was to make sure "no radical changes" were made. It worked—at least for Sanborn's single year as head coach. Carolina again cruised through the Southern Conference undefeated and won the tournament title. There might have been more at work than just athletic ability and solid coaching, however. Apparently a local drunk was telling stories one evening and gave Dodderer a rusty hairpin that the well-lubricated gentleman believed was lucky. Dodderer, not wanting to take any chances, wore the pin through the rear belt loop on his uniform during the 1926 Southern Conference tournament, which Carolina won.

James Ashmore had the misfortune of arriving just after Cobb's graduation. He guided the White Phantoms into the 1930s with a bit of a thud: a 4–7 record and sixteenth-place finish in his fourth year as head coach. A first-round tournament loss to Georgia gave Carolina two first-round Southern Conference losses in Ashmore's first four years; his coaching tenure would last just five years.

As the program entered the 1930s, it wasn't just the on-court dominance that had begun to erode. The foundation of the once-impenetrable Southern Conference was beginning to show the same cracks that would eventually lead to its implosion.

IN A SCATHING FRONT-PAGE STORY, the *New York Times* described college athletics as "over-commercialized" and asserted that several big-name schools were using "slush funds" and illegal recruiting practices to enhance their sports programs. While this sounds like an article that could have been written in 2010, the *New York Times* piece was actually based on an extensive report produced by the Carnegie Foundation for the Advancement of Teaching in 1932.

Within the report's 347 pages, the foundation expressed serious concern about the relationship between big-time college athletics and the universities being represented. The same uneasiness had begun to create a schism in the Southern Conference. On December 9, 1932, at the Farragut Hotel in Knoxville, Tennessee, conference president C.P. Miles of Virginia Tech called the annual league meeting to order. Dr. Sanford, a representative from Georgia, announced that 13 of the league's schools—all from west and south of the Appalachian Mountains—planned to reorganize as the Southeastern Conference. Sanford claimed the withdrawal was made along geographic lines, and Florida's J.J. Tigert added that he believed that the Southern Conference had grown too big. But it was no coincidence that all of the departing schools—Alabama, Alabama Polytechnic Institute (later renamed Auburn), Florida, Georgia, Georgia Tech, Kentucky, Louisiana, Mississippi, Mississippi A&M, University of the South, Tennessee, Tulane, and Vanderbilt—desired to emphasize football.

That left the Southern Conference with just 10 member schools: North Carolina, Clemson, Duke, Maryland, NC State, South Carolina, Virginia, Virginia Military Institute, Virginia Tech, and Washington & Lee. Football remained essential, but the surviving Southern Conference schools definitely leaned toward basketball, which had grown from intramural pastime to athletic-department mainstay in less than three decades.

Within the Chapel Hill academic community, however, there was disagreement about the value of college sports to the university. In 1935 Frank Porter Graham, the first president of the consolidated UNC system, referenced the Carnegie Foundation report in his dramatic reform plan. Under the Graham Plan, which quickly became enormously controversial, every varsity athlete in the Southern Conference would be required to sign an affidavit confirming that he had received no unauthorized financial assistance and that all his scholarship money was based on academic rather than athletic merit.

Graham had athletics in his blood; his brother, Archibald "Moonlight" Graham, had played baseball at Carolina before spending three years in the minor leagues, finally earning a call-up to the New York Giants on May 23, 1905. He played right field for half an inning but never got to bat; his story eventually became famous as part of the W. P. Kinsella novel *Shoeless Joe* and the movie based on it, *Field of Dreams*.

Frank and Archibald's father, Alexander, was a superintendent of schools in North Carolina. According to the *Charlotte Observer*, "perhaps not a man in town was as well-known." The family had deep roots in the state, and the town of Graham was named in their ancestors' honor. All nine of Alexander and Kate Graham's children graduated from college, an extreme rarity in that era. Frank followed in his father's public-service and educational footsteps. He graduated from Carolina in 1909 and served as a high school teacher while earning his law license. In 1930 he was named president of UNC, and in 1932—the same year that the Carnegie report was released—he became president of the consolidated university system.

Graham approached the job as an educator, not as a fan. He found it disturbing that the Southeastern Conference passed a rule in December 1935 allowing financial aid for athletes. He wanted amateur sports to be truly for amateurs, not for dubiously compensated semipros. League members initially agreed with him, ratifying some of his proposals in early February 1936.

But Graham underestimated the hold that college sports had on the alumni of universities across the South. In late February 1936, Carolina alumni passed a resolution against the Graham Plan. The Monogram Club—an on-campus organization made up of athletes—met and went on record in opposition of the plan on the grounds that it discriminated against athletes. Clemson threatened to secede from the Southern Conference if the Graham Plan was adopted leaguewide.

The *Charlotte Observer* reported "Carolina alumni associations all over the State are vigorously voting their disapproval of the Graham Plan for sanitation of college athletics. . . . Nothing that puts a barrier across Carolina's path in beating Duke is expected to stand in much favor with the average University alumni." Forest Fletcher, the president of the Southern Conference, also spoke out against the proposal, calling it "impractical" and "idealistic."

Within a year, the Southern Conference presidents who had first supported the Graham Plan reversed themselves, and by the end of 1936 they had officially removed it from the league's set of standards. Virginia withdrew from the conference as a result, but its reaction was in the distinct minority.

THE CAROLINA FAMILY WOULD EVENTUALLY become one of the defining characteristics of Carolina Basketball. In the 1930s, however, the program decided to literally keep things in the family. Ashmore departed after a disappointing ninth-place Southern Conference finish in 1931. The new head coach was a familiar name: George "Bo" Shepard, the brother of Norman Shepard, who had directed the White Phantoms to an undefeated 1924 season. But in contrast to that high-scoring team, the new coach brought a defensive emphasis to Chapel Hill.

Elsewhere, the game was beginning to change. Midwestern teams were running a more fast-paced style that allowed a guard to direct play rather than the center. In 1932 the ten-second rule for crossing midcourt was implemented, and a new rule was created that gave a post player three seconds to pass or shoot when he touched the ball. In Chapel Hill, however, the head coach wasn't quite ready to transition to a helter-skelter style of play.

"We spent a disproportionate time on defense," Shepard said. "We were never blown out badly. If you scored in the high 30s, you had a real good night in those days. Our goal was to keep the other team from scoring 20 points."

Shepard—who shared a superstition with future Tar Heel head coach Roy Williams about the value of wearing the same clothes while on a winning streak—fortified his defense with some impressive player development. At the close of football season, he typically put out a call for open tryouts, often drawing as many as 100 potential players. The head coach would eventually narrow that pool to 30 players and would dress out as many as 25 players at home and 15 on the road.

"I'd see that they got some kind of scrimmage every day just as a kind of reward for coming out and staying," Shepard said. "I'd have to concentrate on the first 15, but they all got a little bit of attention."

Sometimes the larger traveling party could be a problem. During the 1934 season, which would end with a second-place Southern Conference finish, the team bus broke down outside of Fredericksburg, Virginia. Shepard and his team had to hitchhike into town and locate enough taxis to complete the trip.

Despite such travel difficulties, the basketball team did succeed in avoiding one particular misfortune that befell some members of the football team. In the fall of 1934, six football players suffered accidental poisoning from the dye in the indelible ink used to print numbers on their jerseys. The ink apparently had still been wet and was absorbed into the players' skin.

Shepard proved to be a capable coach and steadily improved his team's Southern Conference finishes. After the second-place finish in 1934, he directed the White Phantoms to a 23–2 overall record in 1935, including a 12–1 record in the league and a Southern Conference tournament title. The centerpiece of that team was 6-foot-4 Ivan "Jack" Glace, who had arrived at Carolina as a gawky freshman with limited athletic skills but departed as an All-Conference senior.

(opposite)
Jim McCachren was one of four brothers to letter in basketball at Carolina in the 1930s and 1940s. (Photo courtesy of UNC Athletic Communications)

"We worked and worked, just [Glace] and myself, just down around the basket . . . working on hook shots," Shepard said. "That was a favorite back in those days. Then we'd run, run, run downcourt, working on footwork. . . . I never did see a boy who loved it more or worked harder than he did."

The city of Charlotte continued to be fertile basketball territory for Carolina, as Glace teamed with Queen City natives Dave and Jim McCachren to return the Phantoms to the top of the league.

"The city of Charlotte furnished a kind of nucleus for our teams, because in those particular years they had a very fine basketball program in the YMCAs there," Shepard said. "And also, Charlotte High School was one of the earliest schools that really went in for basketball hard."

Despite his teams' on-court success, Shepard was battling health problems and resigned at the end of the 1935 season, eventually taking a job in the coal mines. Although that may seem like a hazardous transition, coaching college basketball in that era was actually not without its perils. Smoking cigarettes at Carolina basketball games had become a huge concern. Eventually, just before Shepard's departure, the *Daily Tar Heel* called for a ban on smoking at home games. "Smoke obviously doesn't help a basketeer's vision," an editorial read, "nor does it do his lungs any particular good. And the spectators on the upper tiers can hardly see the court half of the time when the lower-seat smokers lay down a nicotine smoker screen."

Junior varsity coach Walter Skidmore was the next man given the duty of peering through the "nicotine smoker screen" as Carolina's new head coach. Shepard remained a presence on campus, occasionally visiting practice and giving advice to Skidmore.

The new head coach continued to benefit from the Charlotte pipeline, as Jim McCachren earned All-Conference honors in 1936. Although Carolina's results continued to be impressive—a second-place conference finish in 1937 and regular-season championship in 1938—Skidmore did not seem pleased with the direction the game was moving. The center jump after every basket was eliminated in 1938; jump balls were held only at the beginning of each half. "Taking the center jump out of basketball is like taking the kickoff out of football," Skidmore said. "I am against it." His skepticism trickled down to his players, as junior Earl Ruth argued that the change made the game too fast and caused players to become fatigued too quickly.

The new rules left Skidmore melancholy about the start of a new season. "We should have one of the poorest Carolina teams of the past few years," he said before the 1938–39 campaign. The *Daily Tar Heel* sensed some impending trouble. A late December article reported: "Rather downhearted about the whole affair, Walter Skidmore will lead the basketball team. Skidmore still predicts a gloomy season for the team. 'We've improved a lot since the start of practice this fall, but things still look dark.'"

Skidmore's doubts were well-founded. His team struggled to a 10–11 record, the first losing season since 1920. The Phantoms finished seventh in the conference and were ousted

Head coach Bill Lange (in hat) took notes as his 1942 team played at Woollen Gymnasium. (Photo by Hugh Morton; courtesy North Carolina Collection, UNC–Chapel Hill)

in the first round of the league tournament. Shortly after that season-ending 44–43 loss to Clemson, Skidmore resigned without reason. He was replaced by Bill Lange, who planned to play an up-tempo style.

"Basketball can't be changed very much," Lange said. "We try to use a fast break and that means we'll need plenty of men. If we can get enough capable players we will use a fast, wide-open game. But you can't use that kind of game without reserves.

"We will use primarily a set-style offense with a tall center at the foul line and the forwards and guards cutting by him on either side for the goal. But we will also use tip-off plays, out-of-bound plays, fast breaks, in fact, anything that will get us the most shots."

Lange had the good fortune of inheriting George Glamack, who would help lead Carolina to a Southern Conference championship in 1940 and a major milestone—the program's first NCAA Tournament appearance—in 1941. In the late 1930s, the college basketball land-scape had two major postseason tournaments: the National Invitation Tournament in New York City and the National Association of Intercollegiate Athletics event in Kansas City. A trio of head coaches that included Kansas legend Forrest "Phog" Allen proposed that the NCAA hold its own tournament in the spring of 1939.

The NCAA's membership was split into eight districts, with a selection committee in each district responsible for picking that area's tournament representative. The championship game of the first eight-team tournament was held in a nationally central location—North-western University's Patten Gymnasium—and drew a near-capacity crowd of 5,500. Ohio State defeated Oregon, 46–33, in a widely praised championship game. With the National Association of Basketball Coaches overseeing the affair, the 1939 tournament lost $2,531. But it was a well-received event, and the NCAA agreed to oversee all future tournaments.

Despite a Southern Conference tournament championship and a 23–3 record, Carolina did not earn an NCAA bid in 1940. Glamack had an outstanding year, earning National Player of the Year honors from the Helms Foundation. Despite having extremely limited eyesight, Glamack was one of the very first highly recruited Carolina players—and also one of the first to spark a recruiting war between Duke and Carolina.

Glamack, a native of Johnstown, Pennsylvania, was recruited by Billy Carmichael and Bo Shepard to come to UNC. They arranged to meet him in New York City. "It was in a big room in the New York Stock Exchange," Glamack said. "We looked like some executives discussing a big business deal, sitting at a long table with about 100 phones on it." The high-powered meeting couldn't persuade him to come to Chapel Hill, however. Glamack, a dual-sport athlete, initially chose the Blue Devils. But a disagreement with Duke football coach Wallace Wade—Wade wanted Glamack to wear a shirt and tie at all times and Glamack declined—prompted him to switch his commitment to Carolina.

Glamack proceeded to become one of the greatest players in the program's history, earn-ing another Helms Foundation National Player of the Year award in 1941. He averaged 20.6 points per game as a senior, and his star power helped Carolina earn one of the eight slots in the NCAA Tournament that spring. But in the opening-round game, played at Wiscon-sin Field House in Madison, Pittsburgh limited Glamack to just nine points. Carolina lost, 26–20, and then lost to Dartmouth, 60–59, in the consolation game.

AFTER GLAMACK'S GRADUATION, Carolina Basketball required some strategic adjustments. In an early game the next season against St. Joseph's in Philadelphia, UNC played "a new type of game designed by the coaching staff to meet the loss of scoring power from the pivot. Pick-offs, sparkling, air-tight defensive play, lightning speed and unusual accuracy at the foul line have replaced the old 'get it to Glamack' game."

But changes larger than personnel losses and on-court tactics were on the horizon for college basketball. The attack on Pearl Harbor in December 1941 dramatically altered cam-

World War II cadets train in Kenan Stadium on the UNC campus. *(Courtesy North Carolina Collection, UNC–Chapel Hill)*

pus life, as Carolina served as a preflight training base for the military. That brought stars from around the sports world to Chapel Hill, including Ted Williams of the Boston Red Sox. Faced with many lettermen serving overseas, the Southern Conference suspended its eligibility rules to enable athletics to continue. The navy allowed its trainees to compete in intercollegiate athletics—if they were still interested after 12 grueling hours of daily war preparation. Only one letterman was available to the 1943 team, which went 12–10 and did not make the Southern Conference tournament for the first time ever.

"This is a demoralized sport age," Lange said before the 1944 season. "No longer is it possible to arrange schedules a year ahead of time as we have done in the past." Severe travel restrictions were in place: tires and gas were being rationed and naval trainees could only leave campus for a period of 48 hours. Carolina's World War II teams were a mishmash of transfers from Southern and Southwestern Conference schools. The ragtag group eventually won the

(left)
Ben Carnevale led UNC to its first Final Four in 1946 and later was elected to the Naismith Basketball Hall of Fame. (Photo courtesy of UNC Athletic Communications)

(right)
John "Hook" Dillon was a two-time All-America and was credited with having the best hook shot in the college game. (Photo courtesy of UNC Athletic Communications)

(opposite)
"Bones" McKinney and the Tar Heels battled Oklahoma A&M in the 1946 national title game. (Courtesy North Carolina Collection, UNC–Chapel Hill.)

Southern Conference's regular-season title and lost to Duke in the league tournament final. Both squads were approached about participating in the NCAA Tournament, but the 48-hour travel rule made tournament play impossible. As soon as the season ended, team captain Bernie Mock—an NC State transfer—was commissioned to Parris Island. Faced with such difficult obstacles to building a team and a program, Lange resigned in October 1944.

Rather than conduct an extensive coaching search, Carolina chose to hire Ben Carnevale, a former New York University star who was already on campus as the V-12 athletic officer (a role that occasionally required him to serve as a room inspector for nervous cadets). Carnevale essentially volunteered for the job because he knew the program was in dire straits after Lange's early-fall resignation. Building a college basketball program would hardly be his most difficult task; he had served as a gunnery officer on a boat that was torpedoed and spent almost a week adrift with shipmates until their lifeboat landed in the Caribbean.

Pete Mullis, a Carolina star from the late 1930s, became Carnevale's assistant coach. Carnevale and Mullis guided the 1945 team to a 22–6 record, but Carolina again had to turn down NCAA and NIT Tournament bids due to the team's travel restrictions.

One of Carnevale's first official acts as UNC head coach had been the recruitment of John "Hook" Dillon. That paid dividends in 1946, as Dillon provided an inside presence that was complemented by solid perimeter shooters Bones McKinney and Jim Jordan. That trio propelled Carolina to a 13–1 regular-season Southern Conference mark and the near-universal assumption that the Phantoms would win the league tournament title and earn an invitation to a postseason tournament. The second-round Southern Conference opponent was Wake Forest, a team UNC had beaten by 23 and 29 points during the regular season.

"Our ballplayers felt all we had to do was show up and we'd win," Carnevale said. "We played very poorly. It was one of those nights when we weren't hitting anything."

Wake pulled a 31–29 upset, but Carolina's stellar regular season was good enough for the NCAA committee to issue a tournament invitation. Eight teams would be included, but the headliner was Oklahoma A&M's Bob "Foothills" Kurland, a seven-footer—too tall to serve in the armed forces during the war—who averaged nearly 30 points per game.

With the news that an NCAA invitation could be on the way, an Oklahoman living in North Carolina wrote a letter to the *Daily Tar Heel*: "I am writing to let you know I think it is downright silly of Carolina University thinking about playing in the basketball tournament in New York. They don't have a ghost of a chance in beating Oklahoma A & M (the best team). It is the same as throwing money away by going to New York. Just stick to the Southern Conference. A & M is way out of your class."

Carnevale's squad defeated NYU and Ohio State to earn a national championship battle against Kurland and the defending national champions at Madison Square Garden. Tickets were being scalped for as much as $40. Norman Condon, a famous Metropolitan Opera star and native North Carolinian, sang "Hark the Sound" from center court a cappella. The game was even televised locally, as WCBS in New York beamed the game to an estimated audience of 500,000.

But Carnevale didn't have time to enjoy the sideshows; he was too fixated on figuring out how to limit Kurland. "We had good scouting reports from people in Oklahoma who played him often," the head coach said. "He was so big, and he could come out and get the ball and shoot a hook shot. I always paid attention to statistics and who on a team was the poorest shooter. We dropped off their worst shooter and played Bones in front of Kurland and someone behind him."

The strategy worked, as Dillon helped hold Kurland to a manageable 16 points. But Kurland also changed the game defensively, and Carolina could manage just 40 points, eventually falling 43–40.

Less than three weeks later, Carnevale left to take a job at the Naval Academy. His departure was a sign of the times: he accepted the position because of the job opportunity and not the money. But an era was quickly approaching when dollars would play a much greater role in college sports.

Glamack's Braille System

George Glamack, the famous "Blind Bomber" of the early 1940s, has two unique distinctions among Carolina players. First, he is the only one who began his college career at Duke. And second, he had the worst eyesight of anyone to wear a Tar Heel uniform.

Glamack was a two-sport star in his hometown of Johnstown, Pennsylvania. He suffered an injury on the football field at Allentown Prep that left him almost blind in his left eye and weakened in his right one. Despite this handicap, college coaches still regarded him as a top recruit in both football and basketball.

He originally went to Duke to play football, but he left after a week due to differences with Coach Wallace Wade. Carolina had recruited him for basketball, so he moved 10 miles to Chapel Hill.

Glamack's eyesight was so poor that he could not even see the basket while standing in the lane. Glasses had never helped. Duke officials had suggested that he wear contact lenses, but they were huge and painful, and he could barely get them in his eyes. He decided he was better off without them.

Instead, Glamack found spots in the low post where he felt comfortable, and he practiced shooting constantly from those areas. He generally used a hook shot, which he could take with either hand. He practiced so often that he knew how much height and spin to put on each shot. Coming from the 6-foot-6 Glamack, those hook shots were almost unstoppable.

"I designed a Braille system for myself," said Glamack. "I'd look for the black lines near the basket and use them to find my spots. I could barely see the basket. But I'd practiced so much from my spots that I had confidence in my shooting."

Glamack became a star as a junior in 1940. Carolina posted a 23–3 record and finished second in the Southern Conference at 11–1. The Tar Heels then won the league tournament, as Glamack scored 18 points in a 31–27 win over Duke in the finals.

Glamack averaged 17.6 points during the season, including 28 against both Wake Forest and NC State. He had 59 points in three games against Duke. Glamack was a first-team All-America and was named National Player of the Year by the Helms Foundation. Ned Irish, who ran college basketball in Madison Square Garden, came to Chapel Hill to watch Glamack play. He was so impressed that he vowed to make sure Glamack got the Player of the Year award.

Glamack was the main reason Carolina went 19–9 and finished first in the conference with a 14–1 record in his senior season. He had 30 points at Washington & Lee, 31 against NC State, 32 against Wake Forest, and 33 against Lehigh. But his greatest performance came in Woollen Gym on February 10, 1941. He set the Southern Conference scoring record with 45 points against Clemson. That is still the fourth-highest single-game total in school history.

George Glamack remains one of the most famous athletes in Carolina history. Had he gotten along with Wallace Wade at Duke, however, that history would have been quite different.—*Rick Brewer*

George Glamack was Carolina's first two-time National Player of the Year in 1940 and 1941. (Photo courtesy of UNC Athletic Communications)

4 : THE LEAGUE THAT BASKETBALL BUILT

The rapidly expanding bubble of college sports' popularity finally burst in the early 1950s. The rising status of athletics at America's universities had attracted a new fan base. For the most part, that was good news. But on the fringe of that new fan base lurked an unsavory element that caused some problems. A gambling scandal shook college basketball in New York City (and would eventually lead to Carolina's "Underground Railroad" of prep talent from the Big Apple to Chapel Hill). In addition, a cheating episode involving football players at the U.S. Military Academy showed that corruption could happen anywhere.

Many university administrators began to realize that the rapid expansion of their athletic departments could have negative consequences. At the same time, they were aware that big-time sports could mean big-time money. A growing division between larger schools intent on strong athletics and smaller schools that couldn't compete on a national level was emerging within the NCAA.

That schism was especially pronounced in the 17-team Southern Conference. To try and eliminate the temptation to chase the big dollars, the league issued a proclamation on September 28, 1951, forbidding its members from participating in bowl games. "The greatest evil connected with bowl games," wrote Dick Herbert in Raleigh's *News and Observer*, "comes from the large gate receipts the participating colleges divide. That tempts some schools into practices they wouldn't condone otherwise."

Despite the ban, Maryland accepted an invitation to play in the Sugar Bowl, and Clemson agreed to play in the Gator Bowl. The schools formally asked for the conference's approval; when it was denied, they played anyway. "The violation of conference rules has been demonstrable and clear," University of North Carolina president Gordon Gray said. "We must act so that we as a conference may retain the respect of the educational world."

Balancing the respect of the educational world with the athletic ambitions of the sports

Sherman "Nemo" Nearman and Bobby Gersten played at UNC in the 1940s. Nearly 70 years later, they played in an old-timers game at the Smith Center. (Photo by Jeffrey A. Camarati)

world eventually imploded the Southern Conference. Big schools still favored freshman ineligibility. Smaller schools claimed they couldn't compete without eligible freshmen. Eventually, the conflicts became too weighty. A conference trying to balance the needs and goals of a tiny school like Washington & Lee (which, to the consternation of league members, "won" the 1950 football conference title without playing any of the league heavyweights) with those of North Carolina and other larger schools was no longer practical.

On May 8, 1953, representatives from North Carolina, Clemson, Duke, Maryland, NC State, South Carolina, and Wake Forest met at the Sedgefield Inn near Greensboro to announce the formation of a new athletic conference. First, they formally submitted their withdrawal from the Southern Conference. Next, they began drafting a set of bylaws for their yet-to-be-named league. The septet included every big school in the existing league except West Virginia, which was excluded because the other schools believed its location would create insurmountable travel difficulties.

But all the new members also realized the boon that the Southern Conference basketball tournament had been and knew that a seven-team league would make such a tournament difficult to organize. Virginia Tech was mentioned as a possible eighth conference member, but no formal agreement was reached. The *Daily Tar Heel* eulogized the Southern Conference this way: "The split has been discussed for years as a necessary move. The 17-school Southern Conference was spread over a large geographical area, and the size of the member institutions varied greatly. The smaller schools in the conference believed it necessary to use freshmen on varsity teams to insure life of the sports, but larger schools favored freshman teams. Other problems, such as an unwieldy system of choosing a conference champion and the great difference in the wealth and skills of the different members, precipitated the change."

When the seven new members left the Sedgefield, they didn't have a name for the coalition they had just formed. Area newspapers solicited ideas, and some of the best were Dixie, Mid South, Mid Atlantic, East Coast, Seaboard, Colonial, Tobacco, Blue-Gray, Piedmont, Southern Seven, and Shoreline. Maryland, which by now had become accustomed to going against the majority, didn't want a geographic name like "Mid-South" for the league.

On June 14, 1953, administrators from the founding seven schools met in Raleigh. They adopted the bylaws that formed the backbone of the new conference. Duke's Eddie Cameron proposed naming the conference the Atlantic Coast Conference, and the idea was ratified unanimously. Some basic principles for the league's basketball teams were established: a round-robin league schedule would be played during the 1954–55 season, a seven-team ACC Tournament would require the top seed to get a bye into the semifinals, and the winner of the postseason tournament would receive the league's automatic entry into the NCAA Tournament.

Before the meeting adjourned, the charter schools were assessed $200 apiece for league expenses. The Atlantic Coast Conference was officially in business. Six months later, the University of Virginia was added as the league's eighth school.

AFTER BEN CARNEVALE DEPARTED for the Naval Academy, Carolina—for what would not be the last time—looked to Kansas to find a new head coach. Tom Scott was a graduate of Kansas State Teachers College and a longtime high school coach who had spent the previous season directing Central Missouri State to a 13–5 record. He was not particularly charismatic, and after a Southern Conference championship game appearance in his first season as Carolina's coach, his teams failed to advance past the semifinals over the next three seasons. Carolina missed the league tournament entirely in 1951 and 1952.

Carnevale had given Carolina advance warning that their foremost local competition would come from Raleigh. After his departure for Navy, Carnevale penned a letter to the editor of the *Daily Tar Heel*.

"I'll tell you one thing," he wrote. "State College is the team to keep an eye on. . . . They have this fellow Case, coach from Indiana, and he has plenty of material with him." Later, in an interview, Carnevale reasserted his opinion. "I don't know how soon [Case] will be tops, but it won't take long," he said. "If they keep Case down there, State is going to be one of the best teams in the South."

He was right. The Case crew ran the fast break and played an exciting brand of basketball. They pressed defensively all over the court and posted what was at that point the most points ever scored against Carolina in an 81–42 whipping in 1948. The breakneck style of play became NC State's signature.

"Anytime you played an Everett Case team," said Bob Young, a three-time UNC letterman in the mid-1950s, "you knew they were going to press. That was Case's trademark."

"North Carolina wasn't basketball country until Everett Case," said Tom Kearns, a member of the 1957 Tar Heel title team who was also recruited by Case. "He's the guy who got the basketball thing started in the state."

In Chapel Hill, meanwhile, interest in basketball was dwindling. The Tar Heel football program still had the shine of the legendary Charlie "Choo Choo" Justice, who had led Carolina to the 1948 Sugar Bowl and 1949 Cotton Bowl. Justice, a two-time Heisman Trophy runner-up, had even appeared on the cover of *Life* magazine. Carolina's basketball program, meanwhile, rarely filled the 5,000-seat Woollen Gym. The tipping point of Scott's Carolina head-coaching tenure actually came very early, as he benched star John "Hook" Dillon because he believed Dillon's style of play didn't mesh with his teammates. The move prompted letters of complaint to the basketball office, and Scott never won consistently enough to overcome the ill will generated by Dillon's benching.

In 1950 a pep rally was scheduled in advance of the annual home game against the Wolfpack. The event

The Carolina Way

Growing up in North Wilkesboro, I was a huge fan of the Atlantic Coast Conference. From the Dixie Classic to the Big Four and the ACC Tournament, the tradition and history of college basketball ran deep throughout the Tar Heel State, as it does to this day.

I have been fortunate to experience Carolina Basketball from multiple perspectives. As a young kid, I can vividly remember the '57 national championship and being enamored with that first NCAA championship for Carolina as a member of the ACC.

As a high school student-athlete, I was drawn to becoming a Tar Heel because of the university's tremendous success in both academics and athletics. While playing football in Chapel Hill from 1969 to 1971, I was able to follow the basketball team through some tremendous seasons, including the 1972 ACC title and a run in the Final Four of the NCAA Tournament.

It was a great pleasure to return to my alma mater and have the privilege of serving as the director of athletics from 1980 to 1997. And it was an honor to have a man like Dean Smith as our head basketball coach during my entire 17-year tenure as athletic director.

I can tell you that one of the greatest moments in athletics for me was watching Dean cut down the nets in New Orleans after winning his first national championship in 1982. His teams had come close on many occasions; finally, the title was on his resumé, which he so richly deserved. He stands for all that is good about college basketball.

As the commissioner of the ACC, I've also watched the program from yet another perspective. North Carolina has won two more national titles and has continued to set the bar in terms of overall success in college basketball.

As Carolina Basketball celebrates a remarkable 100 years, I think it's only appropriate to mention the importance that the coaches and players of all decades have had on the program's cumulative success. It's truly an all-star list like no other, and the beauty of it all is not just the winning, but also the fact that the extraordinary competitive success has been accomplished in the right way—with integrity and with players who graduate.—*John Swofford*

had been promoted on the front page of the student paper for a week, and the team ended practice early to get there on time. A bell on top of South Building rang for 15 minutes before the scheduled start to alert students of the upcoming event.

The results? Exactly 28 students showed up, where they were outnumbered by the varsity team, the freshman team, and the cheerleaders. Ten minutes after the scheduled start time, a cheerleader called off the pep rally and apologized to Scott, captain Nemo Nearman, and assistant coach Pete Mullis.

"Don't feel bad about it," Nearman responded. "We're sort of getting used to it."

In the summer of 1952, after compiling a 100–62 record over six seasons, Scott suddenly resigned to coach the Phillips 66 Oilers, an AAU team that had won the national title in its division eight of the previous eleven seasons. Calling it a "once-in-a-lifetime opportunity," Scott left with little resistance.

Carolina Basketball was at a turning point. If the next head coach kept the Tar Heels (the nickname "White Phantoms" had slowly fallen out of use around the end of the 1940s, not coincidentally at the same time that UNC's postseason appearances became less frequent) hovering around .500, football would cement its place as the dominant sport in Chapel Hill. NC State was firmly established as the hoops powerhouse of the state, and common wisdom held that there wasn't room for two contenders.

But Carolina was also having trouble maintaining the Justice-era success on the gridiron. Consequently, if the next basketball coach could capture the imagination of the locals, he had an opportunity to create a niche in a small town that valued its sports heroes. The first coaching candidates mentioned included Jim "Pappy" Hamilton, the head coach at Lenoir-Rhyne, who had played under Scott and coached the UNC junior varsity team. Earl Ruth, a three-year letterman from Salisbury, briefly believed he had gotten the job before the search turned elsewhere.

Ironically, it was NC State that dictated the next twist in the coaching search. In the spring of 1952, the Wolfpack hosted the NCAA Tournament at Reynolds Coliseum. Their first-round sacrificial lamb was supposed to be St. John's, but the Redmen upset Everett Case and State and then followed that victory with a win over Adolph Rupp's Kentucky in the next round. While in Raleigh, the charismatic St. John's coach, Frank McGuire, happened to mention that Chapel Hill was still in his blood and he was hard-pressed to get it out.

What could the son of a New York City cop possibly find to love about a small, southern college town? It went back to World War II. At the time, McGuire was the head basketball coach at his prep alma mater, Xavier High School in Brooklyn. But he was called to naval duty, and part of his service time was spent in Chapel Hill as an officer in the V-5 training program. He befriended Y. Z. Cannon, a local barber, and discovered the local high school needed volunteer basketball assistant coaches. He began to develop a rapport with several members of the community.

Five years later, he was back in the area, and this time he had done something much more important than just helping the area's youth: he had demonstrated an ability to beat mighty NC State. Coming during a stretch when Carolina had lost 15 consecutive games to State, this was a notable achievement. McGuire eventually took his 1952 St. John's squad all the way to the NCAA finals, where they lost to a Kansas team that featured a scarcely used reserve named Dean Smith (who'd seen just 37 seconds of action in the title game).

In August 1952 the 42-year-old McGuire was introduced as Carolina's next head coach. It was a bold move, accompanied by a three-year contract at $12,000 per season. In his earliest interviews, McGuire suggested that he hoped to have his new squad competing on a national level by the 1957–58 season. A preseason magazine ranked Carolina a humbling 278th out of 600 NCAA men's basketball teams. McGuire faced a decision about the best way to build his program. Would he continue to use the Charlotte area as a resource and adapt his city style to his new home or import the city to Chapel Hill?

Hall of Fame Coach Frank McGuire piloted the Tar Heels to a perfect 32–0 record and a national championship in 1957. (Photo courtesy of UNC Athletic Communications)

MCGUIRE IMMEDIATELY MADE a five-game improvement, taking the Tar Heels from 12–15 in Scott's final year to 17–10 in his first season. He also rekindled the love for the game on campus. The *Daily Tar Heel* swooned:

> For the past three years the sport has been the disowned daughter of the UNC athletic family. In fact, for the past two years she has been barred from the Southern Conference Tournament door because of infidelity in basketball courting. Her reputation fell to the bottom of the hoop. Carolina fans moaned her misconduct. Then right before she was to go into her fourth year of disgrace she snared a new beau, one Frank McGuire. He coaxed her along for months, made her give up old degrading ways, and then presented her to the family once again for approval. . . . Her courting conduct was a complete reversal over her previous actions, and many people claimed her as a woman changed.

In the first season of ACC competition, Carolina finished fifth. The league winner, somewhat surprisingly, was Duke. NC State finished fourth, narrowly ahead of the Tar Heels. The Wolfpack would, however, claim the inaugural ACC Tournament, along with the next two league regular-season and tournament titles.

McGuire worked with a skeleton staff; he had just one assistant coach, Buck Freeman. But he had important nonstaff contacts in New York City, frequently relying on an area scout named Mike Tynberg to make acquaintances with the area's best prep talent. Tynberg loved Carolina and sometimes even claimed to be a UNC assistant coach. He wasn't, but he served a key function: he scoured the New York private schools for the best talent, made the initial introductions, talked up Chapel Hill, and then reported back to McGuire. Once the top targets were identified, McGuire would swoop in to seal the recruitment.

"When he wanted to be, McGuire was the most charming man I've ever met in my life," said Pete Brennan. "But he could also be as tough as he wanted to be. Maybe that's why he played players from New York. He understood New York kids. He knew they were all from different backgrounds and different religions."

Brennan was enticed by McGuire's magnetism and by the fact that Carolina had already secured a commitment from a post player named Joe Quigg, who was somewhat of a legend in New York City high school basketball.

"Joe was the biggest recruit in the city," said Bob Cunningham. "He was the biggest name, by far, in Catholic high school basketball. We had played against his teams at St. Francis a couple of times and they just crushed us. They had all these Italian guys from Brooklyn and they just whaled on us. Joe was about 6-foot-8 and he was like Mr. Macho. He was terrific. When he announced he was going to the University of North Carolina, I figured that was the start of a pretty good team. His announcement was what really convinced me to go there."

In the spring of 1954, Brennan joined Tommy Kearns, Quigg (who enrolled in January 1954 because of a quirk in the academic calendar), and Cunningham in an all–New York recruiting class. They arrived just in time to watch Lennie Rosenbluth move from the freshman team to the varsity. Rosenbluth was a virtually unknown recruit who had originally committed to NC State. But when he took a visit to campus, which he believed was a mere formality, he discovered that Case had actually intended for him to try out. Rosenbluth, who was not in basketball shape, struggled.

"Son, we only have one scholarship left," Case told the exhausted player, "and we don't want to waste it."

The dismissal of Rosenbluth angered Harry Gotkin, the New York scout who had recommended him. In the intertwined world of 1950s New York basketball, it somehow made sense that Gotkin, who was generally known to favor NC State, was the uncle of Tynberg, who was generally known to favor Carolina. That's how one of the most important recruiting battles in Tar Heel history turned out not to be a battle at all. Carolina didn't really beat out NC State for Rosenbluth; the Wolfpack turned him loose.

Rosenbluth needed a place to play college basketball. He'd worked with a journeyman coach named Buck Freeman during the New York teacher's strike to try and keep his skills sharp. Freeman and Rosenbluth would grab a basketball and find an empty gym and spend the afternoon tweaking Rosenbluth's shot.

Around that same time, St. John's honored Frank McGuire with a testimonial dinner to

Carolina celebrates its 63–55 win over Wake Forest, which clinched the Dixie Classic on December 29, 1956. (Photo courtesy of UNC Athletic Communications)

celebrate his team's journey to the NCAA championship game. Gotkin had been in close contact with McGuire since the botched Rosenbluth visit to Raleigh and was on the verge of switching his scouting allegiances away from the Wolfpack.

"Listen, Lennie, Frank wants you," he told Rosenbluth. "He wants you bad."

"Well, I don't really want to go to St. John's," the player replied.

"Listen to me," Gotkin said with a conspiratorial whisper. "Nobody knows this yet, but Frank is leaving. He's either going to Alabama or North Carolina, and he wants you to go with him. You're his number-one guy."

Jerry Vayda (21), Paul Anisko (34), and Al Lifson from the 1952–53 team. Vayda led the team in scoring the following year; Lifson broke UNC's career scoring record in 1955. (Photo courtesy of UNC Athletic Communications)

Rosenbluth pondered the news, which would not become public knowledge for another three months.

"Okay," he said. "I'll go with Coach McGuire."

He didn't know exactly where he'd be going; he just knew he'd be playing for Frank McGuire. Alabama and North Carolina were both essentially the same place to a kid from New York City—his parents wouldn't be able to watch him play at either place, the people would talk funny, and it would be a long way from home—so he didn't particularly care which school McGuire picked. When he found out he would be a Tar Heel, Rosenbluth knew only that he would be attending the lesser-known of the basketball programs in the state.

"In those days, the Southern Conference and eventually the ACC was all NC State," Rosenbluth said. "If you told somebody you were going to North Carolina, they would think you were going to NC State. No one knew about the University of North Carolina. It wasn't a basketball powerhouse. I wasn't going there for the team. I was going there because of Frank McGuire. It's as simple as that."

McGuire had never seen Rosenbluth play a basketball game. Rosenbluth had never been to the UNC campus. It was a perfect match.

THE NEWLY FORMED ACC had two key ingredients for success: quality coaches and an on-court powerhouse. But the league also needed drama. Watching the rest of the conference play the role of the Washington Generals to NC State's Harlem Globetrotters wouldn't sell tickets. State had constructed a 12,400-seat basketball palace named Reynolds Coliseum that dwarfed every other building in the league. That gave Case an intangible recruiting advantage—come to my school and you'll play in the showplace of the Southeast—and also a tangible edge. When the ACC needed a host for the Dixie Classic and the ACC Tournament, there was only one logical pick: Reynolds.

McGuire believed he had extracted a promise from UNC athletic director Chuck Erickson to build a new on-campus facility within five years of McGuire's hiring. But Erickson balked at the astronomical price tag associated with a new arena: his research projected a cost of $2 million.

Case used his building to his advantage when the coach—about a half century ahead of his time in terms of sports-marketing acumen—created the Dixie Classic in 1949. The three-day, eight-team tournament was designed to fill the void between Christmas and the start of conference play while also throwing a spotlight on college basketball in a time of year traditionally reserved for college football. Many children of the Dixie Classic era fondly remember finding a book of tickets under the Christmas tree.

The genius of the event was the local pride it prompted among fans of the Big Four schools. Carolina, Wake, Duke, and State all participated, and they were joined by four of the best programs from around the country. State won the first three events, and when Duke upset the Wolfpack in 1954, State fans stuck around for the finals to root for the Blue Devils against the invaders from Navy (coached by Ben Carnevale).

The Dixie Classic was a rare example of a college basketball coach creating a stage for programs other than his own. It wasn't just an NC State showcase; it was an opportunity for

Vince Grimaldi, here driving to the basket against Duke, was one of Carolina's top scorers in 1952 and 1953. (Photo by Charles Cooper, Durham Herald Sun)

all four Tobacco Road teams to shine. The image boost was vital, because the prevailing notion was that the most exciting basketball was being played in the Big Ten. As late as 1960, Ohio State was leading the Big Ten with an average of 94 points per game. No one in the ACC averaged even 75. Six Big Ten players averaged more than 20 points; no ACC player averaged that many. The ACC was a defensive league, while other conferences preferred fast-paced offense. Which method was superior? ACC supporters believed the results of the Dixie Classic provided the proof. All 12 Dixie Classics were won by a school from North Carolina, with NC State winning seven, Carolina winning three, and Duke and Wake Forest winning one apiece.

Once the national powerhouses departed and conference play began, however, Case commenced bludgeoning his rivals. McGuire arrived in Chapel Hill at a time when there was serious concern that Carolina might be conceding practically permanent basketball supremacy to the neighbors in Raleigh. As the 1954–55 season began, the Tar Heels had lost 11 of their last 15 Dixie Classic games. A feature in the *Daily Tar Heel* expressed some concern: "The tourney emphasized another point—that Carolina athletic officials are tending to ignore the great interest in basketball which is steadily developing in this state. Carolina has always boasted of a well-rounded athletic program. Of late, basketball seems to have been overlooked in the football fervor. The team has been going down slowly. In fact Carolina hasn't beaten State in four years now. Steps should be taken to restore basketball to its former position of importance on this campus."

In reality, a major step had been taken in the hiring of McGuire. He wasn't quite Case's marketing equal, but he did understand the importance of fan interest and a compelling story line. The first time he coached the Tar Heels against State, he guided his team to a 70–69 upset that snapped the Wolfpack's 15-game winning streak over Carolina. Not satisfied with the milestone achievement, McGuire decided that one final step was necessary: he prompted his team to cut down the nets in Reynolds Coliseum—a direct shot at Case, who had invented the practice of cutting down the nets after championship victories.

Case seethed. His team posted a 21-point rout in the rematch, remaining in full-court pressure defense long after the outcome was decided. Newspaper accounts of most 1950s basketball games rarely included postgame quotes from coaches or players. This time, though, McGuire wanted to make sure his message was heard.

"[Case] ruined the game by using the press," the Carolina coach said. "It was ridiculous. He could beat us by 25 points without doing it, and he comes over here and tries to beat us by 40. If that's the way he wants to play, I'll fight him right back when we get the boys to compete with him.

"I don't mind losing, but when a team takes advantage of your weak spot, especially when it can win by other means, well, that's not cricket in my book. I thought he was my friend, but I know better now. I just can't wait until the day comes when I can meet him on equal terms. I'll get even with that rascal."

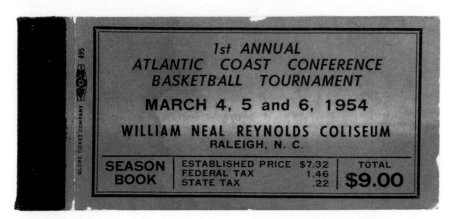

A ticket book for the inaugural ACC Tournament.

With quotes like those, the scribes could only do one thing: race to Case and repeat them word-for-word to get his reaction.

"Since when did he get to the place where he could coach my ballclub?" Case asked in response. "I'll do anything I please as long as it's within the rules."

No one was certain whether the Case-McGuire feud was fueled by genuine animosity or a professional wrestling–style need to have villains and heroes. It grew heated enough in 1954 that the president of the consolidated universities asked the men to meet at the Carolina Inn to make up. According to the *Daily Tar Heel*, the duo "exchanged pleasantries" but "vowed to continue their opposing coaching tactics." Later, McGuire would provide a glimpse into the true nature of the rivalry.

"He'd always say, 'Don't shake hands on the court,'" McGuire said. "He wanted us to let the people think we were mad at each other."

CASE'S PRECONFERENCE CREATION, the Dixie Classic, was a chance for the ACC to feast on national foes. His postseason sweetheart, the ACC Tournament, was a chance for the league members to feast on each other.

After a double-round-robin schedule, the league's eight teams gathered at a "neutral" site—Reynolds Coliseum, of course—to determine the official champion. This struck members of other leagues as a savage way to end a four-month season. They were right—it *was* savage. That's exactly why it caught on with the public, which quickly came to adore the unpredictable finality of a lose-and-go-home tournament.

A sellout crowd of 12,400 packed Reynolds for the first ACC Tournament final, creating a profit of $72,000 for the weekend. This was actually bad news for the league's coaches: in a midseason vote, seven of them (Case was the lone outlier) had voted against making the tournament champion the official league champion. "It's a $60,000 slot machine," one coach grumbled.

The difference was that this slot machine was guaranteed to pay its participants. Even though Carolina lost its first two games in the event, giving the Tar Heels a five-game postseason losing streak that dated back to 1949, the athletic department still profited. Finding ACC Tournament success on the court would require going through NC State and finally edging ahead in the basketball program's first great rivalry.

5 : RIVALRIES
THE PASSION OF THE ACC

t's thrilling to be great. It's even more thrilling to be great against the highest level of competition.

Over the last 100 years, and especially since the formation of the Atlantic Coast Conference, Carolina Basketball has been the program by which every other league foe has measured itself. There have been times when several ACC programs have looked eye to eye with the Tar Heels. But one of the most enduring traits of Carolina hoops is that the Tar Heels always win the staring match, even if it takes a few years to determine the victor—and that is no small achievement.

"It's hard to be good," Phil Ford said. "When you're Muhammad Ali, you get the best shot every time out. When Carolina plays Elon, Elon plays like Duke. Carolina gets that year in and year out. When you get that kind of competition every game and you can sustain your level of excellence, that says a lot about your program."

It's entirely possible that Carolina would have become the best program in the country without the competition provided by the rest of the ACC. But the last 50 years wouldn't have been nearly as much fun. In the mid-1970s, a new species of basketball fan began to emerge: the ABC fan—"Anybody But Carolina." At the ACC Tournament, fans of the other seven (and then eight, and then eleven) schools regularly banded together to cheer against the Tar Heels, regardless of who they were playing. Listen closely enough at traditional ACC venues like those in Winston-Salem or Raleigh and you still might hear a miffed voice decrying "Carolina refs." Winning creates status—and it also creates enemies. Bitter enemies.

Fans accustomed to the Tar Heels being the heavyweight in most rivalries might be surprised to know that Carolina actually began as the ACC's perennial underdog. As the 1940s turned into the 1950s, Carolina Basketball looked nothing like we know it today. Tar Heel teams were an afterthought, even within the state's borders. The unquestioned power was

NC State, which parlayed its hire of Everett Case into Southern Conference—and then ACC—dominance.

In 1948 even the UNC student newspaper was reverential toward State. Somehow, the paper noted, the Raleigh school had managed to turn basketball into a big-time sport at a time when other universities thought the path to top-tier athletics ran only through football.

"The State College coach, active Everett Case, has scoured the eastern parts of the United States," the *Daily Tar Heel* reported, "and his turning over of loose stones and local high schools has allowed the grey-headed gentleman to gather a wealth of talent that turns opponents green with envy and opponents' stomachs from the thought of having to combat this devastating menace which is now in the process of rolling to national honors."

A window of hope opened when State started 6–6 in 1949, but the Wolfpack snapped out of the slump long enough to pummel Carolina, 67–36. The victory was seen as more than just one solitary game; it was also a referendum on the styles played by the two schools. "The game proved one thing rather conclusively to the 3,600 fans present," read the next day's *Daily Tar Heel* summary. "The one-hand push shot and fast-break style offense has antiquated the set-shot offense. The most potent weapon of the current Carolina team is the set shot, and there are good long short artists on the team. . . . But against a polished team like State, it's nearly impossible to get in that extra second it takes to shoot a set shot."

It took Frank McGuire to snap the State stranglehold. He edged them, 70–69, in his first matchup as Carolina's head coach, and the entertaining feud with Case was born. Eventually, McGuire gained the advantage, partially because of Case's mismanagement of the Rosenbluth recruitment and the subsequent crumbling alliance between Case and Harry Gotkin. In the 1954 ACC Tournament, a hard foul by UNC's Tony Radovich and a quick reaction by State's Davey Gotkin led to a brawl between the two teams. Soon, Carolina crept close enough to be considered State's equal. A recruiting scandal surrounding Jackie Moreland, combined with Case's perennial NCAA Tournament struggles, eventually allowed McGuire to pilot his Tar Heels into national prominence.

For almost two decades, the rivalry simmered. Carolina took control in the late 1960s and early 1970s, winning 14 of 15 games against the Wolfpack. But State soon regained the upper hand—in a big way. Their ascension was driven primarily by one recruit: David Thompson, one of the greatest players in college basketball history. Thompson led the Wolfpack to nine straight wins over Carolina, a streak that lasted from 1972 to 1975. It was, by far, the longest State winning streak over UNC in the ACC era. NC State head coach Norm Sloan, weary of the frequent praise for the innovativeness of UNC's coach Dean Smith, chirped, "Some of the coaches can be great when they win, talking about some kind of fancy name for the defense or some kind of inverted something or other for the offense. If you're expecting one from me, I don't have one."

What he did have was Thompson, and that was practically enough. The Wolfpack was

(opposite)
North Carolina natives Walter Davis and David Thompson were two of the finest ACC players ever and competed in a fierce Triangle rivalry in the mid-1970s. (Photo by Hugh Morton; courtesy North Carolina Collection, UNC–Chapel Hill)

Mickey Bell's clutch free throw helped UNC beat David Thompson and NC State, 76–74, on February 25, 1975, to snap UNC's nine-game losing streak against its neighbors from Raleigh. (Photo courtesy of UNC Athletic Communications)

almost unbeatable with the superstar, ultimately winning the NCAA championship in 1974. In Chapel Hill, however, the Tar Heels were about to unleash their own phenom, one who would help them regain control of both the State rivalry and the entire ACC.

Phil Ford's final college choice had come down to State and Carolina. His parents were supportive, and his mother purposely never advised him on which school he should pick. She didn't have to. She had other, more subtle ways of making her opinion known.

"I had grown up a Carolina fan," Ford said. "My mom and dad never told me where to go to school. But they fell in love with Coach Smith. And when Carolina came to visit us in Rocky Mount, we had one of the greatest spreads ever. Potato salad, ham, fried chicken, everything. The fried chicken helped me decide. But also, it's like when you get married. When you meet the right one, you just know."

It quickly became evident that Ford was, indeed, the right one for the Tar Heels. He struggled in his first meeting with State, as the top-ranked Wolfpack took an 82–67 decision in the Big Four tournament. In the next meeting, at Reynolds Coliseum, the Wolfpack needed overtime to escape with an 88–85 win.

Finally, the frustration of the nine-game losing streak against State was released in Carmichael Auditorium on February 25, 1975. Carolina sprinted to an 11-point halftime lead behind 19 points from Ford. The early advantage gave Smith the opportunity to turn the game over to Ford, who led the famed Four Corners spread offense for almost 18 minutes of the second half. Even Thompson's 32-point, 8-rebound performance couldn't bring State all the way back. Mickey Bell hit a clutch free throw for the Tar Heels with 29 seconds remaining to provide the final 76–74 margin of victory. Fans unfurled a sectionwide banner that read, "The Streak Stops Here."

"That was huge for the confidence of our young team," said Ford, who scored 22 points before fouling out. "For us to beat them was a turning point."

"We had struggled against them," said John Kuester, who contributed five points in the

Pulitzer Prize–winning cartoonist Jeff MacNelly was heavily influenced by his formative years as a staff member of the Daily Tar Heel. *(Artwork from Jeff MacNelly)*

win. "But what we had my sophomore year was terrific mental toughness. We had Phil and Walter [Davis] and younger players who could play at a high level against David Thompson and Monte Towe. But our biggest edge was having Dean Smith on our side."

Thompson left State later that spring and Carolina gained firm control of the rivalry. Since Thompson's departure, the Tar Heels have won 73.2% of the subsequent 82 meetings through the 2010 season.

The rivalry with the Wolfpack was largely based on talent and heated competition. But other rivalries—sometimes those that are the most impassioned—are based on cultural differences. That was the case with Wake Forest in the late 1950s. The university had finally completed its relocation from Wake Forest to Winston-Salem in 1956, but the hardwood rivalry was retained despite the move. At that time, McGuire was stocking his Tar Heels with New York City imports. The Wake Forest roster was largely filled with in-state products. The first time the UNC team featuring Pete Brennan, Joe Quigg, Tom Kearns, and Bob Cunningham played at Gore Gym on Wake's campus—"An absolutely terrible place to play, where the fans were so close they would pull the hair on your legs when you were inbounding the ball," said Lennie Rosenbluth—they were greeted with a large banner that read, "Welcome Brooklyn Catholics."

If that sounds like something out of a European soccer rivalry, that's approximately the right tone. The squads had an on-court brawl that both sides attributed to a fight during

"Bones" McKinney played at Carolina and later coached at Wake Forest. (Photo courtesy of UNC Athletic Communications)

the football game earlier in the fall, and when the Carolina freshman team played at Wake in 1955, the team bus was pelted with rocks.

"I think the whole thing stemmed from the coaches," said Harvey Salz (1958–60). "Bones McKinney and Frank McGuire had a little something between them. In the dressing room before the game, Coach McGuire would get us crazy, telling us all kinds of things about Bones McKinney and about how Wake Forest didn't respect us. And I'm sure Bones McKinney was doing the same thing in the Wake Forest locker room."

During the 1956 season, when McKinney was still a Wake assistant under head coach Murray Greason, Brennan went to the free-throw line for a pair of crucial late-game attempts. From the Wake Forest bench, he heard a catcall: "Brennan's going to choke. Brennan's going to choke."

It was coming from McKinney.

Brennan hit both of his free throws. Then he pulled off one of the best comebacks in Tar Heel basketball history. McKinney was known for habitually drinking water out of a pail on the Deacon bench, and as Brennan ran back down the court, he dropped his gum in McKinney's water pail. Brennan then looked at McKinney and said, "Coach, Brennan doesn't choke."

The rivalry, at least between the players, remained fairly healthy. Despite having to fish Brennan's gum out of his water, McKinney consistently supported Brennan for individual honors. And when the Tar Heels advanced to the national semifinals in 1957, they received a long telegram from the entire Wake Forest team wishing them good luck.

That same goodwill never seemed to surface in UNC's battles with South Carolina in the late 1960s and early 1970s. It's probably not a coincidence that that particular rivalry involved Frank McGuire. The head coach had left Chapel Hill for the NBA in 1961, but his tenure in the pros lasted just one season. When the team he coached, the Philadelphia Warriors, moved to San Francisco, McGuire resigned rather than follow the organization. He returned to college basketball in a most unlikely spot: Columbia, South Carolina.

He proceeded to build the Gamecocks by using exactly the same blueprint he'd followed at Carolina: he brought in tough New York City kids who also happened to be talented

Competing against Dean Smith

When you were playing against a Dean Smith–coached team, you had to prepare for everything. They had some set plays that we knew, but he'd throw a little bit of everything at you. He would press you, he would run the motion offense, and you never knew for sure what he might do. The toughest thing to prepare for was the Four Corners. They'd put Phil Ford in the middle and he'd whip you one-on-one. If you helped, he'd dish it to somebody coming from the corner and that guy would dunk on you. Phil Ford was the best. You just couldn't stop him from penetrating.

I tried to recruit Phil, just like I tried to recruit Michael Jordan and James Worthy and Sam Perkins and all of them. When I went to recruit Michael, I went up to his bedroom and he had all this Carolina stuff all over the walls. I said, "Well, he's not coming to Maryland," and that was that.

The only player I ever got that Carolina also wanted was Tom McMillen. His dad didn't want him to go to Carolina. Tom told me his dad used to slide notes under his door that said, "Go anywhere but North Carolina." I finally had to tell Tom, "Dean really isn't that bad. But if you go to Carolina, you're going to make your dad have a nervous breakdown." If his dad hadn't cared where Tom went to school, I know he would have gone to Carolina.

Of course, when you went to play at Carolina, you had to prepare for the heat. Dean turned the heat in Carmichael up to 90 degrees. Sure he did. I always used to ask my managers to try and find where the heat was so we could cut it down. One year, we thought we had found it, but it didn't work out.

Because he beat us all the time on the court and in recruiting, all the other ACC coaches were jealous of Dean. When we had coaches' meetings, we'd all try to jump on him. We'd tease him. At those meetings, everybody would go out at night to go to some club and shag, but of course he wouldn't go. One time when we got back, Terry Holland threw firecrackers at Dean's room.

The truth is that we were all competitors. He was a great coach and a great gentleman. Of all the coaches I competed against, he was by far the toughest to beat.
—Lefty Driesell

Lefty Driesell competed against Dean Smith's teams for more than 20 years at three schools. The two were honored as ACC Legends at the 2008 ACC Tournament in Charlotte. (Photo by Robert Crawford)

Bill Chamberlain earned Most Valuable Player honors in leading UNC to the 1971 NIT championship. (Photo courtesy of UNC Athletic Communications)

basketball players. The product gave South Carolina the most success it ever achieved in the ACC. The Gamecocks had an undefeated league record in 1970 and won the conference tournament in 1971. The battles with North Carolina became fiery.

"One thing about South Carolina is that they were extremely physical, and extremely big," said Bill Chamberlain (1970–72). "They had great guards, and they were all New York City kids. They were Catholics with moxie and they were all disciples of Frank's New York City style."

In 1971 the Tar Heels upset the second-ranked Gamecocks 79–64 at Carmichael. South Carolina players responded by trashing their locker room, breaking mirrors, tearing doors off lockers, and breaking glass in a trophy case. The Carolina athletic department sent McGuire a bill for the damage—and he paid it.

The ringleader of the Gamecocks' style was guard John Roche, who possessed equal measures of basketball talent and feistiness. Roche won back-to-back ACC Player of the Year awards in his first two seasons in the league—although Carolina's Charles Scott had a solid case for winning one of those trophies—but he is better remembered for his ability to rile opponents. After a big win over Duke, Roche proclaimed, "It's all over for the North Carolina schools." His teammate, Tom Owens, once told *Sports Illustrated*, "If we win the national championship, I just want to ride around the state of North Carolina with a megaphone, yelling at everybody, 'Drop dead.' Among other things."

No, it was not exactly a rivalry based on mutual respect. After one South Carolina victory in Columbia, Roche was approached by Dean Smith, who attempted to congratulate the guard on his standout performance. Roche reportedly responded, "Go f— yourself." Roche has never denied making the remark.

*Lefty Driesell's
Maryland teams
were among
Carolina's toughest
opponents during
the 1970s and 1980s.
Even today, Driesell
still refers to Jordan
as "that doggone
Michael Jordan"
because of the
Wilmington native's
heroics against the
Terrapins.*
(Photo by Sally Sather)

Thanks to high-percentage shots like this one against the Terps, Brad Daugherty still ranks third all-time in UNC career field-goal percentage (62.0%). (Photo by Sally Sather)

"When you played them, you knew it was going to be a physical game," said Dick Grubar (1967–69). "I would guard Roche, and I would come out black and blue. They were a guard-oriented offense and Roche was a tough kid. He was a New Yorker, and they are a little more demonstrative. It was easy to not like one person, and he was the one. He was a good player, and he was the key to them winning and losing, but he was the one."

Ten years later, another individual opposing player would define a Carolina rivalry, but this time because of his skill rather than his machismo. Ralph Sampson dominated the paint for Virginia from 1980 to 1983. It was his good fortune—or maybe his misfortune—to compete in the league at the same time as some talent-rich Tar Heel teams. During Sampson's career, Virginia and Carolina met nine times as ranked teams. On four of those occasions, both squads were ranked in the national top three, and another time they met in the Final Four.

"The rivalry with Virginia then was kind of like what it is with Duke now," said Michael Jordan. "There was some distance between us geographically, and Duke wasn't well-liked even then. But Virginia was such a powerhouse in the ACC. Ralph Sampson was dominant, and that's where the rivalry initiated."

Sampson, who had been recruited by both schools, introduced himself to the Tar Heels by scoring 21 points at Charlottesville's University Hall in 1980. Unlike many teams, the Tar Heels didn't assign two men to Sampson, although defenders were supposed to have an awareness of being in front and behind him. Instead, Smith wanted to limit the impact of Sampson's supporting cast. Carolina held the star to 12 points in the rematch at Carmichael. He notched a double-double in the first meeting in 1981, then poured in 32 points with 13 rebounds in a one-point Virginia overtime win in Chapel Hill later that season.

Carolina exacted revenge in the 1981 Final Four with a 78–65 victory. That game served as the preliminary to a terrific stretch of games in 1982 and 1983, with four of the five meetings decided by six points or less.

"They were one of the few teams as talented as we were," said Jim Braddock (1980–83).

J.R. Reid was the subject of a heated recruiting battle between Carolina and Virginia and would later play a key role in the rivalry with Duke. (Photo by Sally Sather)

Ralph Sampson's Virginia Cavaliers were chief rivals of Sam Perkins and Carolina in the early 1980s, playing numerous epic clashes, including the 1982 ACC final. (Photo by Sally Sather)

"People forget that they had a great core around Sampson. Both teams were so balanced, and those games were a lot of fun to play in. We didn't prepare any differently for Virginia, but you could feel it on campus. I'm not going to lie, those games were special."

"The students would line up outside all the way down the street in front of Carmichael," said Buzz Peterson (1982–85). "And we were just as excited. My freshman year, Ralph was outside the lane. He caught the ball, pump-faked James [Worthy], and then leaned over and dunked it. I was like, 'Wow.'"

The most memorable meeting came on February 10, 1983. The Cavaliers had built a 16-point lead in the second half. With 4:12 remaining, Virginia still held a 63–53 lead and had achieved the impossible: they'd silenced Carmichael Auditorium. But spurred by a Braddock three-pointer, the Tar Heel comeback began. Matt Doherty and Sam Perkins each nailed a pair of free throws. Jordan scored on an offensive rebound and then made one of the signature plays of his Carolina career.

Cavalier guard Rick Carlisle brought the ball up the court, and Jordan let Carlisle go by him. As Carlisle approached the midcourt stripe, he appeared to almost forget about Jordan. Jordan quickly closed in, swiped the ball off Carlisle's foot, scooped it up, and then went in for a soaring one-handed dunk that gave Carolina a one-point lead and the eventual margin of victory.

It was a perfect ending to a classic matchup. Well, almost perfect.

"Coach Smith didn't think I was going to make that dunk," Jordan said. "He never wanted to show up the opponent, and he wasn't a big fan of some of the creative dunks. At the time, with that kind of spectacular play, he thought it was showing up the other team."

Almost as soon as Jordan had returned to earth after the slam, the rivalry with Virginia had dissipated. After the two schools met nine times as ranked teams during the Sampson era, Virginia's national prominence became more sporadic; in the past 27 years, the Tar Heels and Cavaliers have played each other only eight times as ranked teams.

Fortunately for college basketball fans, another ACC program was poised to reestablish the most intense rivalry of them all.

6 : UNC-DUKE
AN UNRIVALED RIVALRY

History shows that Carolina Basketball rivalries have waxed and waned. But one school has managed to maintain a consistent—and ferocious—presence on the list of most hated UNC opponents: Duke University.

In addition to overcoming NC State, Frank McGuire also had to stop a disturbing trend against the Blue Devils. By the mid-1950s, Duke was riding a streak of 10 victories in 11 tries against Carolina. It wasn't that the Blue Devils were particularly good, as they were unranked in all but three of those wins. It was that both of the programs had settled firmly behind the Wolfpack, and Duke was a little less behind.

Even 40 years ago, Cameron Indoor Stadium had an unfriendly reputation among visiting teams. Before they were known as the Cameron Crazies, Duke students would come to the Carolina game in suits and slicked-back hair to mimic McGuire. Give them credit for studying the Tar Heel head coach: they even knew how to adjust their tie, a McGuire tic that was usually the only outward sign of nervousness he displayed during the game. The coach, who was extremely conscious of his outward appearance, hated the imitation.

"We won a game at Duke in 1959, and the fans poured onto the court," said Harvey Salz. "McGuire wasn't going to let us walk through the crowd. So he had the Duke officials get police protection for us to leave the court. That's the kind of thing that could create a lot of animosity and rivalry."

"I wanted to play anyplace except Duke," said Hugh Donohue (1959–60, 1962). "Back then, they didn't just paint their faces at Duke. They threw hot pennies."

The physical nature of the rivalry sometimes extended to the court. The conflict began when New York native Art Heyman backed out of a commitment to join McGuire's Tar Heels and instead signed with new Duke head coach Vic Bubas. Thus began a series of physical confrontations, starting with a fight during a freshman game in Siler City.

Larry Brown played and coached at Carolina and was part of the heated rivalry with Duke, which in 1961 even broke out in a full-scale brawl in Durham. (Photo courtesy of UNC Athletic Communications)

The apex came in Durham in February 1961, as a hard Heyman foul on Larry Brown set off what veteran ACC observer Al Featherston called "the ugliest scene in ACC history." It turned into a 10-minute donnybrook involving players, coaches, and fans. The fallout lasted much longer than 10 minutes; at his postgame press conference, Bubas reviewed the game film with writers, and a later report from ACC commissioner Bob Weaver placed the blame for the incident on Brown, teammate Donnie Walsh, and Heyman. All three players were suspended for the remainder of the regular season. The brawl also had a measurable effect on future seasons: because of that fight, team benches were moved from the baseline to the side of the court to prevent reserves from getting involved in heated confrontations under the basket.

"That was a good example of two young guys who went after each other in high school and kept going after each other in college," said York Larese, who played in the 1961 game.

The Brown-Heyman feud set the foundation for a rivalry that would eventually gain national attention. After Heyman's graduation in 1963, Carolina controlled the battles, and

Duke would eventually fall behind NC State in the Triangle hierarchy. The Blue Devils served mainly as the foils for great Carolina exploits, like Phil Ford's heroic Senior Day performance in 1978 (a career-high 34 points) or the legendary 8-point comeback in 17 seconds in 1974—when there was no three-point line.

The almost unbelievable sequence of events for that comeback, which immediately set the standard for Tar Heel end-of-game magic, included:

- 0:17: Bobby Jones hits both ends of a one-and-one. Duke 86, Carolina 80.
- 0:13: John Kuester makes a layup off a botched Duke inbounds pass. Duke 86, Carolina 82.
- 0:06: Another bad inbounds pass by Duke leads to an Ed Stahl miss, but Jones rebounds the miss and scores. Duke 86, Carolina 84.
- 0:04: The Blue Devils finally get the ball inbounds, this time to junior Pete Kramer, who made 82% of his free throws as a sophomore and senior but as a junior was shooting only 57.9%. He clanks the front end of a one-and-one and Stahl grabs the rebound, signaling for a time-out with three seconds remaining.

Phil Ford scored a career-high 34 points on Senior Day in 1978 in his final game against the Blue Devils. (Photo by Sally Sather)

"The whole time the comeback was happening, Coach Smith was very calm in the huddle," Stahl said. "He'd say something like, 'Now fellas, we need to steal the inbounds pass, make a lay-up and call time-out.' And of course, we always did what Coach Smith said to do, so that's what we did.

"He had an uncanny confidence in those situations. He would always say something like, 'Isn't this fun?' And it was. When we broke the huddle, we always had the belief that it would play out the way we had prepared for it to."

In that final time-out, Smith designed a play for Walter Davis. It didn't go exactly as the coach had planned on the chalkboard, but it worked well enough for Davis to bank in the game-tying shot from 25 feet and send Carmichael Auditorium into pandemonium. The Tar Heels had to mount a little comeback in overtime, but they ultimately prevailed, 96–92.

"I Guess I Had Enough Time"

We were down by eight points when Bobby Jones went to the free-throw line for a one-and-one. Coach Smith took a time-out and told us what to do when—not if—Bobby made the free throws. Bobby made both.

Now we're down six. Duke took the ball out of bounds. Ed Stahl was guarding the ball, and Duke tried to pass it through his legs. I stole the ball and passed it to John Kuester for a layup. Now we were down just four, and Coach Smith took another time-out. He told us the same thing: "We're going to press full-court."

Duke threw it away again. I missed a jumper, but Bobby tipped it in. We had made up six points of our deficit in 11 seconds.

We didn't get the steal on the next in-bounds pass, so we fouled right away. In those days, there were no two-shot fouls when it wasn't a shooting foul, so Duke had to take a one-and-one. They missed the first one, and Ed Stahl got the rebound. With three seconds left, Coach Smith called a time-out again. I remember he had a smile on his face the whole time. He kept telling us what was going to happen next, and it always happened exactly like he said. Because he was so confident, we were confident.

In the huddle, Coach drew up the play he wanted us to run. Mitch Kupchak was going to take the ball out of bounds, and I was supposed to start on one side of the court and then run to the side that Mitch was on. Coach wanted me to catch the ball at midcourt. I was afraid that if Mitch had to throw the ball that far, it might be intercepted. So I ran into the backcourt to receive the pass. I took three dribbles and put up a shot. I thought I was close enough that I could try to swish it.

As we all know now, it didn't swish. When it left my hand, I wasn't sure that it was good. I had never really used a bank shot, so it shocked me that it went off the backboard.

Even after it went in, I was still shocked. It was so loud in Carmichael that I couldn't hear the horn, so I wasn't sure if I had gotten the shot off in time. I had to look up at the scoreboard and it said the score was tied. That's when I decided it must have counted. I remember thinking, "I guess I had enough time."

People bring that shot up to me all the time. When I go home, people always come up to me and tell me they were in Carmichael when it happened. Based on how many people have told me they were there, I'd say there were about 25,000 people in Carmichael that day.—*Walter Davis*

For the next decade, Duke joined several excellent ACC foes in rivaling Carolina. A parade of talented contenders, including Ralph Sampson's Virginia and Lefty Driesell's Maryland, tried and failed to overthrow the Tar Heels. But Blue Devil coach Mike Krzyzewski—who had taken over the program in 1980—eventually guided Duke back to the top of the league. The annual clash between UNC and Duke to determine ACC supremacy turned as contentious as anything since the Brown-Heyman scuffle.

In 1989 Carolina was seven years removed from its last Final Four appearance, while the Blue Devils had been to two of the previous three Final Fours. Krzyzewski had won a major head-to-head recruiting battle with Smith, stealing Danny Ferry from the Tar Heels. Ferry was the ACC Tournament MVP in 1988, when Duke earned a "Triple Crown" (three wins and no losses) over Carolina for the first time since 1966.

The teams split their regular-season meetings in 1989, each winning on the other's home court. Both made their way to the ACC Tournament finals, setting the stage for one of the most intense championship games in league history.

"I remember hating everybody at Duke," said Pete Chilcutt, a UNC sophomore in 1989.

(opposite)
Kenny "The Jet" Smith, shown here matched against Duke rival Tommy Amaker, is second all-time for UNC in assists and also ranks as Carolina's second-highest-scoring point guard with 1,636 career points.
(Photo by Sally Sather)

Scott Williams and Christian Laettner square off in the 1989 ACC championship game. Many observers call that game one of the most intense games ever played between the two rivals. (Photo by Hugh Morton; courtesy North Carolina Collection, UNC–Chapel Hill)

"We didn't want to be friends with them. I can't explain why, but it wasn't something I wanted to do. It's not that I thought they were bad people. That was just my attitude. I didn't mind being friends with State or Wake, but Duke wasn't something I would consider. It was a very bitter rivalry. It wasn't good-natured. It was real animosity."

The animosity had several causes. J.R. Reid (1987–89) and Scott Williams (1987–90) saw Ferry as prissy, but Ferry had justifiably earned ACC Player of the Year honors. Smith had caused a front-page controversy by objecting to signs at Cameron Indoor Stadium that he saw as racially motivated. In his frustration, he revealed information about the standardized test scores of several players involved in the rivalry; that move angered Krzyzewski.

The animosity between the two coaches quickly became evident to the sellout crowd at Atlanta's Omni. At one point, Krzyzewski screamed at Williams for rough play under the basket. Smith quickly took exception, yelling at Krzyzewski, "Don't talk to my players!" Phil Henderson would later receive a technical foul and respond by kicking over a chair on the Duke bench.

"There was a lot of trash-talking on the court, but what I remember is that it was probably the most physical game we played during my four years," said Jeff Denny (1987–90). "But our senior leaders, Jeff Lebo and Steve Bucknall, provided the leadership we needed to win the game. I think we knew we were better than they were. We felt like the previous time they had beaten us up a little bit, and we thought maybe it was our turn to beat them up."

Forty-nine fouls were called in the game, and Carolina survived only after a three-quarter-court heave by Ferry bounced off the rim at the buzzer.

The presence of Duke stars Christian Laettner and Bobby Hurley ensured a passionate element to the rivalry's next four years. On February 5, 1992, Carolina toppled an undefeated Duke team in Chapel Hill, prompting the first court storming in Smith Center history. That game is better remembered as the "bloody Montross" game, when sophomore center Eric Montross sustained a pair of cuts on his face. Blood streamed down his face as he made a pair of important late-game free throws, forever searing the image in the minds of Carolina fans. Almost two decades after the game, Montross says he receives far more questions from fans about that game than about his role in the 1993 national championship.

As the attention given to the two teams increased, players began to notice a difference in the way Smith handled the games.

Duke beat Carolina twice in the regular season, but King Rice helped the Tar Heels get the best of Bobby Hurley and the Blue Devils in the 1991 ACC finals. (Photo by Keith Worrell/ Carolina Blue)

"I think Coach Smith appreciated the fact that his players' emotions were so high, that he was going to have a greater tolerance for how the game would be played," said Pearce Landry (1994–95). "If you watch the first ten minutes of most UNC-Duke games, they're pretty ugly. There's a lot of emotion and clanking shots. Coach Smith had done it so many times that he realized when the adrenaline level is that high, you have to let your players play in the moment."

"I loved those games," said Brian Reese (1991–94). "Many times, Coach Smith would want us more structured. But when we played against Duke, he seemed more relaxed. Coach Smith allowed us to go out there and have a little—not a lot—more freedom."

A similar tactical adjustment has proved beneficial for Roy Williams in recent seasons. Under Krzyzewski, Duke has been known for its hard-nosed, man-to-man defense. But when the Tar Heels have had good speed at point guard, the Blue Devils have not always possessed the athleticism to compete in those head-to-head matchups. Their signature is

Ty Lawson's explosive second-half performance at Duke let the basketball world know that the 2009 Tar Heels were the team to beat. (Photo by Bob Leverone/ The Sporting News)

pressure all over the court, stepping into passing lanes even 35 or 40 feet from the basket. That type of risk taking can open driving lanes because there's very little help available to stop the penetrating guard.

One recent result of this advantage in speed was a series of standout performances by point guard Ty Lawson, including a combined 38 points, 14 assists, and 12 rebounds in his final two games against Duke in 2009.

"I felt like I could get to the basket no matter where I was on the court," Lawson said. "So I just kept it going and we were able to keep it rolling."

"I think he got to the point where he felt like he was unguardable," assistant coach C.B. McGrath said. "There were times he knew he could take over the game."

The Tar Heel bench
exploded when Brendan
Haywood's free throws
sealed an 85–83 win
at Cameron Indoor
Stadium in a 4-versus-2
matchup in 2001.
(Photo by Art Tielemans,
Sports Illustrated/Getty
Images)

Deon Thompson celebrates Carolina's
101–87 win at Duke in 2009, the fourth in
a row in Cameron Indoor Stadium for the
Tar Heels. (Photo by Robert Crawford)

True Blue Dislike

I was lucky enough to come along at a time when the Carolina-Duke rivalry was really blowing up into a big rivalry. I'd been coming to games since I was in the seventh or eighth grade, so even though I didn't arrive until the late 1980s, I had seen Carolina play going back to the Carmichael Auditorium era.

For me, the pinnacle of the rivalry was the 1989 ACC Tournament championship game. They had beaten us three times the previous season, and they had just beaten us the week before at the Smith Center. The ACC championship game at the Omni feels like it was yesterday. It was so intense. We wanted to make sure we used that game as a stepping stone, because we felt we were on the way to much bigger things. We didn't want to come out of there hearing about how Duke was better than us. I really wanted to have the feeling of being able to cut down that net at the Omni for Coach Smith and my teammates.

Danny Ferry and I didn't like each other very much. That really came through in that game, but it was something that existed pretty much all the time. In those days, Carolina players didn't go over to Durham and Duke players didn't come to Chapel Hill. When they did—and I remember Greg Koubek and Bobby Hurley made that mistake a couple of times—our guys would make sure they didn't have a good time.

The funny part is that those feelings soften as you get older. I had the chance to go to a big-man camp with Ferry, and we hung out for eight or nine days. You know what I realized? He wasn't as bad as I thought he was when we were on the court. But when you're 19 or 20 years old, they're your hated opponents.—*J.R. Reid*

J.R. Reid battled Duke from 1987 to 1989 and was MVP of the 1989 ACC title game, a bruising 77–74 win over Duke in Atlanta. (Photo by Sally Sather)

(opposite)
Danny Green's one-handed dunk over Greg Paulus in 2008 helped the Tar Heels get their third of four straight wins at Cameron Indoor Stadium. (Photo by Jim Hawkins)

There's a national perception that because of the mere eight-mile distance between the two campuses, the UNC and Duke basketball programs are very similar. During the 1980s and part of the 1990s, that might have been true. Both schools often recruited the same players and were always near the top of the national rankings.

Since then, however, the two programs have rarely been at the pinnacle together. When Williams arrived in 2003, Duke had clearly been dominating the rivalry, winning key recruiting battles and thrashing Carolina on the court. Since then, though, the balance has shifted, and the Tar Heels have had the upper hand both head-to-head and nationally. UNC's dominance included a 4–0 record at Duke from 2006 to 2009, making Tyler Hansbrough and

Dean Smith and Mike Krzyzewski—two of the best coaches in college basketball history—competed against one another 40 times from 1980 to 1997, with Carolina winning 26 times. (Photo by Hugh Morton; courtesy North Carolina Collection, UNC–Chapel Hill)

Danny Green the only Tar Heels in history to play in four straight wins at Cameron Indoor Stadium during the Krzyzewski era.

On campus, the annual meeting with Duke has become the centerpiece of the basketball schedule—almost to the detriment of other home games. While the Tar Heels played in front of less-than-capacity Smith Center crowds in the first three months of the 2009–10 season, tickets for the Duke game were so prized that the annual "What would you do for Duke tickets?" contest had become a regular feature of campus life. Past contestants have taken part in body waxing, Jell-O wrestling, and a variety of food-related competitions that would appeal only to desperate college students.

In 2009 an HBO documentary chronicled what has become generally accepted as the nation's best college basketball rivalry, and at least two popular books have been written exclusively about the enmity between Carolina and Duke.

7 : 1957

TELEVISION STARS

There's plenty to love about Carolina's 1957 national championship team. They beat Wilt Chamberlain and Kansas in the national final, of course. In an era before ESPN and national coverage of college basketball, beating Chamberlain was like uncovering the Loch Ness Monster. That the Tar Heels did it in triple overtime—one day after beating Michigan State in triple overtime—only enhanced the amazement.

There was also the New York angle and Frank McGuire's Underground Railroad. In an era when "Yankee" was still a dirty word in the South, McGuire imported a team full of his home folks and dominated the Atlantic Coast Conference. "New York is my personal territory," McGuire boasted. "Duke can scout in Philadelphia and North Carolina State can have the whole country. But if anybody wants to move into New York, they need a passport from me."

Perfection, of course, is another reason why the 1957 title remains so revered among the Carolina faithful. They're the only Tar Heel NCAA title team to make it through the season without a loss. Modern fans might not fully understand the differences in the game between the late fifties and today, but they understand perfection. On the court 32 times, off the court with 32 victories. No matter what era, that's the type of performance that endures.

But the '57 team hasn't just endured—it has thrived. If anything, the men on that team probably have a higher profile today than they did ten years ago. Why is it that more than a half century later, we're still talking about Lennie Rosenbluth's scoring and Joe Quigg's free throws? At other schools, championships more than 50 years old feel musty and insignificant. McGuire's miracle still seems fresh.

Why?

The 1957 national champions played their home games at Woollen Gym, UNC's hoops home from 1938 to 1965. (Photo courtesy of UNC Athletic Communications)

IN A WORD: television. It wasn't easy to see the 1956–57 Tar Heels play live. Because of Woollen Gym's size, it wasn't especially profitable for Carolina to host games. In the 32-game season, they played just eight contests in Chapel Hill. They played nearly the same number of games (seven) in Raleigh at Reynolds Coliseum, NC State's home court.

The limited on-campus exposure made the quest to find tickets a challenge. A win over Alabama during the 1955–56 season had reignited local interest in college basketball, and by the time Carolina ascended to the number-one national ranking in February 1957, team members were certified stars. The turning point may have been a thrilling double-overtime win in College Park against Maryland. Trailing by four points with two minutes left in regulation, McGuire had effectively conceded defeat. "Our streak had to end sometime, and this looks like it," he told his squad. "So, fellows, let's lose graciously. When the gun goes off, go right over and congratulate those Maryland boys."

"They had us," Bob Cunningham said. "I'm sure Coach was using psychology on us, but it

· · · TELEVISION STARS

No Hesitation

Johnny Green was going to the foul line for Michigan State with a two-point lead and seconds left in double overtime. He was a great jumper and a great defender, but he was not a great shooter. As he went to the line, I told myself that if he missed the first shot and I got the rebound, I had to get down the court as quickly as I could.

He missed the first one, and I was fortunate enough to get the rebound. I was pretty calm, because I'd already thought it through and I knew what I wanted to do. There weren't any alternatives. It wasn't Coach McGuire's way to call a time-out.

I knew there wasn't much time and that I had to get down the court as quickly as I could. For that reason, I knew if I took a shot, there probably wouldn't be enough time to follow it up with another shot. I had always felt very confident in my shot around the free-throw line and to the right or the left of that area. Once I got the rebound, I wanted to dribble as quickly as possible into the front-court. There was no hesitation.

I was coming down the right side, and a couple of my teammates were on the left side. But I felt like I was going forward and they were backing up. If one of them had been cutting to the basket for a layup, I might have passed it to him. But the time was so limited, and I'd already thought about what I was trying to do.

When I got into the frontcourt, there were a couple of Michigan State defenders near me. But I went ahead and took the shot, and, as we all know, it went in. There was a sense of relief when I saw it go into the basket. That took us into another overtime, and eventually we were able to win the game.—*Pete Brennan*

Pete Brennan hit a key shot in the 1957 Final Four and was the ACC Player of the Year a year later. (Photo courtesy of UNC Athletic Communications)

really ticked us off hearing him concede the game. We looked at each other and there was a general consensus of, 'What the hell is he talking about?'"

The Tar Heels battled back to tie the score, and big baskets from point guard Tommy Kearns eventually provided a 65–61 victory. In the locker room, Rosenbluth grinned. His team was 17–0 and ranked number one in the nation. And he knew exactly how many more victories were required to complete the regular season and postseason undefeated.

"Fifteen more to go, Coach," Rosenbluth said to McGuire.

"I wanted to choke him," McGuire remembered later.

Fans had a different reaction. The team traveled home on an overnight train. When the train arrived in Raleigh at 3:00 A.M., groggy players were greeted by a crowd of fans packing the platform to welcome home the team.

"That was the first time I realized something special was happening," said Quigg. "To come back and win a game like that, we felt like we could do anything. And when we got back home, to have people waiting for us was special. It wasn't thousands of people. It was maybe 50 people, some students and some alumni, but they were cheering us on and it made us realize that people were noticing."

The regular season concluded with the traditional finale against Duke. But there was one nontraditional aspect of the game: ticket demand was astronomical. The Woollen Gym bleachers were packed by 6:00 P.M. for the 8:00 P.M. tip-off. To accommodate the fans who wanted to see the game but couldn't score tickets, Broadvision was born.

Sports coverage on television was still in its infancy. The first color broadcast of the World Series had hit the airwaves just 30 months earlier in 1954—the same year that marked the first time revenue for television broadcasts ($593 million) had eclipsed that of radio broadcasts. Any plan to televise a college basketball game, in fact, was usually torpedoed by concerned radio executives. College administrators also had the same question that had been raised by their baseball brethren: if the game was on television, would anyone want to go watch it in person? Numerous baseball owners felt TV would be the end of their ticket revenues.

But Carolina already had a sold-out Woollen Gym, so there wasn't any ticket revenue to lose. At the time, public-television station WUNC Channel 4 was trying to build momentum in the infancy of local television. William Friday, president of the consolidated UNC system, teamed with Billy Carmichael—a former ad executive—to brainstorm about ways to harness some of television's potential.

Their solution combined the best of both TV and radio. The plan for Broadvision was simple: air the video portion of the game on TV but without sound, so fans would be required to simultaneously tune in with their radios to hear the local audio broadcast of the game.

"In view of the fine showing the Big Four teams are making again this year, particularly the first-place Tar Heels, we know there will be an unusual amount of interest in these games

Five against One

My first glimpse of Wilt Chamberlain had come in a summer league in the Catskill Mountains. In those days, players would go to the Catskills and work at hotels, and then the hotels would field teams that would play against each other. You waited tables during the day and played basketball at night. The whole world knew who Wilt was. He was an extraordinary athlete. We knew he was going to Kansas and would probably win three national championships, and then he would move on to pro basketball.

Once we all got to college, it's not like we could keep up with Wilt on *SportsCenter* every night. We were aware Kansas was out there and that they were very good. But Frank McGuire did a great job of keeping us focused on what we were trying to do. We knew eventually we might have the chance to run into them, but we had so much competition in the ACC that we had to focus on what was happening to us.

By the time we made it to the championship game, most of the attention was on Wilt and Kansas. They deserved it. After we beat Michigan State, I stayed around to watch the first half of the Kansas game, and they looked overpowering. I had played maybe the worst game of my career against Michigan State, and now we had to go against this guy who everyone was talking about. The morning of the championship game, I saw Jerry Tax from *Sports Illustrated* in the lobby of the Continental Hotel. I told him that I knew we were underdogs, but that we'd come too far to lose now. We'd won too many games that we should have lost. I didn't think our story could end with a loss. And I told him we were going to win the game that night. I felt like it was our five against their one, and I liked those odds.

At our pregame meal, Coach McGuire said, "Tommy, are you afraid of Chamberlain?" And I said, "No, sir." Coach said, "Good, then you're jumping center against him."

He wanted Wilt to wonder what was going on, and it probably worked. He won the tip, of course. To this day, that's one of the things people remember most about that game. In my obituary, that's probably going to be in there.—*Tommy Kearns*

Two of the giants in college basketball—Lennie Rosenbluth and Wilt Chamberlain—in the 1957 NCAA title game. (Photo courtesy of UNC Athletic Communications)

and we are particularly glad to be able to telecast them," said John Young, the assistant director of WUNC.

The mechanics of implementing the new strategy were complicated. The day of the Duke game, Carmichael and Friday armed themselves with steel chisels and enormous hammers. Their task? To chop a hole big enough to place TV cameras in the wall of Woollen Gym.

"We spent that whole afternoon knocking a hole wide enough for the camera to be able to pan from goal to goal," Friday said. "Around 4:00 P.M. before the game started at 8:00, we finished making the room and carried great big cameras up there and got them into position."

Lennie Rosenbluth was National Player of the Year, ACC Player of the Year, and ACC Male Athlete of the Year in 1957. (Photo courtesy of UNC Athletic Communications)

What those cameras captured changed the way North Carolinians watch basketball. A generation of fans trained to "turn down the sound" was born. Broadvision made such an impact in Chapel Hill that even today, UNC operates an in-stadium radio frequency for basketball fans who feel compelled to listen to their radios while they watch the game in person.

Greensboro entrepreneur C.D. Chesley was the first to realize the potential impact of television on college basketball. After Carolina survived the ACC Tournament to earn an NCAA Tournament bid and then advanced to the national semifinals with wins over Yale, Canisius, and Syracuse, Chesley began searching for a way to televise the matchup with Michigan State. Limited television coverage had been available for the win over Canisius, but he wanted something bigger. A spur-of-the-moment trip to Kansas City to watch the team in person was just a dream for most North Carolinians. But given the way the team had captured the imagination of the public, Chesley knew that thousands of fans would be searching for a way to follow the Tar Heels. He arranged for a five-station network across the state that would broadcast the national semifinal—and, if necessary, the final.

The response was overwhelming. Viewing parties sprouted up all over the state. In Chapel Hill, the Rendezvous Room in the student union set up a 32-inch television (enormous for that era) for students to watch the game. At the Goody Shop on Franklin Street, Spiro Dorton and a host of students packed the off-campus favorite to cheer on the Tar Heels. The picture was not especially sharp, but the fans didn't care—they were able to watch their team, live, as the game was being played in Kansas City. This truly was the miracle of television.

The only dissenting voice came from UNC's student newspaper, where the editorial board fancied itself as the lone source of intellectual reason in the matter. In a page-two staff editorial that ran the morning of the Michigan State game, the writers moaned about a lack of attendance at recent campus events that included speeches by Robert Frost, Dame Edith Sitwell, and Don Shirley. "Not many had enough energy to give education a try," the writers sniffed, "or even to seek a little entertainment more substantial than getting drunk over a winning ball team." For a paper that had agitated just a few years earlier for more attention to basketball, it was a peculiar position to take. Regardless, very few readers heeded the scolding.

Pete Brennan sent the game against the Spartans into triple overtime with his defensive rebound and mad dash into the frontcourt, and the Tar Heels—even with the very limited bench play favored by McGuire—prevailed in the third overtime.

Chesley's network was a huge success. For the championship game, the student union was packed. Several Franklin Street establishments secured a television for the evening. In the Tempo Room, a mellow jazz spot a couple of doors down from the landmark Rathskeller restaurant, there was no jazz; there was just a small television set and a horde of Tar Heel fans.

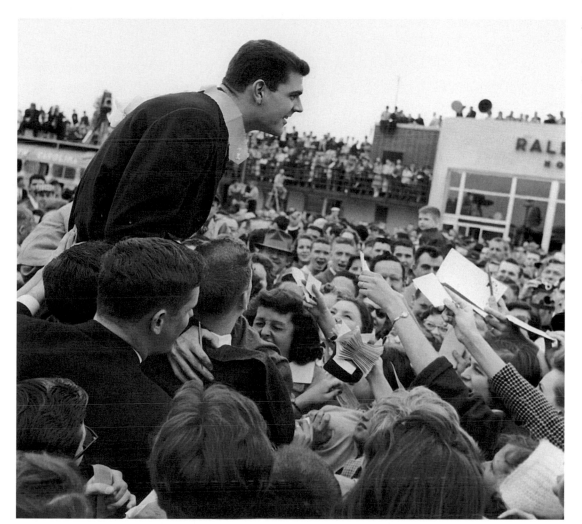

Joe Quigg is greeted by thousands of Carolina fans as the team returns to the airport in Raleigh. (Photo courtesy of UNC Athletic Communications)

The television coverage went beyond North Carolina. In preparation for the clash between the heralded Wilt Chamberlain and the bunch of undefeated New Yorkers, an 11-station national network was arranged. The public-address announcer opened his introductions of the starting lineup by saying, "This is the dream college game of our time."

He was right. Carolina built a 29–22 halftime advantage, but Kansas's perimeter jumpers finally began to fall in the second half. The Jayhawks seized a 40–37 lead with 10 minutes remaining.

"We were in a precarious position," McGuire said. "We had played a triple overtime the night before in the semifinal against Michigan State. The boys were tired. We also had a bad foul situation.

"As I see it, Kansas should have pressed that foul situation and also taken advantage of our weariness. They had the momentum, after eating up our 29–22 halftime lead and going in front themselves."

But Kansas didn't press. Instead, they went into a stall, trying to melt the clock. The Jayhawks held their lead until 1:45 remained, when Rosenbluth fouled out, a seemingly cata-

The '57 Frenzy

It was a Tuesday night, February 5, 1957. The small gym at Albemarle Senior High School was not quite full, but the crowd was excited. The Bulldog boys were putting away another opponent early in the fourth period.

I was there when an older classmate entered the gym and told us, "Carolina is down four in the final minute at Maryland! The streak is about to be broken!"

The streak was 16 straight wins at midseason for Frank McGuire's Tar Heels, who had already survived an overtime at South Carolina and won two games by four and five points.

The gym emptied quickly as the crowd began filing out into the chilly night. Engines were started, exhaust fumes filled the air, windows fogged up, and those inside quickly searched the radio band for the raspy voice of Ray Reeve on the Tobacco Sports Network.

Eventually, the Tar Heels emerged with a 65–61 triumph in two extra periods, and the streak continued. Years later, Pete Brennan said, "We really should have lost the game. We didn't play well, but it was a big lift to us because we were on an opposing team's home court."

I was in Charlotte for the second game of the season and saw the Tar Heels roll over Clemson. After an even bigger win over the Tigers in Chapel Hill, I got to see the two teams play again in the quarterfinals of the ACC Tournament. All-America Lennie Rosenbluth poured in 45 points to spark the Heels' 20-point win.

A 20-point shellacking of South Carolina earned the tournament championship, extended the perfect streak to 27–0, and put the Tar Heels in the NCAA Tournament for the first time since 1946. Regional wins in New York and Philadelphia sent Carolina to Kansas City for the Final Four.

The excitement statewide was at a peak, but the pressure was nerve-wracking for everybody except the

players. Coach McGuire was the apparent reason they felt no pressure. Tommy Kearns said, "He kept everything on an even keel. He was aware a lot more than the players of the stakes."

Only seven teams in the modern era of college basketball have won the national championship with a perfect record. Carolina finished its 32–0 run with triple-overtime thrillers on consecutive nights against Michigan State and Kansas.

To this day, I remember being at a friend's house Friday night and watching Pete Brennan's rebound and jump shot at the end of the second overtime to extend the game against the Spartans. Then, Saturday night my dad and I saw Joe Quigg's free throws and post defense help overcome the Jayhawks. The Tar Heels played the last 17 minutes without Rosenbluth, who fouled out with two minutes left in regulation.

NC State's Everett Case did indeed bring big-time basketball to North Carolina in the late 1940s. There's no argument there. However, the excitement of ACC basketball that we know today was generated by Frank McGuire's miracle Tar Heels in 1957.

I grew up a Carolina football fan, but that excitement also brought me to Carolina Basketball, and to lasting friendships a bit later with the players who made it happen.—*Woody Durham*

Tommy Kearns helped UNC beat South Carolina three times in the perfect season, including an overtime thriller early in the year and a 20-point rout in the ACC Tournament title game.
(Photo courtesy of UNC Athletic Communications)

strophic development. But missed free throws and a timely basket by reserve Bob Young sent the game into overtime.

Back in Chapel Hill, the Tempo Room was silent and tense. In the student union, Carolina students paced around the room to work out their stress. Franklin Street bars were in a bind: the alcohol curfew in Chapel Hill was 11:45 P.M. and they could no longer serve drinks, but no fans were leaving.

The game eventually stretched past midnight into a tension-filled third overtime. With six seconds left and Kansas holding a one-point lead, Quigg was fouled. Oddly, McGuire called a time-out, giving Quigg even more time to think about the magnitude of his upcoming free throws.

"You would think the other team would call time-out there," Rosenbluth said. "But McGuire was thinking all positive, no negative. He wanted to talk about what we would do when Joe made the shots."

The Carolina coaching staff thrived in this type of situation. McGuire was the master psychologist. He knew how to read body language, knew exactly what his team needed and how they would respond to any circumstances. Buck Freeman, the tactician, was already thinking several moves ahead. His mind had already processed every possible permutation.

A 1957 Final Four game program.

McGuire had assembled a team in his own image—a group of brash New Yorkers with plenty of confidence. But after 54 minutes and 54 seconds of basketball, he wondered if he might detect some self-doubt.

Quigg jogged to the huddle.

"I'm going to make them, Coach," he said.

McGuire allowed himself the briefest of smiles. He gathered his team around him, deciding to send Danny Lotz into the game to replace Young.

"All right," he said. "Now, when Joe makes these two shots, this is what we're going to do. They're going to come down the floor and they're going to look for Wilt. Joe, I want you to get behind Wilt, and Danny, you get in front of him. Once Joe makes these free throws, that's what they're going to do."

Quigg did indeed make both free throws—the most significant charity tosses in Tar Heel basketball history. A subsequent deflection by Quigg and steal by Kearns sealed the win, sparking curiously disparate celebrations in Kansas City and Chapel Hill.

In Kansas City, the team that had just completed the perfect season celebrated briefly at center court. A handful of Tar Heel fans stormed the court. Each individual player received a trophy, and then the teams returned to their locker rooms.

And now what? There was no designated team hotel where celebrants could give the Tar Heels a glorious welcome. Their families were not in attendance. Only one player, Lotz, even called his parents. Because of the cramped locker-room facilities, both teams decided to walk back to their hotels before changing clothes. It was after midnight on a rainy Saturday night in Kansas City and suddenly two batches of unusually tall young men were spilling onto the streets.

Several UNC team members tried to stop in a pub near the arena for a quick beer on the way back to the hotel. But the late hour—and the Carolina logo on their jackets—worked against them. The owners first indicated they would stay open, but then they changed their minds and asked the Tar Heels to leave.

That left them with few options. McGuire had invited them to a victory party in his suite at the Continental Hotel. Partying with their head coach wasn't the players' first choice, but it was starting to look like their only choice. After showering and changing into their usual travel uniform of navy blazers and slacks, most of the team assembled in McGuire's room—where a young Air Force assistant named Dean Smith was also present.

In Chapel Hill, the party was much less restrained. Students and alums hadn't just listened to the game—they'd watched it, agonizing over every free throw and marveling at Chamberlain's skills. Reading and hearing about the seven-footer was impressive, but actually seeing him play gave the victory another dimension. Somehow, their Tar Heels had managed to topple a player who was rapidly developing a superherolike reputation.

Two thousand people stormed Franklin Street, and no cars could pass for almost an hour. Students snuck into University United Methodist Church and secured hymnals and chairs to provide fuel for a raging bonfire in the middle of the street. Students were hanging out of trees and from lampposts. Extra police were sent to help control the celebration, but they mostly just looked on in wonder.

Over 50 years later, not everyone can recall the specifics of Quigg's free throws. But everyone remembers where they watched the game and who they watched it with.

"That season captivated the state," said Bill Brown, a Charlotte native who went on to letter for the Tar Heels from 1963 to 1965. "In those days, we didn't stay up for basketball games. But when the games were on TV, you stayed up. It felt like the whole state was awake watching those games in their living room."

A special 45 rpm record celebrating UNC's championship.

(opposite)
Frank McGuire and 1957 starters Pete Brennan (35), Bob Cunningham (32), Tommy Kearns (40), Joe Quigg (41), and Lennie Rosenbluth (10). (Photo courtesy of UNC Athletic Communications)

Masses of boisterous fans welcomed the team home to North Carolina after the 1957 title. (Courtesy North Carolina Collection, UNC–Chapel Hill)

"I was 14 years old," said Mike Cooke (1962–64), a Mount Airy native. "I stayed up and watched it on a fuzzy TV. And it seemed like the whole state turned blue once they watched those games on TV."

The day after the championship, thousands flocked to the airport to welcome home the Tar Heels.

"I was absolutely amazed," said Buzz Merritt, a Carolina sports-information assistant who stayed in Chapel Hill to watch the games and wanted to greet the team at the airport. "I don't even think there had been a concerted effort to get people to go to the airport. It just happened, and that was what made it more amazing. We ended up parking on the side of the highway, leaving our car, and walking the rest of the way to get to the airport."

Associated Press reports would later confirm that by the time the team plane landed, a solid line of cars stretched from the airport back to Chapel Hill. The throng nearly caused the plane to be diverted; pilots briefly considered going to a different airport because the crowd had created safety concerns by surging onto the runway. Eventually, they were persuaded to back up long enough to let the plane land. As the plane puttered low enough to give its passengers a visual of the ground, they gasped.

"The pilot had told us what was going on, but I don't think any of us envisioned what we saw when we looked out the window," Kearns said. "It was extraordinary. We were just kids from New York who played basketball. We went to Chapel Hill, we had a good coach, and all of a sudden we're on TV playing a triple overtime on Friday night and a triple overtime on Saturday night. And we had captured the imagination of these people in North Carolina. Overnight we had gone from being kids from the Bronx and Brooklyn to being heroes."

A Saturday-afternoon ACC television package would soon be created, with the 2:00 P.M. games serving as the centerpiece of sports fans' weekends. College basketball—and more specifically, Carolina Basketball—was becoming a way of life.

8 : DEAN SMITH
CHANGES THE GAME

At the time, it felt like the buzz from the 1957 national championship would last forever. The title team hadn't just won some basketball games; they'd introduced an entire state to a new passion. But less than five years later, the future of Carolina Basketball was being determined by some very important phone calls.

With a haze of grumbling about lavish spending and recruiting expenses trailing him, Frank McGuire departed for the NBA after the 1960–61 season. Chancellor William Aycock asked assistant coach Dean Smith to help prepare presentations for the NCAA infractions committee, which was investigating charges of improper payments by McGuire and shoddy expense keeping. It was an awkward position for Smith: he was being asked to gather information on his athletic mentor at the behest of his academic boss.

The NCAA hearing actually took place during the season. In January 1961, Smith flew to San Francisco with Aycock and athletic director Chuck Erickson. As Smith recalled in his memoir, *A Coach's Life*: "The meeting was run like a court proceeding, and Chancellor Aycock made our case like the brilliant lawyer he was. I simply stood by and handed him the documents to support his argument."

The NCAA eventually dropped a number of the charges, and the NCAA Council responded to Smith's work with the statement, "Let the record show that this board has never heard a more thorough and detailed defense of a university's position."

That was typical Dean Smith. And when McGuire bolted for the pros, with some members of the campus community muttering about the excesses of the basketball program, there was a push to deemphasize the sport. Campus concern was heightened by a point-shaving scandal involving four players from NC State and one from Carolina in the spring of 1961 that forced the end of the Dixie Classic. There was enough widespread alarm about

hardwood overindulgences that the governor of North Carolina, Terry Sanford, became involved and asked UNC system president Bill Friday to reduce the importance of basketball on his campuses.

This time, Carolina would not make a national splash by plucking a well-known head coach from another school. Instead, Aycock and Erickson simply promoted McGuire's assistant Smith. Yes, it was partly a reaction to the pleas to deemphasize the sport. But Aycock had already seen the quality of work Smith was capable of producing. If that same attention to detail could translate to the basketball court, he knew he might have located a capable coach.

"I don't think anybody could've imagined he'd be the greatest," Aycock said. "I just wanted a person who was competent and would obey the rules and get along with his players. Nor was I thinking he'd be here for 36 years. All that he did beyond that was just a plus on our part."

Tar Heel players had also seen the quality of work Smith could produce—with the emphasis on "work." McGuire was an old-school basketball coach. Roll the balls out, let the players choose up sides, usually find a friend or two in the stands and chat with them while the players worked it out on the court. Smith was different. At the time, Carolina players didn't know Smith as a future Hall of Famer. They knew him only as the taskmaster who worked them to exhaustion when the head coach was gone.

When McGuire was on recruiting trips—to New York, of course—Smith was in charge of practice. And that meant lots of defensive drills. Sometimes, he wouldn't even allow the players to shoot the ball at all during practice. Like his eventual protégé Roy Williams, Smith would put rings over the rims to emphasize the insignificance of the result of a shot. Instead, the emphasis was on what happened before the shot, on rotations and communication.

Defensive slides could take up half of practice, with players muttering under their breath throughout the drills.

Those mutterings became louder when Aycock announced Smith's appointment as the new head coach. McGuire's last team had gone 19–4 and won the ACC regular-season cham-

UNIVERSITY OF NORTH CAROLINA
CHAPEL HILL, N. C.

DEPARTMENT OF ATHLETICS

FRANK McGUIRE
HEAD BASKETBALL COACH

August 1, 1961

Chancellor William B. Aycock
University of North Carolina
Chapel Hill, North Carolina

Dear Chancellor Aycock,

I would like to recommend Dean Smith, my assistant the past three years, to replace me as Head Basketball Coach at the University.

There is not the slightest doubt in my mind that Dean can fully accept the responsibilities of the Head Coach and perform the necessary duties in an excellent manner.

He has worked closely with the players in many capacities and is greatly admired by them. Aside from his excellent technical knowledge of basketball itself, Dean has become known in the national basketball circles and is well liked by these people. Even more important he has made many friends with the Faculty, Students and Alumni of our University.

His loyalty to me and the University has been beyond question. I know of no man more capable to lead our basketball program at the University.

Most sincerely,

Frank J. McGuire

Frank McGuire's letter recommending Dean Smith to replace him as head coach, sent to Chancellor William Aycock in August 1961. (Courtesy North Carolina Collection, UNC–Chapel Hill)

(opposite)
Frank McGuire with assistant coaches Dean Smith and Ken Rosemond. (Photo courtesy of UNC Athletic Communications)

Jim Hudock, Larry Brown, and Donnie Walsh were part of Dean Smith's first Tar Heel team in 1961–62. (Photo courtesy of UNC Athletic Communications)

pionship before the NCAA declared it ineligible for postseason play. The core of that team was slated to return for Smith's inaugural season as head coach, but before the final roster was set, several players exchanged phone calls. The key question discussed in those calls: Do we want to play for the rigorous Smith? Are we going to come back? It's hard to imagine now that players would have a problem with *the* Dean Smith. At the time, though, he was simply an unproven assistant who had come to Carolina from the Air Force Academy in 1958. It was the equivalent of replacing Roy Williams with a graduate assistant.

Despite the concern from fans and players alike, some of the players with the privilege of an inside view were more optimistic.

"From the time I was a junior, I knew that if Frank ever left, he'd recommend Dean as the next head coach," said York Larese (1959–61). "The opportunity was fantastic because Dean brought in so many things from the Kansas area where he grew up. He was something to reckon with. He had all the new ideas and he was a disciplinarian."

*Chancellor William Aycock was
willing to pay to attract Dean
Smith to join Frank McGuire's
staff, as this New York Times
article (March 29, 1982) and
Aycock's comments suggest.
(Courtesy North Carolina Collection,
UNC–Chapel Hill)*

McGuire recalled that Carnevale, who coached North Carolina to the N.C.A.A. title game in 1946, said, "Bob here has a young assistant who is about to get out of the Air Force and will be looking for a job."

Spear praised the young man, Dean Smith, and McGuire said: "I come from New York where there are a lot of Smiths. But they're Bill Smith, Sam Smith, Frank Smith. What is this name—Dean? Can't we change it?"

A few days later, McGuire was sold on Dean Smith, name and all, and took him to meet the chancellor of the University of North Carolina, William Aycock.

"I want to hire this man to be an assistant coach," McGuire said. "And

I'd like to start him at $7,500 a year."

"The chancellor said, 'Oh, no, Frank, that's too much.' I said, 'O.K., forget it,' and walked out of the office. Dean said: 'But coach, don't worry about the money. I want the job.' He would have worked for 75 cents."

Ten minutes later, according to McGuire, the chancellor called him in his office and said, "Hire Smith and pay him."

My version of what occurred when Smith was hired as assistant Coach. Coach McGuire came to my office and stated that the Director of Athletics (C.P. Erickson) was unwilling to pay Smith the salary McGuire recommended. My response was that I would talk to Erickson and would get in touch with McGuire. When McGuire left my office I called Erickson. He told me that the salary McGuire recommended was higher than some of the assistant football coaches who were older and more experienced. I explained to Erickson that sometimes it was necessary to temporarily put salaries out of line in order to attract new people. In fact, that we had just done that with some new professors. I made it clear that Erickson should go along with McGuire and that he could, if necessary, place the blame on me. Erickson agreed and I called McGuire in a matter of minutes and informed him that his recommendation had been approved.

William B. Aycock

"I always felt Dean Smith would make a great coach wherever he went," said Harvey Salz. "He was the guy who did the technical part of the game, the real thinking of the game. McGuire gave you the incentive to win, but Dean Smith was so bright."

ONE OF THE FIRST PLAYERS to arrive on campus for a recruiting visit during the new Smith era was Bob Bennett.

"I came down for a weekend visit with my father," Bennett said. "We were shown the library, and Coach Smith knew exactly how many books were in the library. That blew my mind. He took us to meet Chancellor Aycock at Old South. We talked with him for 15 minutes. Almost as an afterthought, Coach Smith showed me the gym and the uniforms we'd wear. The entire time I was with him, his entire recruiting pitch was focused on selling the university as a fine academic institution."

Working under scholarship restrictions left over from the McGuire penalties, Smith built

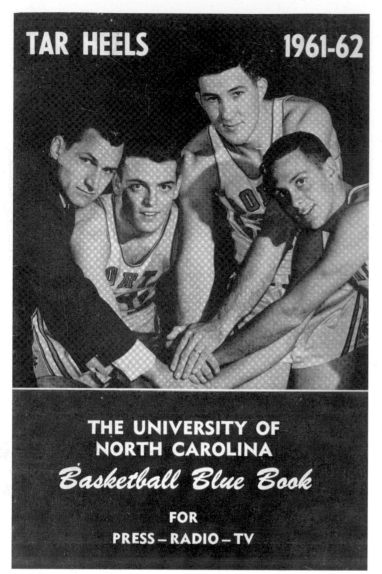

TAR HEELS 1961-62

THE UNIVERSITY OF
NORTH CAROLINA
Basketball Blue Book

FOR
PRESS – RADIO – TV

The cover of the media guide for the 1961–62 season.

his early recruiting classes using a very similar recruiting strategy. One superstar, Brooklyn's Billy Cunningham, was already committed to Carolina and had arrived at midseason of McGuire's final year because of a quirk in the New York school calendar. Cunningham's decision to stick with the Tar Heels instead of going elsewhere after the coaching change was the first turning point of the early part of Smith's head-coaching career. Cunningham was a well-known New York prospect. Losing him would have signaled trouble in Carolina's traditional recruiting pipeline.

Even though Cunningham still attended Carolina, like all freshmen he could not compete with the varsity in his first year. Without him, the Tar Heel varsity went 8–9, playing a limited schedule of 17 games because of the ongoing NCAA restrictions. The new scheduling policy required Carolina to give up all but two of the previously scheduled nonconference games. Employing a philosophy that he would follow for his entire career, Smith chose to keep the two toughest games—a date with Indiana in Greensboro and a Charlotte matchup against Notre Dame. His team split the two contests, beating the Irish, 99–80.

In hindsight, Smith can laugh about his swagger as a young coach. "Keeping those two games didn't mean anything," he said with a smile, "except that I was dumb enough to keep the two toughest games on the schedule."

The Tar Heels did not play a game during the four weeks between the Indiana loss and the Notre Dame victory. For a coach who loved practice like Smith, it was a perfect scenario. His team would also go two weeks without a game in late January, giving him plenty of time in the gym to install new offenses and defenses. He also began to tinker with some new innovations. One of his first creations was the "tired signal," which gave players an opportunity to let the bench know they were tired. When they raised a closed fist, a substitute would enter the game. The player who had given the tired signal could reenter the game when he was rested. The strategy encouraged a player to take himself out of the game rather than remain on the court and make an error in his fatigue.

At the time, however, players didn't ponder the fact that they were witnessing the beginning of a coaching era. They were more concerned about whether they would ever stop practicing and actually play a game again.

"As players, we ended up getting sick of each other," said Mike Cooke. "Coach Smith was a new coach, and like any new coach, he really went to the wall with everything. When you go that long without a game, things can get a little testy. By the end of the season, we were tired of each other."

The scheduling restrictions eased in Smith's second year, allowing him to expand the nonconference schedule. Fortunately, other high-profile coaches were eager to "help" the young head coach. Kentucky's Adolph Rupp, who by that point had already brought four NCAA championships to Lexington, called with an offer of a 10-game series. Of course, Rupp explained that, given the relative profiles of the two programs, six of the games would have to be in Lexington and only four in Chapel Hill. The 1962 Wildcats had reached the NCAA Tournament regional finals and posted a 23–3 record. The outcome of Carolina's 1963 trip to Lexington was not considered to be in doubt.

Kentucky's best player was Cotton Nash, who was coming off a consensus All-America season in 1962. He would go on to become a three-time All-America and was athletic enough to eventually play both professional basketball and professional baseball.

As for Carolina, all those days in the gym practicing multiple defenses paid dividends. Rather than trying to guard the Wildcats man-to-man, Smith designed a box-and-one defense: Yogi Poteet guarded Nash all over the court, while the other four Tar Heels played a point zone. It was one of the first effective examples of the box-and-one.

"When Coach Smith designed that game plan with the box-and-one against Cotton Nash, you could see he had the capability to be a great coach," said Peppy Callahan (1962–63). "You knew that when he started bringing in players, it could be special."

The strategy limited Nash to 3-of-12 shooting from the field and just 12 points. Poteet actually outscored the superstar, tallying 17 points, while Larry Brown added 19 and Billy Cunningham 13. Carolina escaped with a 68–66 victory at Memorial Coliseum, a place where the Wildcats won nearly 90% of their games from 1950 to 1976.

"Coach looked at Yogi Poteet and said, 'Keep Nash from getting the ball,'" said Bill Brown.

More than a Coach

I don't really know why Dean Smith took an interest in me, but he did. I've actually talked to guys who played for him, and it's just his nature.

My father was a teacher at a private school, and Dean Smith reminded me a lot of my father. When I was writing for the *Daily Tar Heel*, he just took an interest. I mean, how many college basketball coaches would do that?

Frank Deford from *Sports Illustrated* was coming in and starting to work on a piece on Coach Smith. Coach Smith got in touch with me and said, "Why don't you come to my office and spend like an hour with Frank Deford? I think it would really be good for you." I don't think I would be doing what I'm doing today if he hadn't given me so much confidence in what I did and made me believe that I actually could be pretty good. So, he had a tremendous influence. I think the world of him.

When Carolina won the national championship in 1982, there was a pitcher for the Red Sox named Billy Mike Smithson, about 6-foot-9. He actually came to my room at a motel in Florida during spring training so he could watch the game. He wanted to be with me when I saw Dean win his first national championship.

When Coach Smith retired, I was in Baltimore covering the play-offs. I was on the field working on some postgame stuff, and one of the Orioles' clubhouse kids came out and said, "B.J. is looking for you." It was B.J. Surhoff, of course, and we sat in the clubhouse until the early hours of the morning talking about Carolina and Coach Smith. That's the way I feel about him.—*Peter Gammons*

"Sure enough, that's what he did. After about five minutes Nash couldn't get the ball, and he basically took himself out of the game. We beat them on their home court, and when it was over, we looked at each other like, 'This guy knows what he is doing.' We got more and more confident."

Smith, assistant coach Ken Rosemond, and trainer John Lacey were so excited after the victory that they walked all the way from Memorial Coliseum to the team hotel. The team spent the night in Lexington, where Brown, Cunningham, and Charlie Shaffer spent some quality time on the phone describing the game to friends and family back home.

The confidence borne of the Kentucky win carried the Tar Heels to a 15–6 overall record and a third-place finish in the ACC. With Cunningham returning, the 1964 season was Smith's first with high expectations. Cunningham was Smith's first great star. He was an All-ACC pick even as a sophomore and would eventually go on to win All-America honors in 1964 and 1965 and ACC Player of the Year in 1965. Cunningham posted 60 career double-doubles (still the UNC career record) out of 69 career games, and his 40 straight double-doubles over two seasons remains an NCAA record (and it's nearly four times longer than UNC's next-longest streak—Doug Moe's 11).

Billy Cunningham grabbed 28 rebounds against Maryland in 1964, second only to Rusty Clark's 30 (1968) on the UNC all-time single-game list. (Photo courtesy of UNC Athletic Communications)

"Billy was a great rebounder, but he was also a great scorer and he could do anything," Bill Brown said. "There were times we'd have trouble bringing the ball up the court and he'd go [do that]. He could do everything, and he was the best player we had."

"What Cunningham did was bring the hero back into play," Mike Cooke said. "We hadn't had that at Carolina since Rosenbluth. We had great players who were heroes to a degree, but they weren't Charlie 'Choo Choo' Justice. Billy was 'Billy the Kid,' and he was a hero."

Smith wasn't particularly impressed by all the awards, and Cunningham never received any favorable off-court treatment. On one occasion, the Carolina bus was packed and loaded for a trip to NC State. Cunningham came strolling across the parking lot for a scheduled 6:30 departure. When Smith's watch showed 6:30 and Cunningham was still lingering outside, Smith shut the bus doors. His star had to find an alternate ride to Reynolds Coliseum.

On the court, though, Smith leaned heavily on Cunningham during the 1964 season. Too heavily, as it turned out.

An early four-game winning streak was promising, but the momentum changed soon afterward. For most of the last three decades, it's been easy to view Smith as the finished product he was for much of his glittering career. But in 1964, he was still a young coach who occasionally had to learn lessons the hard way. A season that would end with a mediocre 12–12 record and a 6–8 mark in the ACC served to teach Smith one of his most enduring on-court principles: team over individuals. Smith bent some of his philosophies to accommo-

*(opposite)
The Kangaroo Kid, Billy Cunningham, holds the NCAA record with 40 consecutive double-doubles. (Photo courtesy of UNC Athletic Communications)*

date Cunningham and conserve his energy; he even instructed the star that he didn't have to run the floor if a teammate took a shot on the fast break before he crossed midcourt. Smith was not pleased with the results.

"I did a lousy job in my third year," Smith said. "I tried different combinations and was really disappointed. I wanted Billy to do everything. I thought we could throw the ball to Billy and he could bring up the ball against the press and do it all. We were team-oriented our first two seasons, but I lost sight of that by trying to use Billy so much."

When Carolina started slowly the next season, including a four-game losing streak in January that dropped the team's record to 6–6, there was some audible grumbling in Chapel Hill. The fourth loss in that stretch was a 107–85 thumping at Wake Forest. When the team bus stopped in front of Woollen Gym to allow the players to disembark, a couple of them noticed a disturbance across the street at Winston Dorm. Fueled by 40 years of retelling, the incident has grown to pitchforks-and-torches status. In reality, it wasn't that substantial. Players whose bus windows had a good view of the dorm eventually had an idea of what was happening. Players across the aisle barely noticed it. The dim light made it impossible to tell that it was anything more than a group of students having some type of meeting.

Rosemond was on the dorm side of the bus. "Look," he said to Smith, "they're hanging you in effigy."

And they were. Smith kept his composure and rose to address the team, giving them the day off the next day but indicating a desire to meet with each of them individually. Then he left the bus.

As soon as Smith was gone, two players sprinted off the bus—Cunningham and fellow Brooklyn product Billy Galantai. The pair had played against each other in high school and shared some of the same fiery New York City temperament. Notably, they had also both committed to Carolina under the McGuire regime but had developed affection for Smith.

"We went over there and basically just told the students, 'Cut this crap out. He's our coach,'" Galantai said. "We never said much more about it."

"We made sure it came down out of the tree," Cunningham said. "We were very upset because we knew it wasn't Coach Smith's fault. We were losing because of the way we were performing."

The story has attained mythical status in Chapel Hill. But at the time, no one on the team realized they'd just witnessed a moment that would be talked about for decades. In fact, had *Daily Tar Heel* writers Curry Kirkpatrick and Peter Gammons not been on the bus, it's entirely possible that the entire evening would have been lost to history. To the players, the notable part was the way their head coach had handled the night—not the implication that his job might be in jeopardy because of a few unruly students.

"Looking back on it, I think everyone on that bus wishes they had realized what was going on," said Bob Bennett. "We all wish we would've gone over there and torn it down. But for whatever reason, it was the two Billys who acted. They were heroes to every single one of us on the team. That one act—and Coach Smith's class in how he handled it—brought us together."

A win over Duke three days later didn't entirely quiet the criticism, as Carolina followed up the victory over the Blue Devils with a 65–62 loss to NC State. Following that defeat, David R. Williams voiced his concerns in the school paper: "It seems to me that we need to give some serious consideration about seeking new leadership, especially for our football and basketball teams. Why should they be coached by men who got their job through their different, but both untimely circumstances? Isn't it time we went out and brought in some outside help? Now I know that both are 'Carolina Gentlemen,' but does mediocrity also have to be a criteria for our coaches?"

THE MID-1960S were a fascinating time in Smith's career. He was receiving significant criticism from UNC students and boosters. It was a situation that would cause most young coaches to eliminate all distractions, focus on the chalkboard, and try to figure out how to win enough games to make the snipers move on to the next target.

Smith did the opposite, however. With almost no personal or professional capital, he became active in several social causes. Most notably, he played a major role in integrating Chapel Hill. Charles Scott was well known for becoming UNC's first black scholarship basketball player, arriving on campus in the fall of 1966. But Smith had actually made efforts to integrate two years earlier, when he placed Willie Cooper on the freshman team. (Cooper eventually chose not to play varsity basketball in order to focus on his academics.) In the fall of 1964, Smith was just a young coach who had never even finished in the top two of the conference. Crossing social barriers was a gamble.

He did it off the basketball court, too. In 1960, while still an assistant coach and before he became one of Chapel Hill's best-known citizens, he helped integrate a Chapel Hill restaurant with Binkley Baptist Church pastor Robert Seymour and a visiting black theology student. The move, in conjunction with similar efforts by other church members throughout the town, eventually helped Chapel Hill earn the progressive label it would carry so proudly into the twenty-first century.

In 1965 Smith helped graduate student Howard Lee purchase a home in an all-white neighborhood. Lee would eventually go on to become mayor of Chapel Hill and one of Smith's closest friends. The next year, Smith's social activity took him back to the basketball court, as Scott enrolled—after a fierce recruiting battle with Lefty Driesell and Davidson—as the first black scholarship athlete at Carolina.

"When we traveled, it was scary how some of the places treated Charlie," said Dick Grubar, who hosted Scott on his recruiting visit and took him to the most liberal and the most conservative fraternities on campus to try and give him an accurate picture of Chapel Hill. "What he went through, no one should have to do. But it was amazing how he handled it. It motivated him to play that much harder."

"It was remarkable how consistent Charlie was," said Jim Delany (1968–70). "He played hard and he was a good leader. He didn't make a big deal to us about the outside stuff. We were aware of it, and so were he and the coaches, but we didn't talk about it much internally. But looking back, an 18- or 19-year-old kid in those circumstances had to be feeling the pressure [because] he was doing something no one had ever done before."

"I made a conscious decision to stay in the South rather than go to the North to play," Scott said. "In the late 1960s, a lot of blacks, including me, were aware of their responsibilities. In those times, if you could do something, you did it. And I wanted to break the color barrier."

Smith made sure he wasn't just tossing Scott into a cauldron of controversy without a well-defined support system. Lee and his wife, Lillian, spent many hours counseling the young Tar Heel at their Chapel Hill home. Howard Lee and Smith had first grown close at Binkley Baptist Church through their work on various community projects. In the late 1960s, the two men worked closely with a local organization in an effort to stimulate a depressed area of western Chapel Hill. The growth of Smith and Lee's relationship mirrored the growth of the community. When they'd first met, it had been a huge step for Lee to buy a home. Less than a decade later, he became Chapel Hill's mayor—the first elected black mayor in a southern town.

Even before he ventured into politics, Lee had a major impact on the town of Chapel Hill and its beloved basketball program: he gave Scott a support system in his new hometown.

"Some people were suggesting to Charlie that he should use his celebrity status to make UNC respond to blacks the way they thought [it] should respond," Lee said. "My advice to him was to endorse a racial issue only if it was good for the masses, not just one single group. I didn't want him to be sucked into a movement that might play a part in reversing the process but painting that reversal as a positive picture."

It was exactly the kind of measured, intelligent advice you'd expect from a member of the Carolina Basketball family—which the Lee family definitely became. Even before his program was on a completely solid foundation, Smith had already found ways to make long-lasting changes in the Chapel Hill landscape. Shortly, he was about to make a similar impact on the basketball world.

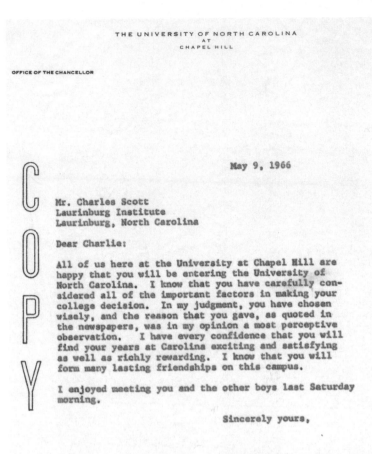

THE UNIVERSITY OF NORTH CAROLINA
AT
CHAPEL HILL

OFFICE OF THE CHANCELLOR

May 9, 1966

Mr. Charles Scott
Laurinburg Institute
Laurinburg, North Carolina

Dear Charlie:

All of us here at the University at Chapel Hill are happy that you will be entering the University of North Carolina. I know that you have carefully considered all of the important factors in making your college decision. In my judgment, you have chosen wisely, and the reason that you gave, as quoted in the newspapers, was in my opinion a most perceptive observation. I have every confidence that you will find your years at Carolina exciting and satisfying as well as richly rewarding. I know that you will form many lasting friendships on this campus.

I enjoyed meeting you and the other boys last Saturday morning.

Sincerely yours,

J. Carlyle Sitterson

JCS:jb

cc: Coach Dean Smith

Chancellor J. Carlyle Sitterson's welcome letter to Charles Scott. (Courtesy North Carolina Collection, UNC–Chapel Hill)

(opposite)

Charles Scott, Carolina's first black scholarship player, earned All-America honors on the court and Academic All-America honors in the classroom. (Photo by Hugh Morton; courtesy North Carolina Collection, UNC–Chapel Hill)

9 : TAR HEELS AT THE TOP

Carolina Basketball would never again be mediocre under Smith's direction. The Tar Heels eventually finished second in the ACC in 1965 and third in 1966. Smith also found success on the recruiting trail, wresting Larry Miller away from Duke in the first big recruiting victory of his tenure.

"The Miller recruitment was when everybody started believing, 'Hey, this guy can coach and he can recruit,'" said longtime Tar Heel radio announcer Woody Durham.

Although Miller was a marquee addition, Smith's first signature recruiting class came before the 1967 season, when he landed guard Dick Grubar and post man Rusty Clark—one of the first true big men to pick the Tar Heels under Smith.

Clark's addition transformed Carolina from a scrappy, undersized team to a group with good size at every position. Instead of having to play Miller at power forward, the Tar Heels now had the ability to complement the scoring of Miller and Bob Lewis with Clark's inside skills and rebounding. The NCAA's freshman ineligibility rules kept Grubar and Clark on the bench in 1966, but after they made their varsity debut in 1967, it was again a trip to Kentucky that proved to be a turning point.

The Tar Heels entered the season with the first top-10 ranking of the Smith era and carried a 3–0 record into Lexington for the meeting with the fourth-ranked Wildcats. Carolina again had good defensive success against a high-scoring UK star, harassing Pat Riley into a 2-for-14 effort. Miller scored 24 points to go with 10 each from Lewis and Clark, and Clark's 11 rebounds helped the Tar Heels dominate the rebounding battle, 41–24. The 64–55 win snapped a four-game, two-season losing streak to ranked programs.

"We still had questions going into that game, especially the sophomores," Grubar said. "We were wondering how good we could be. Going in there and beating Kentucky at Ken-

94

tucky meant we beat a team that we put on a pedestal. When we beat them there, we started thinking, 'We're pretty good.'"

Grubar was right. Carolina eventually climbed as high as second in the country, trailing only the dynasty of UCLA. Miller had his best scoring season as a Tar Heel, averaging 22.4 points per game, and Lewis added 18.5 points per game. Although it was Miller who was perhaps better known, Lewis had set the UNC single-game scoring record (which still stands) with 49 points against Florida State as a junior.

"Larry Miller had just come up from the freshman class," Lewis said about his historic performance. "We had lost Billy Cunningham to graduation. So at that time, I was the main scorer. I just had a hot game. Everything seemed to go in. I got an opportunity to stay in the game more than players today would. I was hot."

Building off a tobacco advertisement, the "L&M Boys" became one of Tobacco Road's best-known hoops combinations. In fact, they became so popular that other tobacco companies surreptitiously complained to UNC about the nickname, thinking that it was providing free advertising to Liggett and Myers. Fans from Miller's hometown of Catasaqua, Pennsylvania, raised $4,000 in advertising to get Carolina games broadcast on a Pennsylvania radio station. The duo even earned a *Sports Illustrated* profile by Frank Deford.

Dick Grubar started on three consecutive Tar Heel teams that won ACC titles and played in the Final Four from 1967 to 1969. (Photo courtesy of UNC Athletic Communications)

Lewis' uniform does not fit as snugly as those of his teammates. He is best described by his father, John Lewis, an electrical engineer, as "poor old skinny Bob." He eats well enough, but "the nervous energy just sort of runs out of me," he says, and his weight seldom goes above 175. His cheeks are hollowed, and his eyes are surrounded by great dark circles; since the eyes are precisely the color of the Carolina-blue ring that he wears, they shine like two mountain lakes in a dark forest. He even stammers a little, just enough to make him more appealing in his deceptively anxious way. Actually, his nervous energy comes out mostly as confidence.

Rusty Clark was a rebounding force in the late 1960s and holds UNC's single-game record for rebounds with 30. (Photo courtesy of UNC Athletic Communications)

Miller, if it is possible, is even more sure of himself, but then his faith is founded on more substantial ground. For if Lewis is the soft pack, Miller is a hard, flip-top box. He has cut his weight to about 200—which serves to make his muscles more revealingly awesome. When he came to Chapel Hill, he favored a motorcycle-rider hairdo—close on top, long sides brushed back (and he had clothes to match)—but now as a junior he wears a proper brushover collegiate cut. Miller is a lefty who parts his hair on the right; Lewis is right-handed and parts his hair on the left. They are also mama's boys, since Mrs. Virginia Lewis played semipro basketball and Mrs. Magdaline Miller played semipro soft-ball.

Miller and Lewis were usually lumped together on the court. Off it, however, they were opposites. "Bobby was a guy with no airs," Jim Delany said. "He could get along with anyone. He was low-key and low-stress. Larry was a different guy. He was very intense. He was still good to his teammates, though."

The pair each possessed some of that only-in-the-sixties earnestness. Delany went home with Miller one Thanksgiving to Catasaqua. With beds at a premium, the All-American superstar slept on the floor because he refused to allow his guest to be uncomfortable. Lewis—moved to the backcourt as a senior after the Grubar, Clark, and Bill Bunting recruiting class had given the Tar Heels more flexibility—saw his shots drop by about six per game.

Smith posted this aphorism in the UNC locker room: "The main ingredient of stardom is the rest of the team."

"I have scored," Lewis said. "I have scored 27 points per game, and that's a lot of points. Now I want to show I can do everything else."

He still flashed his shooting touch when it was needed. Lewis scored 31 points against Boston College in the East Regional final, earning MVP honors and sending Smith to his first Final Four and the Tar Heels to their first Final Four since the 1957 championship season.

Then, even without Lewis, Carolina did it again in 1968, winning the ACC regular-season and tournament titles and advancing to the Final Four. This time, they won the national semifinal matchup before encountering the perpetual champion, UCLA, in the finals. The Bruins won a 78–55 decision. Carolina fans chanted "We'll be back!" Somewhat ominously, UCLA fans responded, "So will we!"

With Grubar, Clark, and Bunting as seniors, plus the addition of Charles Scott, players believed the 1969 team might have been the best of Smith's three straight Final Four squads. Carolina dashed to an 18–1 record in mid-February and climbed to second in the country. They entered the ACC Tournament ranked fourth and advanced to the tournament title game against Duke—where head coach Vic Bubas had just announced his impending retirement. The unranked Blue Devils had just pulled an 87–81 upset of Carolina in the regular-season finale.

Duke jumped to a 43–34 halftime lead, a problem compounded by Grubar's knee injury late in the first half. The injury ended his season and would have major ramifications in the NCAA Tournament.

To advance to the NCAA postseason, however, Carolina would have to first come back against Duke. Sophomore Lee Dedmon contributed 19 points and 11 rebounds off the bench, but the second half belonged to Scott, who made 13 of his 14 field-goal attempts. He finished with 40 points—28 in the second half—and sealed the Tar Heel win with a leaping three-point play over Duke's 6-foot-11 Randy Denton.

The cover of Smith's Basketball: Multiple Offense and Defense.

"With Dick out, I felt like the burden was on me," Scott said. "I started hitting shots and demanding the ball. Sometimes you get into a rhythm where you can't do anything wrong. I felt like everything was going in."

Grubar's absence proved pivotal in the NCAA Tournament. Carolina scraped by Duquesne, 79–78, and survived Davidson, 87–85, on another heroic Scott effort. But without Grubar's sticky defense, Purdue's Rick Mount scored 36 points in the national semifinals, depriving the Tar Heels of another shot at UCLA in the national title game.

One of the golden eras of Carolina Basketball had ended. As the program moved into the 1970s, Smith had guided the Tar Heels from deemphasizing basketball at the start of the decade to being nationally competitive at the end of it. Now came an even tougher challenge: maintaining the excellence.

THE MACHINELIKE CONSISTENCY of the UNC basketball program was in stark contrast to the turmoil affecting the rest of campus. Chapel Hill was a typical college environment in the late 1960s and early 1970s. Game reports from the latest basketball triumph often shared the front page with news of the latest student protests. Civil rights leader Reverend Ralph Abernathy, the president of the Southern Christian Leadership Conference, traveled to Chapel Hill in December 1969 to support striking cafeteria workers, walking arm in arm with picketers. Chapel Hill mayor Howard Lee ordered the Chapel Hill police to leave the campus after officers fought with some of the striking workers.

The front page of the *Daily Tar Heel* on December 7, 1969, contained four main stories: a report on Abernathy's visit, the sale of bus tickets to a Vietnam War protest in Fayetteville, N.C., the addition of three African Studies classes to the UNC course catalog, and a preview of the basketball team's upcoming trip to Kentucky.

In an era when the Black Power salutes of U.S. track stars Tommie Smith and John Carlos at the 1968 Olympics had raised the profile of athletes making social statements, Carolina basketball players were similarly engaged. In the spring of 1969, Scott and Bill Chamberlain appeared onstage at a Black Student Movement (BSM) rally. Amid meetings with Chancellor Carlyle Sitterson, the BSM had become an important campus force. Student Reggie Hawkins had recently told the *Daily Tar Heel* that if Sitterson was not responsive to the BSM's demands for formal recognition, "Our tactics will change from reform to revolutionary." A few days later, Chamberlain addressed the crowd at a BSM rally. Scott was well aware that as a Carolina basketball player, his mere presence carried some significance.

"What Scott and Chamberlain are now doing in connection with BSM will be unpopular in many quarters," Owen Davis wrote in the *Daily Tar Heel*. "They will be branded as troublemakers, as have others in the civil rights movement for years."

But Davis was wrong.

"People were very accepting of me," Chamberlain said. "I was warmly embraced by the current team and the student body. Race was a factor sometimes when we traveled, especially below the Mason-Dixon Line, but if the team had a reservation at a place that wouldn't serve us, Coach Smith would cancel the reservation."

Quietly, Smith was one of the most influential people in the Chapel Hill civil rights movement. He didn't make speeches or stage rallies. Newspapers rarely included his opinion on social matters. But as the head basketball coach, his beliefs mattered. And his beliefs were never in doubt.

"We talked about difficult and controversial issues during my recruiting process," Chamberlain said. "He was very forthright about his position on civil rights and equality of treatment. It wasn't some recruiting scheme for him. His staff, including John Lotz, was the same way. It wasn't just a fad for them."

(opposite)
The L&M Boys: Bob Lewis (right) and Larry Miller starred on Dean Smith's first ACC championship and Final Four teams. (Photo courtesy of UNC Athletic Communications)

Larry Miller, here making a pass against Wake Forest, is one of only four players in ACC history to twice win MVP honors at the ACC Tournament. (Photo by UNC Athletic Communications)

THE ON-COURT SUCCESS was as consistent as the campus was unsettled. The trips to the Final Four earned Smith some recruiting cachet. He was no longer the young coach trying to prove himself. Carolina certainly wasn't on the level of UCLA yet—no one was, as the Bruins were in a stretch of winning 10 national championships in 12 seasons—but they were climbing into the tier of teams that posed an annual threat to the dynasty.

"When I was being recruited, Carolina was coming off several Final Fours," said Mitch Kupchak (1973–76). "It wasn't a program that was just starting out. It was established, and I think Coach Smith had been established as a young coach with a very bright future. From my point of view, it wasn't a question of whether the coach and program were going to be successful. I thought they already were."

Basketball was also becoming an essential part of the Chapel Hill student experience. On February 9, 1968, transfer student Mary Righton wrote an editorial in the *Daily Tar Heel* describing the moment she knew she was a Tar Heel.

It happened to me in the middle of the game. It started out to be another game, another team, another night to be a semi-supporter, a pseudo-fan. I was sitting and yawning. The 26-point lead had killed the excitement of a close game. I realized I was a Tar Heel!

(opposite)
Bob Lewis averaged 27.4 points in 1965–66, the second-highest single-season average in UNC history. (Photo courtesy of UNC Athletic Communications)

This was my team—mine as much as anybody's. It was third best in the nation and it was beating Virginia by 44 points. . . . I wanted to kick everybody that yawned, got bored or left early. I wanted to show them how it feels to suddenly realize you're a part of something like this school.

By 1972, ticket campouts were a regular feature of campus life. In early January of that year, five freshmen girls camped out over 24 hours for tickets to a home game against Wake Forest.

Carolina's ascension suffered two setbacks when Tom McMillen picked Maryland and David Thompson spurned UNC and Duke for NC State. (The Blue Devils and Wolfpack would eventually receive NCAA penalties for incidents in Thompson's recruitment.) Carolina missed the NCAA Tournament in 1970 but won the NIT—in the days when the NIT was a legitimate consolation prize to the NCAA Tournament—in 1971.

"People in Madison Square Garden for the NIT were astounded because of our style of play," Chamberlain said. "We ran and ran, and we played everybody. We'd play 10 or 11 guys and run people into the ground. Then, at time-outs we'd run to the bench. The New York papers were calling us the 'Running Tar Heels.'"

After two more NIT appearances, Carolina survived the Thompson era and returned to the NCAA Tournament in 1975 by virtue of an ACC Tournament championship win over the Wolfpack. They would return every season for the next 27 years, a remarkable string that remains the all-time record.

Smith developed into a coach who was capable of instructing without embarrassing. He was certainly capable of a sharp one-line critique in practice, but his players remember other ways that he made his point.

"We were watching film of a game and I caught a rebound and threw an outlet pass," remembered Ed Stahl (1973–75). "I hit the ground running and passed everybody. It was a pretty good play on my part. Coach Smith said, 'Run it forward, run it back.' I was getting a big head watching this because every time we ran it back, it was a good play. He finally said, 'Stop the film. Turn on the lights.'

"He looked at me and said, 'Ed, that is one of the best moves and the fastest I've ever seen a big guy run on a play.' He's building me up and I'm getting all pumped up. He says, 'Let me ask you a question. Why don't you do that every time?' His point was that he didn't show me Bobby Jones and say, 'Why can't you be like Bobby?' He showed me a benchmark [of my own] excellence, and it was something I had already shown I could do. He never expected more of you than you could give, but he never expected less, either."

Smith reversed the previous recruiting trend by winning a key in-state battle for Phil Ford, who became the first player to start in his first game as a freshman at Carolina (freshmen had become eligible to play in 1972). Ford's outstanding career ended in 1978, but it helped propel the Tar Heels into the 1980s, when two more in-state standouts, James Wor-

(opposite)
Dean Smith and his assistant coaches playing golf with Mildred the Bear. (Photo by Hugh Morton; courtesy North Carolina Collection, UNC–Chapel Hill)

Father, Brother, Friend

After every loss, Coach Smith would take the blame. He never said it was our fault—even though it was, because it was a case of us not executing what we had practiced. But when we won, we were the ones who got the credit. In every game, we always believed that if we did what Coach Smith told us to do, we would win the game.

One of the great tributes to Coach Smith is that no matter how many games he won, he impacted even more people off the basketball court than he did on the court. Even kids whose careers at Carolina didn't work out and transferred to another school, those guys still talk about how much Coach Smith means to them. We all realize how blessed we were to have someone like him in our lives. Yes, he was the best basketball mind and he was teaching us and making us better. But he also cared for us as people. I would talk to players on other teams, and their relationships with their coaches were different. Coach Smith was that stern teacher who also really cares for you.

There was nothing I was embarrassed to go to Coach Smith about. I'd go by his office just to talk. It was not unusual for me to spend an hour in there when I was playing. We didn't just talk about basketball. We could talk about anything. We'd talk about music or race relations. I enjoyed being around our coaches. Guys at other schools sometimes would tell me they didn't like their coaches. I didn't understand that. Why would you go to school somewhere you didn't like being around the coaches? Not everybody can be as lucky as a Carolina basketball player, I guess.

I can't put his impact on me into words. I don't know where I'd be without him in my life. He's been such an influence—a friend, a brother, and a father figure. But it's not just me who feels that way. All the guys who played for him would tell you the same thing. Way back when I was being recruited, my mom told me it would be that way. She thought Coach Smith would be a friend for life. Women have that intuition, and I'm happy to say she was exactly right. He's been a friend to me and much more.—*Phil Ford*

thy and Michael Jordan, brought Smith his first national title in 1982. By then, UCLA's dynasty was a distant memory and Carolina was perched on top of the college basketball landscape.

Given the significant changes that had preceded it (conference realignments, freshman ineligibility, rules changes) and would follow it (media-coverage explosion, even more conference realignments), the era from the mid-1970s to mid-1980s was a relatively stable time. Part of that stability could be found at the top of the ACC, where Carolina won the league regular-season or tournament title in 10 of the 11 seasons from 1975 through 1985.

Similarly, basketball settled in as a centerpiece of the town of Chapel Hill. By the mid-1970s, town administrators were forced to plan for basketball in the way that other towns planned for Fourth of July parades or holiday events. The difference was that basketball seized control of the town 10 or 15 times per season for home games, plus must-watch road games and postseason events. Parking was a constant concern; accommodating the thousands of fans streaming into town became an important issue both for visitors and for year-round residents. The town of Chapel Hill and the University of North Carolina were created on the same day—October 12, 1793, when lots were sold and the cornerstone was laid for Old East. Smith once famously commented, "Athletics is to the university what the front porch is to a home. It is the most visible part, yet certainly not the most important." Maybe not, but nearly 200 years after the the town and school were created, basketball had gained the most prominent place on Chapel Hill's front porch.

Players became local celebrities largely because they were so familiar. In an era when many schools set up athletic dormitories, Tar Heel basketball players lived in Avery Dorm or Granville Towers, mixed in with their classmates. They played on intramural sports teams—the basketball team fielded a particularly formidable softball team in the early 1980s—and hit all the Franklin Street hot spots. Even Marvin Williams, in his only season as a

Tar Heel, spent most of his freshman year riding a bike around campus like a typical college freshman.

On the court, even with the advent of rules that detractors predicted would lead to the downfall of the Tar Heels—Smith was incorrectly seen as being an opponent of the three-point shot and shot clock, when in fact his teams used the three-pointer more effectively than most teams in the league—the reign continued. Facing an uncharacteristic Final Four drought that stretched from 1982 to 1991, Smith went out and landed one of the best recruiting classes in school history. The group that arrived on campus in the fall of 1990, which included Pat Sullivan, Brian Reese, Derrick Phelps, Eric Montross, and Clifford Rozier, would team with a core of talented seniors—Rick Fox, King Rice, and Pete Chilcutt—to return Carolina to the Final Four in 1991. Two years later, the freshmen-turned-juniors would make another Final Four trip, this time claiming a national title.

"The best part of playing for Carolina in those days was you always knew somebody was going to step up and take a big shot or be willing to guard the best player on the other team," said Kevin Madden (1986, 1988–90). "Just about every guy on the team was a high school All-American. So that means you were the best player in your area. And you bring all those guys in from different areas with different attitudes and different backgrounds, and Coach Smith molded them into one unit that wasn't concerned about stats."

WHILE PLAYERS CAME TO AND LEFT Chapel Hill in four-year bursts, Smith had extraordinary success in building the stability of his coaching staff. He'd shown a talent for picking assistant coaches from the very beginning. Ken Rosemond—who would go on to become head coach at Georgia—was a key part of Smith's first UNC staff. Donnie Walsh was also an early assistant; he was replaced by Larry Brown for two seasons in the mid-1960s.

"I always knew I wanted to coach," Brown said. "I had a good background, because I had a great high school coach and I played for Coach McGuire. What I found when I became a head coach was that everything I was doing I learned when I was Coach Smith's assistant. The values I learned from Coach Smith were the things I believed in. When I became coach of the freshman team, I found that the things I was trying to express to those young players were the things I had learned from Coach Smith. To this day, nothing has changed.

"Every day, I write on the board, 'Play hard, play unselfishly, play smart, and have fun.' Then I always end with, 'Let's rebound and defend a little bit.' Those are things Coach Smith instilled in me. He would challenge you. He was very fair and probably the greatest innovator in our sport."

After Brown left Carolina, a revolving assistant-coaching door was closed by the arrival of Bill Guthridge. A fellow Kansan, Guthridge was the perfect complement to Smith. His dry humor added some levity to the Tar Heel program; it wasn't unusual for him to respond "Hello, Player" to a player who greeted him in the hall with "Hey, Coach."

But Guthridge, who joined John Lotz—an eventual SEC Coach of the Year at the Univer-

*Dean Smith
talks to his team
during a time-out.
(Photo courtesy of
UNC Athletic
Communications)*

sity of Florida—on the UNC staff, was more than just a comedian. He earned a reputation as one of the best big-man coaches in college basketball, turning a parade of sometimes-gawky Tar Heels into solid contributors.

"When you think back, it's funny because he helped so many big men but he wasn't a big man," said Stahl. "It was kind of funny. He'd box you out, but instead of his butt coming at you where a normal competitor's would, his would be at my knees. He was always anxious and willing to spend time with the big guys. You knew he would always work with you."

In 1978 Guthridge nearly left Carolina to accept the head-coaching job at Penn State. But just as he prepared to tell his team, the Tar Heels lost to San Francisco in the NCAA Tournament. He couldn't bear to leave Chapel Hill under those conditions, with Phil Ford graduating and a new host of rivals eager to topple the Fordless Tar Heels. So he apologized to the Nittany Lions and turned down the job, while also deciding he'd been on his last head-coaching interview.

"Penn State was a good situation," Guthridge said. "But I already had a better job than that and I was happy here. So why leave?"

His decision highlighted a deep love for the program and for Smith that most of the public had never realized. When Smith was ejected from the 1991 Final Four scmifinal game against Kansas, it was Guthridge who rebuked the offending official in a tunnel of the Hoosier Dome after the game. And when Lefty Driesell declined to shake Smith's hand after a particularly tough Maryland win over the Tar Heels, it was Guthridge who was the most incensed.

Guthridge's loyalty preserved arguably the best coaching staff in Carolina history. From 1979 through 1986, the Carolina staff included Smith, Guthridge, Eddie Fogler, and Roy Williams. All four would eventually earn at least one National Coach of the Year award as a head coach.

"Everything I do on the basketball court and everything I do with the players, I was taught by Coach Smith, Coach Guthridge, and Coach Fogler," Williams said. "I was taught to run a program, not just coach a team."

AS BROWN SAID, the architect of those staffs was an innovator. By the end of Smith's career, he was sometimes characterized as the rigid dictator of the Carolina system, but that label is not accurate. Smith created the tired signal, the Four Corners, huddles at the foul line, and pointing to the passer after made baskets. *Basketball: Multiple Offenses and Defenses*, a coaching textbook he authored that remains relevant three decades later, is perfectly titled because of the way it captures his philosophy. Call a time-out to game-plan against Smith and it was entirely likely he'd change his offense or defense during the time-out.

But the beauty of Smith's coaching came in the final two minutes of a game, which often seemed to last forever. He would hoard his time-outs, of course, saving them until they were most necessary. Late-game comebacks became a Carolina signature. Opponents sometimes

The Meaning of Argyle

I have the perhaps dubious distinction of being the only person in college basketball who had to try out in the pros first. I had designed the uniforms for the NBA's Charlotte Hornets two years before Dean Smith called and asked me about designing uniforms for Carolina. As I have often said, it was like God phoning from heaven to say, "We need new halos for the archangels." If I screwed it up, I knew I could never go home again.

The first step was to think about fabric. A lot of the players were wearing T-shirts underneath their jerseys in those days, and that's because the jerseys were like sandpaper. I wanted a material that would be comfortable but that also had a wicking capability.

Many people don't realize that we also changed the color. In those days, Carolina wore "TV Blue." It wasn't Carolina blue. Because of the primitive color reception on television sets in the late 1970s and early 1980s, the team had changed to a deeper color because Carolina blue almost looked gray on television. But by the time I was working on the jerseys, television sets had improved enough that you could show the real color. That's how we changed back to a true Carolina blue.

I have a long history of using argyles as a signature motif. It's a timeless design that appeals to men and women simultaneously. What I was looking for with the uniforms was something timeless, fashionable and something that represented what Carolina was: a class act.

With the design, I was sending ideas from my studio in Connecticut to Chapel Hill and also to Chicago—for Michael Jordan. We had three or four conference calls with Coach Smith and Michael when we would discuss what we had in front of us. Michael liked the argyle and so did Dean. It didn't hurt that Michael endorsed it or advocated for it.

It turned out to be something kind of lucky for me. The most pervasive point about the argyle was that it was classy and timeless, and it was different from what anybody else was doing.—*Alexander Julian*

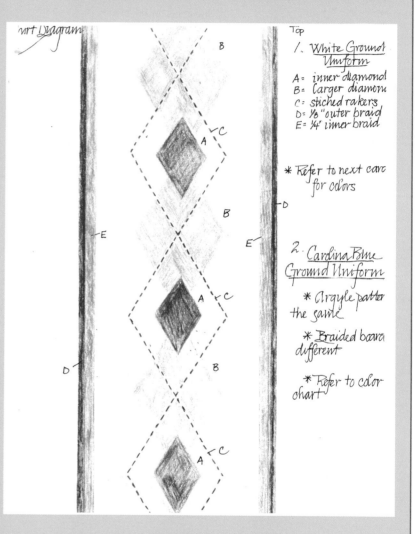

Court Diagram

Top

1. White Ground Uniform
A = inner diamond
B = larger diamond
C = stiched rakers
D = 1/8" outer braid
E = 1/4" inner braid

* Refer to next card for colors

2. Carolina Blue Ground Uniform

* Argyle pattern the same

* Braided board different

* Refer to color chart

Sketch of UNC uniform designs by Alexander Julian.

called them lucky. But as a pattern began to emerge, it became obvious that good fortune wasn't the only thing at work.

In 1967 Utah built a 17-point second-half lead against the Tar Heels in the Far West Classic. Mixing defenses and getting timely baskets from Charles Scott, Larry Miller, and Dick Grubar, Carolina came all the way back for an 84–82 win. It was the first of what became

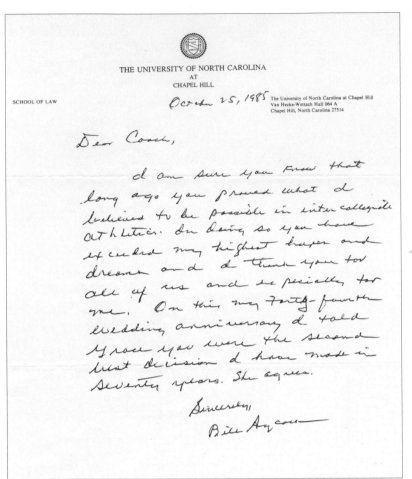

THE UNIVERSITY OF NORTH CAROLINA
AT
CHAPEL HILL

SCHOOL OF LAW

October 25, 1985

The University of North Carolina at Chapel Hill
Van Hecke-Wettach Hall 064 A
Chapel Hill, North Carolina 27514

Dear Coach,

I am sure you know that long ago you proved what I believed to be possible in intercollegiate athletics. In doing so you have exceeded my highest hopes and dreams and I thank you for all of us and especially for me. On this my forty-fourth wedding anniversary I told Grace you were the second best decision I have made in seventy years. She agrees.

Sincerely,
Bill Aycock

Letter from former chancellor William Aycock to Dean Smith, October 1985. (Courtesy North Carolina Collection, UNC–Chapel Hill)

almost regular comeback occurrences. Scott did it again in the 1969 ACC Tournament final, then beat Davidson almost single-handedly the next weekend. Two months before the famous 8-points-in-17-seconds game, Carolina needed a steal and a layup from Bobby Jones to beat the Blue Devils at Cameron Indoor Stadium. In 1975 Ford, Kupchak, and Walter Davis helped eliminate an 8-point deficit to Wake Forest in 50 seconds.

Even today, you can feel an impending sense of doom in opposing arenas when the home team builds a lead against Carolina. It's jubilation at the lead . . . but also a bit of foreboding. The run, you can feel them thinking, is coming.

"We were all in awe of Coach Smith," Ford said. "We thought he was the greatest thing in coaching. We always thought that if we did what Coach Smith told us to do, we would win the game. He was so cool and calm. I've never seen anything like that in my whole life. There was nothing that could happen in a basketball game that we hadn't practiced. He'd come up with these scenarios in practice and I'd think, 'No way this could happen in a game.' But then it would come up later, and we had already worked on it."

As Smith built the program, the Tar Heels eventually reached the status of perennial favorites. They rarely had the opportunity to be underdogs, but when they did, they were perhaps even more dangerous than when they were favored. In 1987 a depleted Carolina team upset top-ranked Syracuse in the season opener. In 1988, with most of the college basketball world infatuated with Loyola Marymount's high-octane offense, the Tar Heels blistered them, 123–97, in an NCAA second-round game. In 1990 eighth-seeded Carolina upset top-ranked Oklahoma in the second round of the NCAA Tournament. And in 1995, with Kentucky head coach Rick Pitino already planning his team's postgame celebration party, the Tar Heels won a trip to the Final Four with a 74–61 victory in front of a partisan Wildcat crowd in Birmingham.

"When your coach is calm and collected, it wears off on you," said Antawn Jamison (1996–98). "In practice, he might have gotten on us. But at game time, no matter how good or bad things were going, he stayed even-keeled. He'd draw something up and you would think, 'Will that work?' And then in the game it would work every time."

"We had practiced so many situations," Pete Chilcutt said. "In that Syracuse game, he was

"If I could go up and sky and dunk one, I'd scream, too," Dean Smith said of Rasheed Wallace's reactions—this one to a dunk against NCAA rival Kentucky in the 1995 NCAA Tournament. (Photo by Doug Behar; courtesy of UNC Athletic Communications)

sitting over there rubbing his hands together saying, 'Isn't this fun?' When the coach acts that way, it gives you a better comfort level as a player. I never saw him lose his calm or not know what to do. He relished situations where we had to do something in the final 30 seconds of a game."

During Smith's head-coaching career, his teams won 102 games by three points or less. Almost two-thirds of the time that a Smith-coached team played a game decided by three points or less, they won it.

"What we figured out was that late in the game, you better listen to him," said Buzz Peterson. "His mind was three or four minutes ahead of the game. You knew he had everything planned out, so just do what he asked. He'd get out the pen and paper, and your job was to follow your line as best you could."

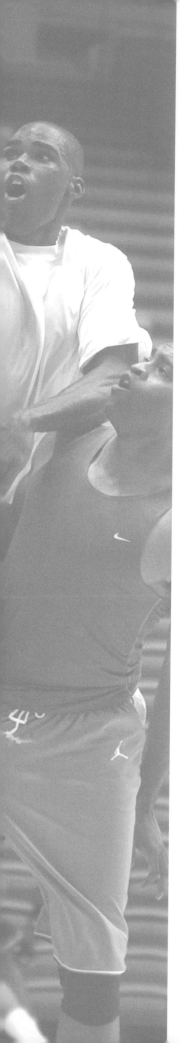

10 : FAMILY ACROSS THE DECADES

Dean Smith's technical knowledge of basketball was widely respected. He was a brilliant coach and an unsurpassed recruiter. Year in and year out, he brought a bevy of quality players to Chapel Hill and formed them into an outstanding team. And fan support for Carolina, of course, was consistently tremendous.

The numbers show, however, that UCLA has more national championships than UNC. Kentucky does, too. And James Naismith, the inventor of the game, coached at Kansas—another traditional hoops powerhouse.

What is it, then, that separates North Carolina from these and other historically elite basketball programs across the nation? Is there one characteristic that sets Carolina Basketball apart, defines it as something much more than a long series of highly successful teams?

Many believe that there is, and they point to Smith as the person who put it in place.

"The thing that's different about Carolina is that when we talk about a family, it's not just talk," said Phil Ford. "It is a real feeling of togetherness. I never played with Lennie Rosenbluth, but when we get together we have a good time. I enjoy meeting the newest freshmen. I like welcoming them to North Carolina and telling them how happy I am that they're part of our team. It's important for people to know how close-knit our basketball family is."

There's that word—family. It can't be quantified in a stat sheet or a record book, but it's possibly the most important trait of Carolina Basketball. Those of us who are Tar Heel fans assume that everywhere is like Chapel Hill. Former players come back for summer pickup games on all campuses, right? No matter where they might live in the United States, former players always make an effort to come to the game whenever their school plays nearby. The head coach always takes the time to visit with any former player who comes to town. These

Dozens of former players turned out at the 2009 Final Four in Detroit, including Phil Ford, Makhtar Ndiaye, and Julius Peppers, shown here at the 2009 pro alumni game. (Photo by Jeffrey A. Camarati)

traditions seem obvious to us, as fundamental to building a basketball program as hiring assistant coaches, recruiting players, and making sure the basketballs are filled with air.

But here's the real truth: other schools are different.

"It's absolutely different," said Mitch Kupchak, who deals with programs across the country in his role as general manager of the Los Angeles Lakers. "I run into people who come from storied programs, and we'll get into heated debates about whether UCLA or Indiana or Carolina is the better program. But I think most people that have gone through college basketball look at Carolina and get a feeling that something special goes on there."

"I'm pretty sure people from outside Carolina hate the Carolina Family," Michael Jordan said. "They don't understand the unity and bond that is established in the short time you are at the University of North Carolina. You leave there, and you find yourself taking care of family members. It's hard for people who haven't been a part of it to understand it. But as long as those of us within it understand, it's something we will cherish no matter what happens to us or where we go."

That's what compelled numerous Tar Heels, including Vince Carter (1996–98), Antawn

National Players of the Year Lennie Rosenbluth (1957) and Sean May (2005) at a lettermen's reunion in Chapel Hill. (Photo by Robert Crawford)

Jamison, Julius Peppers (2000–2001), and others, to make a special effort to journey to Detroit for Carolina's thumping of Michigan State in the 2009 national championship game. It's what prompted nearly 100% participation in the program's first-ever professional alumni game in September 2009. Not only did players flock back to Chapel Hill, but most of them also stayed an extra day or two. Carter, Jamison, Ademola Okulaja (1996–99), and Makhtar Ndiaye (1997–98) spent time just strolling down Franklin Street, reflecting on how things had—and hadn't—changed since their last visit.

The alumni game happened to coincide with the annual coaching-tree summit in Chapel Hill. Since the Smith era, all the coaches in the Carolina Family have convened for a day or two of hard-core basketball discussion. Everyone from longtime head coach Larry Brown to practically brand-new assistant coach Wes Miller (2005–07) returned.

The coaches met from 8:00 A.M. to 5:00 P.M., breaking down a series of concepts and ideas for the upcoming season. It's not a lecture-oriented event, with one coach presenting to the group. Instead, it's more like a forum, with Roy Williams throwing out a topic—how to defend a screen on the ball, for example—and everyone offering suggestions.

When the session ended, all the eligible coaches—current Tar Heel coaches weren't allowed due to NCAA rules—walked down to the Smith Center court, where a host of former players had convened for pickup games. Usually, those games are competitive. Since Williams's return to Chapel Hill, he has emphasized the importance of competing in every situation, and the annual summer-camp games that match current players against former players have become battles. This time, though, the game was secondary to the reunion. Along the sidelines, Matt Doherty was hugging Jackie Manuel (2002–05), and John Kuester was catching up with Sean May (2003–05). Even the players who weren't particularly well acquainted greeted each other with a hug.

"There is no place like this," Brown said. "The relationships we have with one another, the loyalty we have to players and coaches that have been here is unsurpassed. I've been able to participate in a lot of NBA All-Star games. Because of the relationships we've been able to have, there's always a sense of pride among the Carolina guys there. And there's a sense of envy among everyone else."

The cornerstone of the Carolina Family is Dean Smith. It began immediately upon his ar-

National champion point guards Ty Lawson and Raymond Felton joke during the 2009 pro alumni game in the Smith Center. (Photo by J.D. Lyon Jr.)

rival in Chapel Hill, before he had even manned the bench for his first game as head coach. One of Frank McGuire's players, Harvey Salz, had completed his eligibility in 1960 and wanted to continue his basketball career. Smith contacted an AAU team in Denver and sent clippings and photos of Salz. A few days later, the team offered a contract.

"Coach Smith was the guy who did that for me," Salz said. "I didn't think I was good enough to play pro ball in those days. But he went out of his way to try and help me."

Some of Smith's personal and intellectual gifts were natural. His phenomenal memory enabled him to recall names and ages of his players' wives and children decades after the players had departed Chapel Hill. But he also worked at it. When other coaches were on the golf course or taking a weekend at the beach, Smith was signing letters or mailing media guides.

"What's so hard to replicate is the time it takes to create the family feeling," said Eddie Fogler (1968–70), who went on to serve as head coach at three different schools. "He spent

Michael Jordan visited a UNC practice in 2004 and posed with Roy Williams and Dean Smith. (Photo by Jeffrey A. Camarati)

so much time putting the pieces together into building that feeling. No one has created that kind of family concept that sustained itself over a long period of time."

Smith made a habit of going out of his way during his coaching career. When Charles Scott was contemplating breaking the scholarship-athlete color barrier at Carolina, Smith brought him to church with him on his recruiting visit to allow him to get a feel for the reception he might receive in town. As Scott noted, none of the other coaches recruiting him did the same thing.

A man with many demands on his time, Smith made it clear that current or former players were at the top of his priority list. Basketball-office staffers knew that the coach could be interrupted in any meeting if a player needed his help with a problem. Numerous lettermen say they wouldn't make a key decision in their lives without consulting him first.

"I wasn't even a player when Coach Smith did the greatest thing he ever did for me," said Brad Hoffman (1973–75). "My wife and I experienced the loss of a child. We were really struggling financially and mentally and physically. We were living in California, but Coach Smith stepped in—all the way across the country—and helped support us in many ways. This was two years after I left the program, and he was still there. It's the first thing I think about when I think about Coach Smith. He impacted the life of myself and my family more than he'll ever know."

Smith's attention to his former players wasn't limited to emergencies. When Mitch Kupchak arrives at the office on the first day of the NBA season, he knows a fax will be waiting for him from the Carolina Basketball office. It's been there every year of his NBA career—just a few short words wishing him luck in the new season and letting him know that someone back in Chapel Hill is paying attention.

Every year, every letterman gets a media guide and a letter thanking him for his contribution to the program. Ticket requests, even for the toughest games, are usually honored. It's Roy Williams at the head of the organization now, but he's following the same principles he was taught by Smith. As Williams said at his introductory UNC press conference, "I was taught to run a program, not just coach a team."

"I think Coach Smith genuinely cares about his players," Mike Cooke said. "He cares about what they're doing. He cares about their careers. He keeps in touch. Every year of my life, I've gotten a letter or a note from him. And it's not just me getting those. It's everybody."

The continuity created by passing the coaching reins from Smith to Guthridge to Doherty to Williams is an essential aspect of the Carolina program. Since 1961, and with only a few exceptions, players who have played for UNC have had the same experiences. They've been

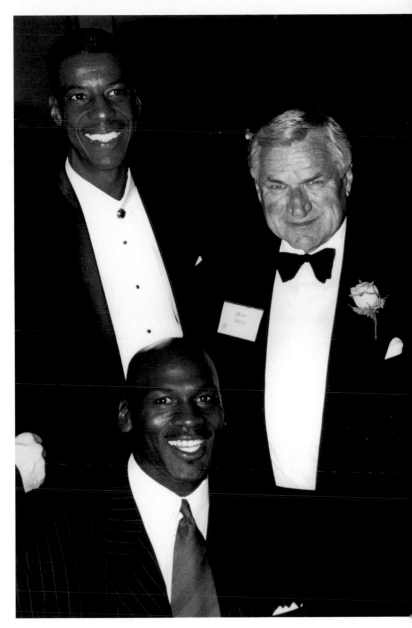

Tar Heels from different eras: Charles Scott and Michael Jordan are united by Dean Smith and the Carolina Family.
(Photo by Hugh Morton; courtesy North Carolina Collection, UNC–Chapel Hill)

taught the same fundamentals, been through the same practice drills. When they get together, all of those experiences are the common language that allows them to speak the same way to a player who came decades before them as they would to one of their teammates.

"When someone gets here as a freshman, I know immediately what they're going through," Brian Reese said. "I know what they're trying to build. As soon as the new class comes in, we show them how to respect the program and understand the way we do things here. We look out for each other. Whether a guy was on the 1957 team or the 2009 team, I can honestly say I have some kind of relationship with them. We know each other and we respect each other, and we look out for our own."

Ironically, it's often the current players who have the least understanding of the value of the Carolina Family. They're too close—or perhaps too young—to see it or fully understand it. It's the only college basketball experience they've known, so to them it may seem almost routine.

Roy Williams casts an especially wide recruiting net, with the West Coast connections he built at Kansas providing a Pacific time zone recruiting bed more developed than any previous Carolina coach. Already under Williams, four West Coast players—Marvin Williams (Bremerton, Wash.), Deon Thompson (Torrance, Calif.), Quentin Thomas (Oakland, Calif.), and Larry Drew II (Encino, Calif.)—have earned national championship rings.

The new recruiting territory gave Carolina a nationwide flavor it had rarely had before. But it also required some indoctrination into the value of Tar Heel basketball.

"It's been an education for me," said Thompson. "Growing up, I knew James Worthy because he played for the Lakers. When I got here, I started to learn more about Phil Ford, Mitch Kupchak, and many of the other great players from previous years. I'm thankful to be part of this history."

Even as they learn about the players who came before them, current Tar Heels don't always understand the value it will have for them later in life. When Danny Green, Ty Lawson, and Wayne Ellington tested the waters of the NBA Draft after the 2008 season, they did so because they wanted to research their professional stock. Eventually, all three discovered they would be better served by coming back to college.

But part of the draft research process involved visiting numerous NBA teams, conducting

Marvin Williams was the ACC Rookie of the Year and the second pick of the NBA Draft in 2005. (Photo by Peyton Williams)

(opposite)
Jordan and Worthy returned to play an NBA exhibition game in the Smith Center in October 1986. (Photo by Sally Sather)

interviews with front-office personnel, and going through workouts for coaching staffs. That's when the trio realized what their pedigree meant.

"Everywhere you go, people say, 'Here comes a Carolina guy,'" Ellington said. "They would always tell us how Carolina is taking over the NBA. It's really cool to be part of the Carolina Family when you go into the pro world, because everybody knows you as a Carolina guy."

"I didn't realize how big the Carolina Family was until I went through that," Green said. "It seemed like everyone I talked to was either from Carolina, graduated from Carolina, or knew somebody from Carolina. Everyone knows who you are when you're from Carolina. It let me know how deep the family goes and how widespread it is throughout the nation."

In the era of one-and-done superstars, it's reasonable to wonder if that same family feeling can be preserved. Part of the feeling was built on the natural progression of a Carolina basketball player through his four years at UNC. As a freshman, you chase down the loose balls during practice and pickup games (yes, they still do that). By the time you're a senior, you're the one who delights in yelling "Freshman!" when the ball rolls out of bounds.

In an unusual twist, however, it's often those who leave early who seem to have the deepest attachment to Chapel Hill. It's almost as if by giving up their last year of eligibility (or two years, or three), they've gained a richer understanding of what they missed. Jerry Stackhouse (1994–95) and Antawn Jamison, who departed for the NBA in the mid-1990s, graduated on the same day in 2000. On May 20, 2001, Vince Carter attended his UNC graduation in Chapel Hill. Later that day, he played in game seven of an NBA playoff series against the Philadelphia 76ers. One-year players Brandan Wright and Marvin Williams both returned for the alumni game in 2009, and Williams has spent part of every offseason in Chapel Hill attending classes and training with strength coach Jonas Sahratian.

"When I got to the NBA, what I found out was that everyone else wants to ask about Carolina," Jamison said. "They ask lots of questions about it. 'How do you guys have that family thing? What's so special about Carolina?' Sometimes it's hard to explain. It's the guys who

*Antawn Jamison
and Vince Carter
played pickup
hoops in the
Smith Center the
day before the
2009 pro alumni
game. (Photo by
Jeffrey A. Camarati)*

"If you're a Carolina guy, you've been taught the right way and you know the fundamentals," said Jerry Stackhouse.

(Photo by Doug Behar; courtesy of UNC Athletic Communications)

played before me and the guys who are playing now. We all realize we went through the same things. We wore that 'North Carolina' on our jersey and every single person was treated the same way.

"When you're in college, you appreciate it because it's fun. But when you leave, you appreciate it because you realize the bond you have with your teammates is the same bond you'll have with the guys who came before and after you."

"When you're going through it as a freshman, you don't understand why Coach Smith is making you run stairs with a weighted vest on your back," George Lynch (1990–93) said. "You don't understand why when the pros come back it's so competitive. You think it's just another hell week. But when you're finished, you've left the blood and the sweat on the floor and you appreciate and value what you went through. Guys before you and after you will go through the same thing. When you watch Carolina games, you see them playing the same way you played. That means more to me than anything. I can sit with my son, and if I'm trying to explain how to play good basketball, we turn on a Carolina game."

The Tar Heels who play in the NBA are only the most visible members of the family. Outsiders may hear Jordan or Ford or Tyler Hansbrough praise the Carolina Way and mistakenly believe their goodwill exists because they were superstars. The truth is that the same treatment is afforded a player who has a career scoring total of two points as one with his jersey in the rafters.

"It is such a unique feeling," said Bill Harrison (1964), who made exactly one basket in his Carolina career before giving up his scholarship to focus on academic endeavors. "It becomes more unique as you get older because you realize Carolina is unusual in its culture. Coach Smith embraced very strongly the idea of staying in touch with lettermen and making them feel part of the tradition. The basketball relationship transcends a whole lot of things in terms of a connection with the university. Chancellors retire and professors move on, but basketball remains an anchor point. They stay in touch with you, and everyone wants to be part of a family like that."

Former players know they've gotten something from the program, but they also feel an obligation to give something back. In 2002 the Tar Heels were going through what would eventually become the worst season in program history. Any chance at an ACC title was gone. The NCAA Tournament was out of the question. Even an NIT appearance was impossible.

With Carolina sitting at an unthinkable 6–16, longtime basketball staffer Kay Thomas had one of her regular phone conversations with Mike Cooke. The pair commiserated about the pounding the program was taking in the press, and finally they decided to do something about it. With a home game against Florida State in less than a week, Cooke began to make calls to lettermen to round up a group willing to attend the game and make a visible sign of support for the current players, who had begun to feel that they might be letting down the program.

By game day, 13 players—Cooke, Joe Brown, Bill Bunting, Dave Colescott, Jeff Denny, Eric Harry, Kim Huband, Jim Hudock, Kevin Madden, Warren Martin, Mike Pepper, Ray Respess, and Al Wood—had come to Chapel Hill, some traveling across several states to be there. They addressed the team in the locker room before the game. The gesture both encouraged the young players and strengthened their bond with the past, which had grown somewhat shaky.

"Coach Smith would constantly talk about some of the older guys when I played," Matt Doherty said. "He would stop practice and say that Bobby Jones was the best he'd ever seen at reversing the basketball at the top of the key or that Mitch Kupchak worked so hard in practice. Deep down, you wanted to be one of those guys. You wanted to be talked about in that light when your career was finished."

Roy Williams and Billy Cunningham at the Celebration of a Century reunion in February 2010. (Photo by Jeffrey A. Camarati)

The message connected with the current Tar Heels, who posted a win over Florida State in front of the alums.

"For those guys to be there and tell us they believed in us and showed the loyalty and what a family it is to be part of Carolina Basketball, it made everything worthwhile," Jason Capel said. "As long as everybody who has put on that Carolina uniform is loyal to you, that's all that matters."

It's that belief that forms the core of the Carolina Family. In animated conversations, former players may jab each other about accomplishments or championships or banners. That's what family members do. But the foundation of their relationship is built on mutual respect and an understanding of a common experience.

"The Carolina Family is so much a part of my identity as a person," said Bill Chambers

More than 100 former players honored Coach Smith by joining him at center court at the Celebration of a Century event on February 12, 2010. (Photo by Jeffrey A. Camarati)

(1973–76), now a high school coach. "I've tried to impart the knowledge Coach Smith and Coach Guthridge gave me. I've tried to do things the Carolina Way. Real families don't seem to exist anymore, but it exists at Carolina. It's genuine."

"Carolina was the best four years of my life," said Walter Davis. "Playing for Coach Smith, going to the University of North Carolina, playing in Carmichael. All of that was awesome. And the best thing was that I got an education from the University of North Carolina and I shared experiences with coaches and players. The Carolina Family means everything to me."

11 : 1982

MAKING LEGENDS

n a famous Nike commercial released late in his NBA career, Michael Jordan offered some insight into his personal motivation.

"I've missed more than 9,000 shots in my career," intoned Jordan's voice-over as images of the superstar arriving at an arena played across the screen. "I've lost almost 300 games. Twenty-six times I've been trusted to take the game-winning shot and missed. I've failed over and over and over again in my life, and that is why I succeed."

Sure, by that time, Jordan had a half dozen world-championship rings, so we all recognized that if he missed his next game-winning shot opportunity, it wouldn't diminish his legend. Once upon a time, though, he had to take his *first* big shot—the first one with a national-television audience watching and the important outcome resting only on his fingertips. Win or lose, hero or goat—all would be determined by whether the ball dropped through the 18-inch-diameter rim. If he'd failed on that first try, perhaps, the consequences for Jordan—and for many other people—would have been very different.

In 1982 Dean Smith was two decades into his Chapel Hill tenure. John Wooden had retired at UCLA after the 1974–75 season. That left Smith, Indiana's Bobby Knight, and Louisville's Denny Crum as college basketball's coaching elite. Smith had already guided Carolina to six Final Fours. Just one year earlier, the Tar Heels had advanced to the national championship game. Playing on a strange day that also saw an assassination attempt against President Ronald Reagan, Carolina lost to Knight's Hoosiers, 63–50.

This was the era before the Internet and nonstop sports talk radio. But it was one of the golden ages of newspaper columnists, and a popular sentiment had begun to emerge about Carolina's head coach: for all his attributes and accomplishments, Dean Smith couldn't win

The 1982 team huddles. (Photo by Hugh Morton; courtesy North Carolina Collection, UNC–Chapel Hill)

the big one. It's hard for Tar Heel fans of the twenty-first century to appreciate just how widespread that belief was among non–Tar Heels in the late 1970s and early 1980s. As early as April 1977, following a disappointing Carolina loss to Marquette in the NCAA finals, a *Gastonia Gazette* editorial speculated that Smith might be overpaid at $100,000 per year.

The Four Corners offense employed in that loss was a late-seventies and early-eighties flash point. Tar Heels saw it as making the best use of the rules to win the game; opponents saw it as a maddening stall. In the summer of 1977, Cleveland Cavaliers head coach Bill Fitch said, "I've seen so much of the four-corner stall I've become nauseated. It's spreading like a cancer. It doesn't take any skill to play it. You can take kids off the street and teach it to them in a few minutes. It's not a game. It's not basketball." A few months later, when the Tar Heels defeated sixth-ranked Cincinnati, 67–59, Bearcats head coach Gale Catlett (a good friend of Virginia coach Terry Holland, an outspoken opponent of the Four Corners) said, "If Carolina had played ball in the last seven minutes, instead of the Four Corners, we would have won."

The detractors' theory was that the strategy somehow made Smith a lesser coach, unable to aggressively force the action in the biggest games. That theory conveniently overlooked one key achievement of Smith's career. He had been handpicked to coach the 1976 U.S. Olympic team. That was the squad that followed the 1972 team's controversial loss in Munich. In an era when the Olympics dominated the sports world—which was much less saturated with a variety of sports options—the head coach of the Olympic basketball team in an absolute must-win situation had one of the most pressure-packed jobs in athletics. In the 1970s, the Olympics were not only a test of physical competition but also a referendum on the political and social worth of the participating countries. Losing another gold medal in a sport invented in America would have been as damaging to the United States as the 1980 hockey loss was to the Soviet Union.

To help win back the gold in Montreal, Smith stocked his roster with four Tar Heels—Phil Ford, Tom LaGarde, Walter Davis, and Mitch Kupchak—and three other Atlantic Coast Conference representatives. Bill Guthridge, as usual, was a member of the coaching staff. The squad's only near upset was a 95–94 win over Puerto Rico, and the Americans won the gold medal with a 95–77 victory over Canada.

"People said we weren't old enough or tough enough to compete," Ford said. "But I knew our guys. I knew how tough they were. If there was someone tougher than them, I didn't want to see them.

"At Carolina, we always talked about doing the best we could, and that if we did the best we could, winning would probably be the outcome. The Olympics was the only time that Coach Smith ever talked solely about winning. We all understood that winning was the only thing that would make that team successful."

So Smith obviously was capable of winning the biggest of "big ones"—when victory was the only possible option. But by 1982, the Olympic triumph was a distant memory for the

The emotion of a 1 versus-2 victory over Virginia in 1982 is etched on the faces of (from left) Michael Jordan, Sam Perkins, Jim Braddock, Matt Doherty, and James Worthy. (Photo by Manny Millan, Sports Illustrated/ Getty Images)

national sporting public. It had been replaced by Carolina's 1977 upset by Marquette in the national title game—a Marquette team led by Butch Lee, the same player who'd nearly engineered Puerto Rico's Olympic upset—and 1981's disappointment against Indiana.

By the time Carolina arrived in New Orleans for a Final Four matchup with Houston, Smith's championship quest had become a dominant story line. The players were aware of the criticism. While waiting on a team flight during the 1981 season, several Tar Heels browsing in an airport bookstore had noticed a story focusing on Carolina's national title drought. After the conclusion of that season, the returning players met as a group and made a commitment to take the title in 1982. They knew quality players returned—Player of the Year candidate James Worthy, steady point guard Jimmy Black, do-it-all forward Matt Doherty, and rising sophomore big man Sam Perkins—and there was substantial incoming talent, including the North Carolina prep Player of the Year, Buzz Peterson, and the runner-up for that award, Mike Jordan.

Despite the loss of high-scoring Al Wood, the returning core felt that the talent was in place to win a national title. As a team, they agreed to pay more attention to some of the

· · · MAKING LEGENDS

details that they might have ignored during the 1981 campaign, such as better conditioning, better eating habits, and fewer late nights on Franklin Street. Jimmy Braddock went home that summer in 1981 and told his parents, "We're going to win the national title next year."

They wanted to do it for themselves, of course. But there was another source of motivation.

"We'd like to do something about Coach Smith not winning a championship," Black said at a press conference before the Houston game. "Every time we read a story about him, they say what a good coach he is but that he chokes in the Final Four. I'm tired of that, and I think he'd tell you he is, too."

Actually, before winning the title, Smith probably wouldn't have admitted that unless under oath. The UNC head coach was almost incapable of talking about himself, unless it was to take the blame after a rare Tar Heel defeat. In fact, Smith didn't even fly home with the team after the 1982 championship victory. Instead, he chose to hunt down a red-eye flight that forced him to connect through Miami to get to Raleigh-Durham Airport. The head coach also thought his presence at the raucous reception awaiting the team at Kenan Stadium might detract from the attention given to the players. While 25,000 fans assembled at Kenan, Smith took his daughter for a walk around the neighborhood. He'd tried to impart a similar sense of perspective to his team. In the moments following the on-court celebration in New Orleans, as his squad gathered in the locker room, he repeated a frequent mantra: millions of people in China had no idea the game had been played.

Senior point guard Jimmy Black and the Tar Heels won the 1982 ACC championship before advancing to win the NCAA title three weeks later. (Photo by Scott Sharpe)

Smith's avoidance of the spotlight didn't mean he was ignoring the commentary on his lack of a title. He actually had an impressive ability to remember perceived slights that dated all the way back to his effigy days. ("I can't," he told a crowd of students asking him to address them after a big win over Duke a few days after the effigy incident. "There's something tight around my neck that keeps me from speaking.") Immediately after the championship victory, he made a pointed remark aimed at a Charlotte sportswriter who had written that the Carolina "system" prevented the program from playing well in big games. Smith, who hated the negative implications of the word "system," never publicly commented on the story when it was released; instead, he filed it away for later use.

So Smith was aware of the speculation about his inability to win a title. But that was only part of the story after Carolina advanced to face Georgetown in the national championship game. The contest would match Smith against one of his closest coaching friends, John

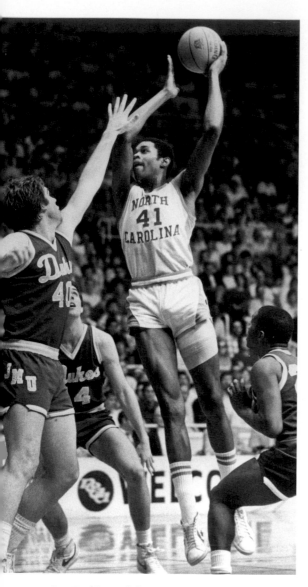

Sam Perkins and the Tar Heels barely escaped James Madison in the second round of the NCAA Tournament. (Photo by Sally Sather)

Thompson, who had served as an assistant on the 1976 Olympic team. The relationship between the two men would have a significant impact on the game. With Carolina leading, 63–62 and just seconds remaining, Thompson decided not to call a time-out to set up a final play. His reasoning? "I wouldn't have known what kind of defense Dean was going to use," said Thompson, who was well aware that the master of multiple defenses would have switched strategies after a time-out. "So I would have wasted my time setting up a play." Without the time-out, Thompson's Hoyas looked slightly confused and committed a fateful turnover.

The two teams assembled an impressive collection of talent, led by Carolina's Perkins, Worthy, and Jordan and Georgetown's Patrick Ewing and Sleepy Floyd—five players on the court who later had decade-plus NBA careers. The game, which was played on the same night as the Academy Awards (*Chariots of Fire* took Best Picture in a huge upset; Henry Fonda and Katharine Hepburn won the major acting awards for *On Golden Pond*), was almost as star-studded as the Hollywood festivities.

Ewing, one of the most dominant college centers of the 1980s, was called for goaltending five times in the first half. If nothing else, it was an impressive display of defensive bravado: Carolina had played against Ralph Sampson, but here was a freshman with reckless disregard for the rules of goaltending. On one play, Ewing caught a Tar Heel shot attempt, bringing it down with one huge hand and drawing yet another violation. Carolina continued to challenge him—the Tar Heels didn't actually put the ball through the basket on a field goal until eight minutes had elapsed, instead scoring off Ewing's goaltending violations—and the Georgetown big man continued to play aggressive defense. Undoubtedly, Jordan's most memorable play came with 17 seconds left, but the play with the most foreshadowing regarding his abilities probably came three minutes earlier, when he took the ball to the rim against Ewing and laid it high off the glass with his left hand over the seven-footer's outstretched reach. It was exactly the kind of daredevil maneuver that would make him an icon.

Jordan's history-making jumper, though, is what grabbed the headlines. With no shot clock and his team facing a 62–61 deficit, Smith called his first time-out with 32 seconds remaining. With the Hoyas in a zone, he knew the potential game-winner would probably have to be a jump shot. Jordan was, at best, the second offensive threat on the floor, and Georgetown covered him appropriately. Naturally, Smith went over practically every variable in the huddle.

"Normally, our [number] two play from the zone offense was a lob from Jimmy Black to James Worthy," Smith said. "But we knew Georgetown knew that, too, so we wanted to get

130   · · · MAKING LEGENDS

At the time, the title-game crowd of 61,612 at the Louisiana Superdome was the largest to see a basketball game in the Western Hemisphere. (Photo by Hugh Morton; courtesy North Carolina Collection, UNC–Chapel Hill)

it behind Worthy to Michael Jordan. With Georgetown in the zone, Jordan, or anybody, was to shoot as soon as he got a good shot. As the second alternate, the big men want to work the boards for a rebound. As the third alternate, if the first two missed, we wanted to foul at once."

"In that time-out, I saw a look on their faces that bothered me," said assistant coach Roy Williams. "It was the first time I actually thought we could lose. Coach Smith was so calm. He said, 'I'd much rather be in our shoes than theirs. We're in the driver's seat. Michael will get it and knock it in. If he misses, don't worry because we'll have inside rebounding position.'"

As Smith noted immediately after the game, both Worthy and Perkins had worked inside for quality rebounding position. That duo would've battled Ewing for anything coming off the rim. Had they failed, the result would have most likely been an immediate foul of Ewing, who shot 61.7% from the free-throw line as a freshman. No three-point line existed in the college game in 1982, so making both free throws would likely have sealed the game for the Hoyas. Smith did have four time-outs remaining and would have stretched the final 15 seconds as long as possible.

Had Ewing made one of two and Carolina managed to tie the game, overtime would have

favored the Tar Heels. Three Hoyas had four fouls: Ewing, Fred Brown, and Eric Smith (who ultimately fouled out after Brown threw a horrendous pass to Worthy on the final possession). Neither team had a particularly deep bench, and losing any starters would have been crippling.

The possible combinations are endless. Maybe Carolina still would have found a way to win. Maybe Georgetown would have sealed the game with free throws.

But all of that is speculation. Jordan made the jumper, as everyone even remotely connected to college basketball knows. Dean Smith's Tar Heels were, at long last, national champions.

Even Jordan didn't seem to immediately understand the magnitude of the play he'd made. He told reporters afterward that he hadn't watched the ball go in. Observing the young rookie handling the bright lights, assistant coach Eddie Fogler said, "Look at him. Does he know what he's done?"

At that time, he didn't. The direct ramifications were not about the impending superstardom for the freshman from Wilmington. They were about the changed perception of Dean Smith, and even a quarter of a century later, players from the 1982 team cite that as one of the most satisfying aspects of the championship.

(left)
Perkins and Worthy celebrate with the national championship hardware.
(Photo by Sally Sather)

(right)
Dean Smith and John Thompson's strong friendship began years before the national championship game.
(Photo by Hugh Morton; courtesy North Carolina Collection, UNC–Chapel Hill)

(opposite)
James Worthy earned Final Four Most Outstanding Player honors after scoring 28 points against Georgetown.
(Photo by Sally Sather)

"Finally we got that monkey off Coach Smith's back," Perkins said. "We had lost in 1981 and were very disappointed. To win it in '82 made '81 seem okay, like we had gotten a reprieve. If we had lost again, we would have been very disappointed, not just for ourselves but also for Coach Smith."

In some ways, Jordan's shot has obscured Worthy's greatness as a collegian. As Jordan's fame grew, the role of other players on the 1982 team became secondary. Casual fans assumed Jordan had always been the superstar on any team on which he played. In reality, Worthy was the superstar of that team. His 28 points in the national championship game remain one of the best performances in Carolina history. His matchup with fellow Gastonia native Sleepy Floyd was called "the biggest thing to happen to Gastonia since the textile workers went on strike in 1929" in a CBS News feature that ran in advance of the game. And although Floyd did score 18 points and went on to a 13-year professional career, it was clear Worthy was the superior player. His second-half, one-handed, fast-break dunk over Floyd—"It was Gastonia on Gastonia," as Woody Durham described it to his radio listeners—is one of the most ferocious dunks in Tar Heel history.

Jordan was a quality freshman and won the ACC Rookie of the Year award handily over Maryland's Adrian Branch. He did not, however, make either of the All-ACC teams (Perkins and Worthy each made the first team). The 1982 season might be remembered today as Jordan's year, but it was really Worthy's team.

So the question remains: what becomes of Jordan if one of his most notable failures happens in his thirty-fourth game as a collegian on the biggest stage imaginable? To that point in his career, he hadn't been entrusted with many opportunities to take a last shot.

Matt Doberty and the Tar Heels rode on top of the team bus along Franklin Street to the welcome-home celebration at Kenan Stadium. (Photo courtesy of UNC Athletic Communications)

"You look at turning points in lives. . . . That was a turning point in my life," Jordan said. "If I missed it, I don't know where I would have been. That's the day my name went from Mike Jordan to Michael Jordan. If it had remained Mike Jordan, I don't know where I would have been."

At lcast two Tar Heels disagree.

"I never thought that shot made Michael Jordan into Michael Jordan," Braddock said. "He was Michael Jordan before that shot. He was going to be one of the greatest players ever to play the game regardless of that shot.

"As a matter of fact, if he had missed it, he might have been even better. Because he would have spent the entire summer shooting jump shots. He was going to work his tail off no matter what. There's no way to know for sure. But his competitive fire was so great that I can't imagine him letting a missed shot—even that missed shot—change what he was going to be."

Fogler agreed: "Michael was going to be Michael whether that shot went in or not. It gave him some fame as a college player, but he was going to eventually be the same player."

With that in mind, Fogler speculated that the famous shot may have benefited Dean Smith even more than it did Michael Jordan.

"Where that shot changed things," Fogler said, "is that it put the stamp on Coach Smith's résumé. Coach Smith wouldn't agree with this, but once he had won that national title, it solidified him as one of the greatest coaches of all time."

12 : EIGHT FOR THE AGES

Jordan's shot set him on a course to become one of Carolina's most honored players. Some schools memorialize greats with a hall of fame or a ring of honor. In Chapel Hill, such accolades hang above the court in the form of honored jerseys.

Forty-seven players earned honored-jersey recognition during the first century of Carolina Basketball. It was quite a confusing mix, however, with some numbers honored multiple times and minimal distinction between honored and retired jerseys in the Smith Center's rafters. But in 2006, assistant coach Jerod Haase and associate athletic director for communications Steve Kirschner sought to remedy some of the confusion by clarifying the recognition process. They designed a new banner plan that included a blue background for retired jerseys and a white background for honored jerseys. The net effect was a more-organized Smith Center and a clearer acknowledgment of the program's all-time greats.

Today, earning jersey retirement means meeting stringent criteria, as players must be a consensus National Player of the Year. Over the last 100 years, only eight Carolina players have earned this distinction. Not coincidentally, five of the eight also played on national championship teams. As Roy Williams likes to say, "Winners deserve the awards and rewards." A few members of the elite eight were obvious picks to rise to the rafters from the moment they set foot on campus for basketball camp as seventh graders. Others just wanted to have a place on the team. But despite their differences, all eight had something very important in common: as a group, they make up the best players in the first 100 years of Carolina Basketball.

The first player to have his number retired didn't even wear a number. Jack Cobb played

George Glamack, the National Player of the Year for both 1940 and 1941. (Photo by Hugh Morton; courtesy North Carolina Collection, UNC–Chapel Hill)

(opposite)
Lennie Rosenbluth led the Tar Heels to the 1957 NCAA title, the first in ACC basketball history. (Photo courtesy of UNC Athletic Communications)

at UNC before numbers on jerseys were common, so a simple interlocking NC adorns his shirt.

Cobb played in a time when his 6-foot-2 height allowed him to play forward. He was raised in Durham but came to Carolina by way of Woodberry Forest High School in Virginia. In the undefeated season of 1924, he averaged 15 points per game—nearly half of the team's total of 36.8 points per game.

After graduation, Cobb expected to go into coaching. But he lost his lower right leg in a 1929 auto accident and chose to enter the business world. He did continue to be involved in Little League coaching and died in 1966 at the age of 62.

It would be 20 years after Cobb's achievements before another Carolina player earned National Player of the Year honors. It just so happened that the next honoree, George Glamack (#20), also possessed one of the best nicknames in Tar Heel history. Today, however, most fans have little idea how accurate the "Blind Bomber" moniker was. It wasn't just a cute case of alliteration. The 6-foot-6 Glamack, a native of Johnstown, Pennsylvania, was poked in the eye during a sandlot football game as a child. His mother applied a salt solution to the eye that saved some of his sight, but he had a "bubble" on the eye for the rest of his life.

Even while playing basketball, Glamack wore huge eyeglasses. When he was very young, other children laughed him off the court, but he developed a lethal hook shot—he aimed using the lines on the floor rather than eyeballing the hoop—that he could shoot with either hand, eventually becoming one of the first great Tar Heel offensive weapons. Even the supposedly friendly *Daily Tar Heel* had a hard time believing the physical characteristics of the school's new star. "Often it would be funny if it weren't so pathetic to see the big giant rub and squint his eyes, or lose his balance and go sprawling, for the simple reason that he cannot see," a story read.

Head coach Bill Lange spent endless hours working with Glamack in Woollen Gym, and although the vision difficulties would still sometimes prompt Glamack to mishandle an easy pass or miss a point-blank shot, he became a two-time All-America and two-time National Player of the Year. After predicting he would break the league scoring record against NC State, he actually did it one game earlier. In February 1941 he scored 45 points against

Clemson—a Southern Conference record at the time and still the fourth-best individual scoring mark in Tar Heel history. The *Daily Tar Heel* reported that Glamack received "the greatest ovation any athlete has ever received in Woollen Gym."

Clad in their striking all-navy uniforms with Carolina-blue letters, Glamack and his teammates took Carolina to the first NCAA Tournament in school history in 1941. During that event, Glamack scored 31 points against Dartmouth, the most points scored in NCAA play until 1952.

Glamack played five pro seasons, leading the Rochester Royals to two National Basketball League titles. He died on March 10, 1987.

Unlike Glamack, Lennie Rosenbluth (#10) never had a widely accepted nickname. Among his teammates, however, he did have one particular moniker. As Carolina motored toward a perfect season and a national championship in 1957, players joked that they had one primary offensive set: Feed the Monster. The Monster was Rosenbluth, who had slipped through the New York City prep ranks virtually unnoticed because he played for a public school rather than in the better-known, private-school leagues. He soon joined forces with a team full of other Big Apple products to produce the Carolina basketball team that captured the imagination of the entire state. The centerpiece of that team was Rosenbluth, who averaged 28.0 points per game as a senior.

"The acknowledgement was that Lennie was the guy who was going to get the ball," said Joe Quigg. "Coach McGuire made that clear. He could go any place on the court that he wanted to go. Our job wasn't to go out and be high scorers on our own. Our job was to work with Lennie and get him the ball."

Getting Rosenbluth the ball almost anywhere led to baskets. At 6-foot-5, he was comfortable both in the post and on the perimeter.

Still a Tar Heel

It's amazing how much the 1957 team is still remembered. We played over 50 years ago, but we're still treated so warmly anywhere we go in Chapel Hill. That's different for us, because the kind of attention college basketball received in the 1950s was very different from what it receives now.

People don't realize what basketball was like at North Carolina before Frank McGuire got there. It was a nothing sport. You couldn't give the tickets away. It was not a basketball school. My very first game, when I was on the freshman team, I got there a little bit early. I was so excited, because I thought Woollen Gym was the nicest gym I had ever seen. It had a square glass backboard, which was a big deal to me. In New York, we had played on wooden backboards and at prep school we had a fan-shaped backboard, so this seemed like the big time.

But the door was locked. I stood outside in the cold trying to get in, and people passing by must have wondered why this guy was standing outside Woollen Gym rattling the door. Finally, about 10 minutes before tip-off, someone showed up to let us in. For my very first freshman game, we played in front of 15 fans.

The crowds got bigger as my freshman season progressed, and eventually we started playing in front of crowds that were close to capacity. Sometimes, they would come to watch the freshman game and then leave before the varsity game.

We didn't have ESPN, of course. We didn't play on national television. Until we won the championship, it was much more of a local type of attention. When we went to eat at the Goody Shop on Franklin Street, I'd just sign the tabs. When my allowance came from my mother and father, I'd pay the bills. When I married Pat, Spiro Dorton, the owner of the Goody Shop, tried to give us all those signed tabs as a wedding present. Pat gave them to her little brother, and now her little brother had a bunch of Lennie Rosenbluth autographs. He took them out in the neighborhood and sold them for a quarter apiece. I thought that was the most autograph attention I'd ever get.

But even today, almost 55 years later, I still get autograph requests regularly in the mail. And they send a card or a magazine or an article for me to sign. I had no idea that playing basketball at North Carolina would be something that people still remember so many years later. When I go back to games—and I try to go back as much as I possibly can—it's like I never left. Coach Williams treats all of us who played like we're still on the team today.
—Lennie Rosenbluth

"In terms of shooting, Lennie was extraordinary," Tommy Kearns said. "If you got into a jam, you tried to get him the ball, and he delivered so many times for us. He had a little flip hook, which was a great shot that won the game for us against Wake Forest in the ACC Tournament. He could knock down 30 in a row with his one-handed shot. He had a God-given talent and touch on a basketball that I have rarely seen. You put the ball in his hands and it was magic. He wasn't particularly fast, and he couldn't jump particularly high, and he couldn't defend particularly well, but he had an extraordinary talent to hit a shot from anywhere on the floor, and we all knew it."

Fans began to notice Rosenbluth as soon as he played for the Carolina freshman team. It wasn't unusual for several thousand fans to pack Woollen Gym for Rosenbluth's game. Then, as soon as it concluded, half the crowd would sometimes leave before the varsity contest started.

"I think people liked the way I scored and they liked the way I rebounded," Rosenbluth said. "I would get up and pull the rebound down with one hand and cradle the ball in my arm. And offensively, I would shoot every shot. You name it, I shot it. Whether it was a hook shot, a jump shot, a two-handed set shot, I shot them all. In New York, we always played against older guys, so I had to develop all these different shots."

As Rosenbluth's stellar senior season progressed, opponents eventually focused on him with box-and-one defenses. He consistently maintained that he was only a cog in a very good team, and his assertion was proven true when he fouled out in regulation of the triple-overtime national championship game against Kansas.

"I never had any hesitation in my mind we were going to win the game," Rosenbluth said. "There were so many times when I didn't play well and other players stepped up. As soon as Bob Young came in for me in the championship game, he scored two points right away."

Remarkably, even though Rosenbluth played just three seasons because of freshman ineligibility, he still ranks first in UNC history for most points in a season (895); first, fourth, and sixth for highest scoring average in a season; fourth in career points scored (2,045); and fourth in career rebounding average (10.4).

Rosenbluth's pro career included two seasons with the Philadelphia Warriors. After basketball, he became a successful high school teacher and basketball coach, winning a state championship and coaching future NC State point guard Chris Corchiani. Today he lives in Florida with his wife, Pat—the couple met at The Goody Shop on Franklin Street while Rosenbluth was a UNC undergrad—and makes frequent trips back to Chapel Hill to watch home games.

Rosenbluth had the benefit of getting his college basketball introduction on the Tar Heel freshman team. Two decades later, Phil Ford (#12) wouldn't be given the same opportunity. And as he remembers it, he didn't have a very auspicious debut for the Tar Heels in the fall of 1974.

"I was awful at the start," Ford said of the beginning of his Carolina career, when he was the first freshman to start his first game under Dean Smith. "I was so excited to be at Carolina, and I couldn't believe I had the opportunity to play here. I wanted to do so well, and I

Phil Ford remains perhaps the greatest point guard in ACC history. (Photo by Hugh Morton; courtesy North Carolina Collection, UNC–Chapel Hill)

I'M FROM FORD CORNERS N.C. —DEAN SMITH, Mayor

A popular bumper sticker from the Phil Ford era.

couldn't do anything right. I dribbled the ball out of bounds off my foot with no one around me. I missed layups. I did all kinds of things I had never done before."

After committing 63 turnovers in his first 14 games, including 10 in his first game against Duke, Ford even made tearful phone calls home to Rocky Mount, wondering if perhaps he wasn't good enough to play in Chapel Hill. His teammates, however, had no doubt about his skill level.

"From the moment we had been recruiting him the previous spring, it was clear he was the guy we needed," Mitch Kupchak said. "We were in an era when NC State had David Thompson and Maryland had Len Elmore and John Lucas and Tom McMillen. We always won 20 or 25 games, but we couldn't quite turn the corner. To me, I thought Phil was the guy who would help us turn the corner.

"From the very beginning it was clear he was the best player I'd ever seen at the point guard position. He was born with some gifts, like speed and quickness. He also had leadership ability and an understanding of how to play the game. He was coachable, and he was an extension of Dean Smith on the court."

Ford eventually recovered from his shaky freshman start, becoming the first freshman to win the ACC Tournament MVP trophy. Over the last eight games of the year, he averaged 22.1 points per game and finished second on the team in scoring on a squad that included Kupchak, Walter Davis, and Tom LaGarde.

But Ford's most impressive progress came in game management. "What I realized is that as a point guard at Carolina, you had a lot of responsibilities," he said. "So you were constantly looking over at the bench to see what Coach Smith is calling. The day you looked over to the bench and it was time to make a call and Coach Smith sat back and crossed his arms, you had arrived. That meant you had gotten on the same page of knowing exactly what he would call in a certain situation. He did that for me late in my sophomore year or early in my junior year, and it was a good feeling."

Many times, that call from the bench was for the Four Corners, a trademark offense that was as closely tied to Ford as any offense has ever been to a specific Tar Heel. He was mesmerizing with the basketball, and when Carolina grabbed a late-game lead and spread the floor with Ford with the ball in the middle, the game was essentially over. The strategy was maddening to opponents and delightful to the Tar Heels.

"People thought the Four Corners meant we weren't trying to score," Ford said. "That was totally wrong. We were trying to spread the court. We were trying to get an easy basket or a backdoor cut or a foul. Eventually, the other team would get frustrated. You would start to see some antsiness in them, and if we had patience, eventually it would snowball on them."

Ford would eventually become perhaps the most beloved player in Carolina history. A generation of fans grew up mimicking his trademark four-fingered call for the Four Corners, and anytime he returns to campus—as he did when Tyler Hansbrough broke his UNC career scoring record in December 2008—he is still greeted with a standing ovation. Tar Heel fans loved him for his skills and his scoring, but they also loved him for his passion for Carolina. Ford memorably broke down in tears on his Senior Day before going out and helping beat the Blue Devils with 34 points.

The bond between Smith and Ford extended off the court. The Tar Heel head coach was an integral part of Ford's later battle with alcoholism. "I can't put his impact on me into words," Ford said. "I don't know where I would have been without him in my life."

After a successful NBA career—he was the 1979 Rookie of the Year—Ford turned to coaching, serving as a Tar Heel assistant from 1988 to 2000. He is currently an assistant coach with the Charlotte Bobcats.

Over the first sixty years of Tar Heel basketball, players earned National Player of the Year honors only about once per generation. That began to change in the early 1980s, when for the first time, two Tar Heels who would eventually have their number retired played on the same team.

James Worthy and his trademark finger roll on the way to the 1982 NCAA championship.

(Photo by Sally Sather)

James Worthy (#52) arrived at Carolina basketball camp as an eighth grader and made an immediate impression.

"The way he carried himself and his maturity level at that age was beyond his years," Eddie Fogler said. "You could see stardom written all over him at a young age. A lot of that goes back to his mom and dad and family, because they made him a conscientious, motivated, mature, talent-oriented kid. Combine that with the God-given talents and it was obvious he was headed for stardom even when he was young."

"I knew as a freshman he would be a pro," Smith said.

In many ways, Worthy was a generation ahead of his time. At 6-foot-8, he had the height of a power forward mixed with the athleticism of a small forward. He ran the floor brilliantly and could explode to the basket on the fast break. His freshman season was ended after just 14 games because of a broken ankle, and that ankle continued to bother him throughout his sophomore season. As a junior, however, he stayed healthy all season and won virtually every available award: MVP of the ACC Tournament, MVP of the NCAA East Regional, and Most Outstanding Player of the Final Four.

It was Worthy who broke tradition and forbade his teammates from cutting down the nets in Raleigh after the East Regional win. "Those aren't the nets we want," he told them. "The nets we want are in New Orleans"—the site of the Final Four.

"Worthy was a heck of a player," said Maryland's Lefty Driesell. "He had this move that I tried to copy with my guys. He'd catch the ball midway from the corner, and he had this spin move that he'd use. I called it, 'The Worthy Move,' and I'd try to teach our players the Worthy Move."

Worthy took that move to the pros after a terrific performance in the 1982 championship game. He was the overall top pick and played his entire career with the Los Angeles Lakers. He was named one of the 50 greatest players in NBA history and one of the 50 best players in ACC history in 2002, and he was inducted into the Naismith Basketball Hall of Fame. Worthy still lives in Los Angeles, where he does television work on Lakers broadcasts.

(opposite) ESPN named Michael Jordan the greatest athlete of the twentieth century in 2000. (Photo by Bob Donnan)

There are two common misconceptions about the college career of Worthy's 1982 team-mate Michael Jordan (#23): first, that the game-winning shot against Georgetown was his only notable play as a Tar Heel; and second, that he wasn't that special as a collegian and gained most of his fame because of his success with the Chicago Bulls.

Both of these fallacies can be disproved by simple facts. It's true that Jordan's 17-foot jumper for the NCAA championship was the most significant play of his first season at UNC, which started with Smith leaving him off a preseason *Sports Illustrated* cover in an effort to avoid focusing too much attention on a freshman. But that shot was just the beginning of a spectacular college career. As a sophomore, Jordan helped send a game against Tulane into overtime with a steal and a long jumper, and he was instrumental in Carolina's 10-point comeback in the final four minutes against Virginia at Carmichael Auditorium. He had a pair of 32-point games against Duke in 1983 and also poured in 39 against Georgia Tech. His heroics earned him National Player of the Year honors from *The Sporting News*.

That turned into the consensus opinion during his junior year, when he led the Tar Heels to a 21–0 start and won every major basketball-related award. Outsiders would also get a glimpse of his famous competitiveness, as Jordan was the first player to step toward Louisiana State's John Tudor when a hard foul by Tudor broke Kenny Smith's wrist.

That was exactly the attitude Jordan's teammates saw every day in practice.

"He didn't just want to beat you," Jim Braddock said. "He wanted to beat you bad. In practice, he was awesome. I'd walk to class and people would say, 'Wow, what a great dunk by Michael last night.' I'd say, 'That dunk? He does eight or nine of those every day in practice.'"

At Smith's urging, Jordan turned pro after his junior season. "I totally regret missing my senior year," Jordan said. "I was looking forward to all the things that go along with being a senior at Carolina."

Fortunately, his decision proved to be a pretty good one. Jordan was picked third overall in the NBA Draft by the Chicago Bulls and went on to become a six-time world champion, a two-time Olympic gold medalist, a Naismith Hall of Fame inductee, and the universally acknowledged best player in the history of the sport.

"Since the day I left, all the successes I have had are because of the University of North Carolina," Jordan said.

With Smith in charge, Carolina dominated in-state recruiting. Ford (Rocky Mount), Worthy (Gastonia), and Jordan (Wilmington) were all in-state products, and Smith found another gem in Charlotte's Antawn Jamison (#33). Unlike some of his predecessors, Jamison was not expected to play right away. He was recruited with the idea that he'd sit for a season behind Rasheed Wallace. But Wallace turned pro after his sophomore season, forcing Jamison— and his more-heralded freshman classmate, Vince Carter—into the spotlight a season early. Along with classmate Ademola Okulaja and guards Shammond Williams and Ed Cota, Jamison played on some of the most entertaining Tar Heel teams of the first century.

The 6-foot-9 Jamison made an immediate impression, becoming the first freshman to lead the ACC in field-goal percentage (62.4%) and the first Tar Heel freshman to earn first-team All-ACC recognition. His next two seasons ended with ACC Tournament championships—the 1998 game was a pulsating win over Duke—and trips to the Final Four. Jamison dominated the Blue Devils in Chapel Hill during his career, averaging 30.3 points and 12.0 rebounds against Duke in the Smith Center.

Unlike some of his peers, Jamison never really had a signature shot. He couldn't jump as high as Jordan or power through a defender like Worthy. But he could get off the floor more quickly than any of them. Even as he became a National Player of the Year candidate, he still seemed to take defenders by surprise with the way he could get off the floor seemingly without having his feet under him.

"He had the ability to jump a second time faster than most guys could jump once," Smith said. "He had an uncanny ability to go after the ball."

Over the last decade, Jamison has also become the veteran standard-bearer for Carolina players in the NBA. He's the first to greet a fellow Tar Heel before a pro game, and he's developed a keen sense of appreciation for what his three years in Chapel Hill meant.

"When I look back, I know what kind of platform Carolina gave me to reach my goals," he said. "I was able to come here and be a part of this special university. If it wasn't for Carolina, I wouldn't be where I am right now.

"And to know that no one else can wear my jersey, it's indescribable for me. Every time I come back to Chapel Hill, it's like the first time. I learned so much in Chapel Hill."

After kissing the Alamodome floor in his final game as a Tar Heel, Jamison left college early and became an NBA lottery pick. He recently completed his eleventh year in the NBA and is a two-time All-Star selection.

Jamison spanned the Smith-Guthridge era. The first retired jersey from the Roy Williams era belongs to Tyler Hansbrough (#50), a player who ended one of his first visits to Chapel Hill nearly in tears. In the era when private planes were still allowed to be used for recruiting visits, the native of Poplar Bluff, Missouri, was on his way to Chapel Hill when the small jet he was in encountered some rough weather. Hansbrough had very little flying experience, and when the plane finally touched down safely, his eyes were moist.

At the annual meeting of the Carolina coaching tree in the fall of 2005, Williams described his strategy for the upcoming season. Much of it revolved around Hansbrough—a freshman. Jeff Lebo, then the head coach at Auburn, was skeptical of such heavy reliance on a rookie. The skepticism was natural. At first glance, Hansbrough didn't appear to be the freshman centerpiece of an elite college basketball team.

A Carolina legend executing a Carolina trademark: Antawn Jamison thanks the passer. (Photo by Craig Jones, Getty Images)

(opposite)
Antawn Jamison earned consensus National Player of the Year honors in 1998. (Photo by Robert Crawford)

A Dream Come True

The first time I became aware of the importance of those jerseys in the rafters was when I was playing. Phil Ford was one of our coaches, and of course his jersey hangs in that retired row. We'd be going through a tough practice, and he'd say, "Hey, I used to do the exact things you guys are doing now." And he'd look up in the rafters and point at his jersey. What else could you say to that? The man had his number retired and it was hanging right over your head.

Every kid who plays any game, whether it's basketball or football or baseball or anything else, knows that having your number retired solidifies that you were pretty good at the game you played. Every time I come in the Smith Center, I sneak a look up there every couple of minutes. I just have to make sure it's still up there, that the big number 33 is still hanging. When I see it up there, it takes me back to coming into Carolina with a bald head and a little moustache. I'd come down to the Smith Center at 1:00 or 2:00 in the morning with Vince Carter or Ade Okulaja, and we'd shoot until late at night. Even at the time, you knew you were going to treasure these memories forever. But I never thought about all those guys who came before me and all the guys who would come after me. Seeing my name and number up there with them means a lot to me.

The first time I saw a Carolina game in person was in high school. It was in the Smith Center, and I was so happy just to get to see a North Carolina basketball jersey in person. I remember thinking, "I would like to wear that jersey." I would like to be one of the elite players who has come through North Carolina. Being able to wear the jersey at all means so much to my family and me. I dreamed about getting to hang a banner—any kind of banner—in the rafters. That would be something that would be here long after I wasn't playing here anymore.

When I came back for the alumni game, I thought about how lucky I was to get to wear a Carolina jersey at all. And I'm one of the very few who can say that my jersey will never be worn again. Can you imagine what that feels like? When I was walking off the court that night, I grabbed my son and took a second and pointed out that jersey with "Jamison" on the banner. There are no words to describe what that felt like. I felt like I was showing him the past and the future all at the same time. For the rest of my life, every time I walk into the Smith Center, I'm going to sneak a glance up there. It's still unbelievable to me.

—*Antawn Jamison*

But a few months later, after watching Hansbrough's first couple of months of college competition, Lebo called and left Williams a voice mail: "Coach, you were right. Hansbrough is everything you said he was."

In reality, Hansbrough probably turned out to be even greater than Williams expected, eventually becoming one of the most accomplished players in college basketball history. He did it all: he stayed four years, set likely unbreakable records, won a national championship, and drained the marrow out of the college experience in an era when some players seem to only see college as a required stopover on the way to the NBA. In many ways, Hansbrough was his generation's Phil Ford. And just as Ford was deeply connected to Smith, Hansbrough felt a unique personal bond with Williams.

"When I was being recruited, some teams said, 'If you come here, you'll start and you'll play this much and score a lot,'" Hansbrough said. "When Coach Williams recruited me, he said, 'I won't guarantee you'll start. You have to work for it.' Things like that make playing for Coach Williams special, because you respect that he makes you that much better. Even when you think you're playing well, he was always the first to tell you how you could improve."

(opposite)
Tyler Hansbrough is the first ACC player in history to earn first-team All-Conference and All-America honors four times.
(*Photo by Grant Halverson*)

Tyler Hansbrough and Michael Jordan shake hands before the UNC pro alumni game in Chapel Hill in September 2009. (Photo by Jeffrey A. Camarati)

And Hansbrough did improve, even when it looked like it might not be possible for him to get any better. He progressively collected more achievements every season, eventually adding a reliable jump shot and improved defensive skills to the potent scoring package he flashed as a freshman. He was the first player in ACC history to be voted first-team All-America four times; he owns Carolina's all-time scoring and rebounding marks; and he is the conference's all-time leading scorer.

He capped off his career with the 2009 national championship, giving him virtually every possible honor a University of North Carolina basketball player could have.

"You're not going to talk about North Carolina basketball very much anymore unless you mention Phil Ford and Tyler Hansbrough," Williams said.

13 : 1993

A TRUE TEAM

For 17 years, there's been a suspicion that Carolina facing Michigan in the Rainbow Classic in December 1992 might have had an intangible benefit when the two teams met again in the national championship game a few months later in April. As it turns out, the benefit was actually quite tangible.

An impressive season for Carolina—which included an ACC regular-season championship and the second Final Four appearance in three years—came down to 19 seconds. With that much time on the clock, Pat Sullivan hit one of two free throws to give Carolina a 73–71 edge.

"In some ways, I was more scared to pass the ball than I was to get fouled and have to shoot the free throws," Sullivan said. "I trusted my ability to shoot the ball. Then I looked over and saw the guys on the bench holding hands and I thought, 'Oh man, I can't let these guys down.'"

After Sullivan nailed the first one, Michigan's Jalen Rose stepped in front of him. "This is for the national championship," Rose said.

The second free throw felt good off Sullivan's fingertips, but it sailed long. And as Chris Webber pulled down the rebound, the need for Rose to pay more attention to the game's details and less attention to his trash-talking became very evident.

RARELY HAS THERE BEEN an NCAA championship game more defined by a clash of styles than the 1993 game in New Orleans. The Michigan Wolverines were rock stars. Webber, Rose, Juwan Howard, Ray Jackson, and Jimmy King had arrived the season before as the "Fab Five" and advanced to the 1992 title game—the first all-freshman starting five to reach the Final Four—before losing to a far superior Duke squad in one of the most-watched college basketball games of all time. They returned intact for their sophomore season, which was widely expected to be a coronation.

In a year when Carolina hadn't yet made the much-discussed switch to Nike—the Tar Heels wore Converse, the shoe of Magic Johnson and Larry Bird, who had been cutting-edge a decade earlier but now seemed archaic—the Wolverines were intriguing. It was hard not to admire them, even if you had to do so while pretending to disapprove. Their celebrations might have occasionally been excessive, but it sure looked like they had fun on the basketball court.

The Wolverines' swagger had a financial impact. Sales of clothing with the Michigan logo spiked; the Michigan athletic royalties as reported by the Collegiate Licensing Company were $6.2 million during the 1993–94 school year, triple what they had been just three years earlier and double what they were by the end of the 1990s. The Fab Five captivated Wolverine fans, but they also fascinated the casual fan. Detroit columnist Mitch Albom wrote a book on the Fab Five that was published a few months after the national title loss to the Tar Heels. The title said it all: *Fab Five: Basketball, Trash Talk, the American Dream.*

"They started all the trends," said George Lynch. "They had the black shoes, the black socks, the baggy shorts, the flashy plays and celebrating afterward."

And the 1993 edition of the Tar Heels?

"We were just Carolina," Lynch said. "We were blue-collar and we were under the radar. For some of our younger guys, it was nice that Michigan was getting all the attention. And for me as a senior, I enjoyed the fact that I knew how hard I was working but they were getting all the publicity. It was an opportunity to come in with no one knowing who we were."

When a newspaper took an informal survey of players and coaches across the basketball world prior to the title game, J.R. Rider of UNLV was the only individual to pick Carolina. The rest of the nation thought it was a simple case of star power: Michigan had it, Carolina didn't. The only Tar Heels on the three All-ACC teams were Lynch and Eric Montross. Duke and Florida State had more representatives; Clemson (5–11 in the ACC) and Wake Forest had the same number.

But more than any of the other Carolina national champions, 1993 was a team where the whole was greater than the sum of the individuals. Look at the better-known, more-aggressive opponents dispatched on the way to the title: Nolan Richardson and Arkansas's "Forty Minutes of Hell," Cincinnati's Nick Van Exel, and the Fab Five. Carolina didn't have

George Lynch's steal and dunk capped a 21-point second-half comeback against Florida State.
(Photo by Grant Halverson)

a catchy nickname. Even today, it's probably the Tar Heel national championship team that's least familiar to Carolina fans. Collectively, the entire roster played in zero NBA All-Star games. So what made that group national champions over competition that was more physically talented?

"From top to bottom, every single person bought into our goal to be in the Superdome at the end of the year," Montross said. "When we played, you never second-guessed whether it would be anything other than a complete team effort. We interacted as a group and we trusted each other. More than any other team I've been a part of, that team was selfless."

It wasn't that they weren't talented. Some heated recruiting battles had to be won to build the foundation of the team. Montross was picked out of Indianapolis and wooed away from Michigan, where both of his parents had lettered. Brian Reese, Derrick Phelps, and Sullivan were spirited out of Carolina's traditional recruiting grounds in New York. Lynch's brother loved the idea of Lynch playing with Alonzo Mourning at Georgetown.

But perhaps the toughest battle was for a shooter who lived less than an hour from the UNC campus. Donald Williams grew up an NC State fan in an era when the Wolfpack was a legitimate Carolina competitor. But the Jim Valvano controversy plus a terrific recruiting visit to Chapel Hill swayed Williams to the Tar Heels.

"I was very close to going to State," Williams said. "I played pickup games in the summer with their players, and I was close with them. But I had no idea what Carolina Basketball was about until I made my visit, and that changed everything."

Leadership Lessons

I learned a lot about leadership in 1991 as a sophomore. We went to the Final Four and had five seniors that year, and I learned a lot about how to be a leader at a program like North Carolina.

I learned that it involved being responsible for the younger guys. Things that might have seemed like little things—meeting curfew, paying attention to strength and conditioning—were important in building a championship team. You have to be committed in everything you do to winning a championship. That's especially true in Chapel Hill, because when you have North Carolina on your chest, you are going to get the best possible shot from every team you play, whether it's the first game of the season or the national championship game. Playing against Carolina matters to people. That's the message I wanted to get across to our younger players in 1993.

But I also learned that there are some things you can't control. There might be injuries. You might have some bad luck. There will be some things that you can't prepare for, and those things may go against you. It's so important to maximize the chance you're getting to play on a high-quality team and do the very best you can. There's no guarantee that you're going to get back there, and we wanted to play with an understanding of that sense of urgency.—*George Lynch*

Williams was the only underclassman in a rotation made up almost exclusively of juniors and seniors. The core of the team had played in the 1991 Final Four together, where they suffered a disappointing 79–73 loss to Kansas. That experience became important in 1993. Instead of simply being happy to be in the national semifinals, the Tar Heels arrived in New Orleans eager to complete a mission.

Before the first day of practice, Smith had ordered a doctored photo of the Superdome scoreboard from 1982. Instead of "North Carolina 1982 national champions," the photo now read, "North Carolina 1993 national champions." A copy of the new and improved picture was placed in every player's locker.

"In 1991 we learned how to play together as a team," Reese said. "In 1993 we had just one

Derrick Phelps's defense on Cincinnati point guard Nick Van Exel sent the Tar Heels to the 1993 Final Four. (Photo by Andrew Cline)

common goal: win a national championship. In '91 we were just freshmen, we didn't know what we had to contribute to reach that goal. When we were juniors, we were more comfortable with the idea of being a team."

Their comfort level off the court carried over on the court. Until the criteria changed in the summer of 2009 and Donald Williams was added, the 1993 team had fewer players honored with jerseys in the Smith Center rafters than any other Carolina title squad. Somehow, though, the pieces fit.

The signature regular-season win was a dramatic home comeback against Florida State. The Seminoles led by as many as 21 points in the second half, but Henrik Rödl ignited a comeback with a pair of three-pointers. Lynch's steal and dunk gave the Tar Heels the lead and remains one of the single loudest moments in Smith Center history.

Carolina closed the regular season with a nine-game winning streak and won the ACC regular-season race by two full games over FSU. Only an injury to Derrick Phelps prevented them from adding the league tournament title. The Tar Heels' average margin of victory was 17.8 points per game, tied for the widest scoring margin in program history. Their season rebounding total (third) and steals total (second) still ranks in the top three all-time among Carolina teams.

"As a team, that group played together as well as any team we've ever had at North Carolina," said Phil Ford, an assistant coach on the 1993 team. "They could read each other. Henrik Rödl was so smart. The big guys, Kevin Salvadori and Eric Montross, could play off each other. And with George and Derrick Phelps, we had two defenders who could [make quick adjustments]. . . . We'd call one thing, Derrick would see something and run something totally different, and everyone else would pick up on it."

Lynch was the unquestioned leader, the senior capable of blistering a teammate for a mistake and then encouraging the same teammate on the very next possession. While in Hawaii for the Rainbow Classic in December, Lynch had gotten in a wrestling match on the beach and injured his shoulder. He didn't bother to tell anyone and averaged a double-double in the three games in Hawaii. Ford began calling Lynch "Mangani" because of his toughness.

"George was just a tough, warriorlike dude," Ford said. "He wasn't just a warrior in the game. He was a warrior in practice, a warrior in the dorm, a warrior walking down the beach."

After a dominant 8–0 start to the season that included an average margin of victory of 28.3 points, the Tar Heels lost a one-point decision to Michigan in the Rainbow Classic on a Jalen Rose tip-in. The loss miffed the perfectionist Tar Heels, but it also provided an important tidbit for a team that thrived on the game's subtleties.

Donald Williams helped UNC beat Cincinnati and then made 10 three-pointers in two Final Four games the next weekend. (Photo courtesy of UNC Athletic Communications)

"When we played them in Hawaii, I noticed they let Webber handle the ball a lot in the backcourt," Lynch said. "He didn't always make the right decisions, and sometimes they would have Rose taking the ball out to throw it in to Webber. In Hawaii, I mentioned to Derrick that when Rose took the ball out, we could try some pressure to take some time off the clock or even get a 10-second call."

That eye for detail became very important three months later in New Orleans. Williams, who was sporting a freshly shaved head for the Final Four, carried the Tar Heels through a back-and-forth first 39 minutes, swishing five three-pointers for the second straight game.

"When I think about Donald, I think about a pure shooter," Montross said. "He elevated so high, and every time he shot it, he had that perfect follow-through. The ball had perfect spin, and his eyes were on the front of the rim. Sometimes shooters change their form with every shot. He didn't. He was perfect every time."

Williams's backcourt partner was Phelps, who attempted the fewest number of shots of anyone in the starting lineup against the Wolverines. But he also defended the wiry Rose, forcing the sophomore point guard into a 5-for-12 performance with six turnovers.

Part of Phelps's defensive prowess was physical. Listed at 6-foot-3, he seemed to have the wingspan of a taller player. He combined that spidery reach with an advanced knowledge of how to defend.

"It all goes back to Coach Smith and the way he recruited," Williams said. "He knew how to put a puzzle together. Derrick was perfect for that team. He had such good instincts and he did all the things you can't teach. I had to go against him in practice when I was playing some point guard as a freshman, and I thought I was a pretty good offensive player. He would shut me down every day. My freshman year, he made life miserable for me. I wanted to fight him every day."

Rose might have felt the same way, and by the time less than 20 seconds were left in the national championship game, Michigan was clearly more rattled than Carolina. Webber's first instinct after grabbing the rebound after Pat Sullivan's missed free throw was to call a time-out. Realizing the Wolverines had used them all and trying to grant the player a favor, the official looked the other way. That left Webber looking for an outlet, but Lynch hung

Playing the '93 Heels

Twice in my career, I coached against North Carolina and Coach Smith. It was awkward, but at least both games were in the Final Four. Kansas won in 1991, but two years later, the Tar Heels not only beat us, they also took home the national championship by beating Michigan's Fab Five.

The 1993 game was a little easier on both Coach Smith and me because we did a better job of telling the media, "We are going to answer these questions one time and get it over with." We tried in 1991 to make it about our teams, but no one would let us get by with that. Motivation turned out to be a huge negative for Kansas the second time. Henrik Rödl told me that losing in '91 was a huge source of motivation for the Carolina players. He said they'd heard all the stories about what a great guy Coach Williams is, and then they got beat, so they were not going to let that happen again.

I loved the '93 Carolina team—it mirrored what we had at Kansas. Both programs had very good players but no superstar. I was most impressed with how hard they worked, how together they were, the chemistry they had, and how, even from 1,119 miles away in Lawrence, Kansas, I could see that winning was the only thing important to them.

They didn't care how many points they scored or how many rebounds they got as individuals. From the start of the season, Carolina was a *team* that only cared about the final result.

They had great size and experience, would get after you defensively, and had great inside-outside balance on offense. When we scouted them, we had a tremendous concern about their inside strength and felt we did not have the kind of size, experience, and ability to handle Eric Montross and George Lynch. If Donald Williams was making three-point shots, their balance was a huge problem because you couldn't double down on George and Eric.

Donald started to have some big games before the ACC Tournament, and he was really a major factor at the start of the NCAA Tournament. He gave them a balance that is always more difficult to cover. You can smother someone inside or cover the three-point shot, but it is very difficult to do both. Offensive balance was more prominent of a concern in playing the '93 Carolina team than any one team I can remember coaching against.

Throughout that season, each of the Tar Heels found their right role offensively and understood how to play to their strengths. It was for Donald to shoot the ball, for George and Eric to score inside, for Derrick Phelps to distribute, for Henrik to give them ballhandling and another shooter, for Brian Reese to give them a little bit of everything, and for Pat Sullivan to give them steady play and hustle.

But Lynch was the key. He was a gifted rebounder and defender who could score and do a little of everything. His greatest strength was his leadership and the emotion he got everybody to play with. He wasn't a rah-rah guy, but he set a great example. I remember asking Coach Smith once why George went to double-team on a certain play. Coach Smith said, "I don't know, George just decided to go do it." And we laughed about it. Sometimes they would press just because George would press. But Coach Smith trusted him.

They hurt us that night in New Orleans with their size—they had 20 second-chance points—and Donald hit five threes, which gave them that inside-outside threat. I felt bad for my team, but on Monday night, I was an alumnus again. I sat in the Carolina section, waved my blue pom-poms, and watched Coach Smith win a second national championship. That was a title won by a great team that exemplified hard work, character, and unselfish play.—*Roy Williams*

back to apply token pressure on Rose—just as he had learned to do in Hawaii. That cut off Webber's passing lane, forcing him to drag his pivot foot.

"I had confidence in Derrick's ball pressure," Lynch said. "I knew it was a gamble, but I was willing to take it. If it had been Rose bringing the ball up, I wouldn't have hung back there. But when I saw Webber with the ball, I liked my chances."

It was the kind of nuanced game-winning play the 1993 team always seemed to make, and

Eric Montross scores in the national championship game against Michigan. (Photo by Hugh Morton; courtesy North Carolina Collection, UNC–Chapel Hill)

Lynch could have easily been the hero if Webber had been called for traveling. But the whistle didn't blow, so Webber dashed up the court. Now trailing the Wolverine big man, Lynch had to hustle into the frontcourt to keep up with the play.

A trap hadn't been called from the bench. But Carolina had a basic defensive principle that any time a player saw an opponent's numbers—meaning the opponent had his back to them—while dribbling the ball, it was acceptable to try and create a trap. That was even more suitable when the dribbler was next to the sideline or the baseline, because the boundary provided an extra defender. Phelps funneled Webber to the sideline in front of the Michigan bench. Sprinting back upcourt, Lynch came from behind to apply a double-team.

That left Webber trapped between Carolina's two best defenders. In the frenzied final seconds of the national title game, he thought his best option was to call a time-out.

But what if he hadn't?

Howard was trying to get free near the free-throw line, but Sullivan had rotated over and was in position to get a deflection if the pass went there. Williams was under the basket blanketing King. Rose had jogged across midcourt and was open, but Lynch's trap prevented Webber from making an easy pass.

In the previous time-out, Smith had instructed his veteran team that they still had fouls to give; with fewer than seven team fouls, Carolina could commit a nonshooting foul without sending the Wolverines to the free-throw line. If Webber had not called a time-out, that fact would have been important. Only 12 seconds remained by the time he advanced the ball to the frontcourt. If he'd found Rose, the clock likely would have been at around 10 seconds.

"Under those circumstances, I think we absolutely would have used the foul we had to give," Montross said. "We would have wanted them to take as much time off as possible and then stop it with a foul."

"Chris was away from the basket, and I think we would've tried to play them straight up," Lynch said. "We were always told never to foul if we had someone trapped. If they had gotten the ball under the basket or if someone was beaten off the dribble, then maybe we give the foul.

"The whole thing is that we were so well coached. We knew if we kept it close, we had the better coach on our sideline. And that's what happened."

Eric Montross's jump hook over Chris Webber graced the cover of Sports Illustrated's *issue on the 1993 title game. (Photo by David E. Klutho, Sports Illustrated/Getty Images)*

The banners from the 1992 and 1993 Final Fours no longer hang in Michigan's Crisler Arena due to NCAA sanctions.

In Chapel Hill, however, the 1993 national championship banner still waves, perhaps the most improbable of any of the six national title memorials in the rafters of the Smith Center.

"At the time, I had no idea what a big deal it was to win a national championship," Montross said. "I knew it was a big deal. But I didn't know how hard it was to do. I just had the expectation that you come to Carolina and you go to the Final Four. I took it for granted. My senior year, it became apparent that it was something really special.

"It wasn't until I watched Michigan State win it in 2000 that I finally started to have enough distance between our success and someone else's success to appreciate how hard it was. Mateen Cleaves, from that MSU team, was drafted to the Pistons, where I was playing at the time. To be around him and see how much he appreciated it really opened my eyes. You start to realize how many great teams never get the chance to get there, and seven years later it finally sunk in that it must be quite an accomplishment to win a national championship."

(left)
Final Four Most Outstanding Player Donald Williams cuts down the nets in New Orleans. (Photo by Hugh Morton; courtesy North Carolina Collection, UNC–Chapel Hill)

(right)
Dean Smith won his second NCAA title in 1993 and would go on to make two more Final Four appearances before retiring in 1997. (Photo by Hugh Morton; courtesy North Carolina Collection, UNC– Chapel Hill)

14 : HOME-COURT ADVANTAGES

The 1993 team was responsible for adding another national championship banner to the Smith Center rafters. But that group also played in an era that saw some dramatic changes in the way fans enjoyed—and helped influence—games in Carolina's home facility. It marked the continual progression of the Tar Heels' home court, which has developed from finding any spare 94-foot surface on campus to one of the country's best basketball venues.

Today, addressing the comfort of fans in modern arenas means high-definition televisions and elaborate concessions. In the formative years of Carolina Basketball, however, fan comfort had more to do with finding a comfortable temperature inside the arena.

Finding a place to play might seem like an elementary part of fielding a competitive basketball team, but it actually was one of the primary reasons why Carolina didn't have a team until 1910. The on-campus Bynum Gymnasium was a possibility, but it was also committed to more important functions, such as housing daily gymnastics work by students.

The *Tar Heel* addressed the issue before the first intercollegiate season.

So far, the basketball team has not become a reality. There seems to be only one reason why it has not—the inability of those interested to secure a suitable place to play. Are we really under the handicap of not having a fit place to play a game of basketball, or are we simply neglecting the places we do have? Certainly no one could wish for a better place for basketball than the gymnasium. Of course the gym is primarily for other uses, and basketball could not be allowed to interfere with the regular gym exercises. But the gym is used for nothing at night, and basketball could be practiced then. . . . With the players wearing gym shoes, as of course they would, the building would not necessarily be damaged any more by a game of basketball than by the daily gym work.

Desperate to find a home for the team, the *Tar Heel* even came up with an unusual suggestion.

"What would be the objection to playing in Memorial Hall?" the paper asked, referring to the facility that had been built in 1885. "At present, the building is used on only two or three occasions per year. . . . Memorial Hall is a monument to distinguished alumni and benefactors of the University and is regarded as being of a more sacred character than other buildings on campus, but surely it would be no desecration of the place to play the innocent game of basketball there."

Desecration of the building might not have been the primary concern; Memorial Hall was declared structurally unsound and razed in 1929.

Carolina's home games moved to the Tin Can in 1924. (Photo by the Yackety Yack)

By then, though, Carolina had already played 13 seasons in Bynum Gym. It was not a showplace. Early Carolina players complained that the backboards were "a good deal liver" than they had been accustomed to in high school, the floors were too slick, and the lighting was bad. The facility also had its quirks, as a second-floor running track hung over the playing surface. Practicing under the questionable conditions must have had its benefits, however, because Carolina amassed a 62–11 record in Bynum.

With basketball's profile on campus increasing, basketball home games moved to the Tin Can in 1924. Two thousand fans turned out for the inaugural game, a 34–23 win over Mercer that opened a 10-game home slate during the undefeated 1924 campaign. Almost as soon as basketball had moved into the gym—which had been constructed at a cost of $6,741.72—there were issues. To hold down construction costs, the Tin Can did not include a heating system and had been built of steel. That created some heating problems for a sport played in the winter. By 1927, players had taken to wearing three sweatshirts and gloves during warm-ups, and they complained of shooting with numb hands. Even after central heating was added in 1929, players and coaches continued to moan about the temperature.

Potbellied stoves were used for heat, and high-wattage light bulbs were placed under the players' benches to provide some warmth. By the time the players had arrived at the Tin Can for a game or a practice, however, it was almost too late: since there were no dressing facilities on site, players had to dress at Emerson Stadium and make the chilly 300-yard walk in their uniforms.

Woollen Gym, then, seemed like a palace when UNC began playing there on January 4, 1938, with a 47–20 victory over Barton. This time, the construction cost was $646,000, which included an adjacent swimming pool. Seating capacity climbed to over 6,000.

Compared to the rest of the Southern Conference and then the ACC, Woollen gave Carolina a high-quality facility. Virginia—which still featured a track ringing the second floor

above the court, which could prove perilous for jump shooters—was acknowledged as having the worst place to play in the league.

"Woollen was a good setup for us," said coach Ben Carnevale. "We had a good student body, and the stands were full or even overcrowded most of the time."

Even with the 1949 opening of NC State's Reynolds Coliseum, which had double the capacity of most existing basketball venues, Woollen remained nice enough to impress wide-eyed recruits. That was especially true of the New York City products that Frank McGuire targeted. Most of those players were accustomed to high school gymnasiums that sat fewer than 500 fans. For them, walking into the "spacious" Woollen was eye-opening.

"You know what I remember about Woollen Gym?" Lennie Rosenbluth said. "It had glass backboards. In New York, only the parochial schools had glass backboards. In the public schools, we played on wooden backboards. I thought it was the greatest thing ever.

"Then, in my very first freshman game, I'm excited to get to play at home, and we couldn't even get in the gym. The door was locked. By the time we found a way to get it open, there were about 15 people in the stands for my first freshman game. But I was in college and playing in this great place, and I didn't care how many people were in the stands."

Thanks largely to Rosenbluth and his 1957-era teammates, attendance never dipped to as low as 20 again. McGuire had been agitating for a new arena since the day he was hired, and while he thought he'd received some promises for new construction, nothing happened.

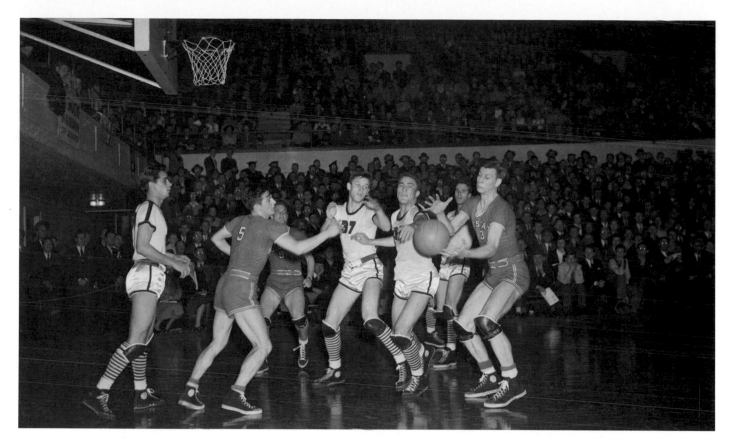

Capacity crowds and well-dressed fans were the norm in Woollen Gymnasium, including this 1942 victory over NC State. (Photo by Hugh Morton; courtesy North Carolina Collection, UNC–Chapel Hill)

Soon, the success of his teams on the court made the lack of a new building problematic. Administrators were forced to devise an alphabetical ticketing system. Students with last names beginning with *A* through *M* were eligible for tickets for the first game, and those with last names beginning with *N* through *Z* were eligible for the next home game. The rotation continued throughout the season, so students who wanted to see every home game had to get creative to find ways to beat the policy.

Because the small capacity and intense demand limited the number of tickets available to visiting teams, visitors rarely wanted to come to Chapel Hill. Carolina administrators soon learned that more money could be made by moving high-demand games to Greensboro or Charlotte, venues with larger seating capacities and fewer ticket requests from students—which meant that more tickets could be sold to the public. Despite a 24-game home winning streak that stretched over three seasons, the Tar Heels played just eight home games per season in 1957 and 1958, six home games in 1959 and 1960, and seven home games in 1961. They would lose just three of those 35 games.

"The fan support we had in Woollen was unbelievable," said Bob Cunningham. "It was a madhouse. They'd let about 500 visiting fans in, and the rest of the place was just students. You could hear them a mile away. It was bedlam."

A gaudy winning percentage wasn't enough for the basketball program to claim Woollen as their own, however. Basketball practices were often conducted at the same time as

Billy Cunningham and Bobby Lewis pose during the construction of Carmichael Auditorium. (Photo courtesy of UNC Athletic Communications)

intramurals, and it wasn't unusual for a volleyball to come skipping across the court in the middle of one of McGuire's lectures. That forced the team into some inventive attempts at avoiding distractions. In 1956 the varsity basketball team practiced at night to try to avoid intramurals, and during part of another season, a curtain was rigged around the court to isolate the team.

Part of the Woollen advantage was familiarity. The same court that was installed in 1938 was used throughout the life of the building as the home of the basketball team, so players knew the location of every dead spot. And the fans who ringed the court were more like friends than spectators. "It was very intimate," said Joe Quigg. "It felt like you knew everyone who was there. At that time, Carolina wasn't a huge school. We'd be playing a game, and a couple of my fraternity brothers would be sitting under the basket. They'd say, 'Hey Joe, shoot a hook shot.' So the next time down, if we had a lead, I'd take a hook shot for them."

There were problems with Woollen that went beyond the court. For a short time, McGuire and head football coach Jim Tatum shared an office suite—a situation that proved untenable for a duo that had little in common other than a creeping jealousy of the other. Tatum, of course, had the larger office. McGuire's office was so small it could not accommodate two guests at the same time. Assistant coach Buck Freeman used a ticket office shelf as a desk. Freeman, who had a reputation as a basketball-obsessive gym rat, didn't seem particularly

concerned, however. He actually lived in a 200-square-foot apartment in the back of Woollen throughout his UNC coaching tenure.

But most coaches were less enamored of Woollen than Freeman. The state of North Carolina refused to help build a completely new arena, so UNC administrators came up with an ingenious plan: they built a new facility as an "annex" to Woollen. The new Carmichael Auditorium—named in honor of William Donald Carmichael, a popular former school vice president and the brother of Cartwright Carmichael—shared Woollen's western wall.

After almost 60 years of UNC basketball, the move to Carmichael in 1965 finally put Carolina into the perfect facility. The arena was small enough to maintain feverish ticket demand and big enough to generate plenty of noise. The tiled concourse and the brick wall against Woollen meant noise stayed inside the building and low to the court. Finally, the Tar Heels had a facility that was a suitable rival to Reynolds.

James Worthy, Michael Jordan, and Jimmy Black stand for the national anthem in Carmichael Auditorium in 1982. (Photo by Sally Sather)

Dean - Bill - Eddie - Roy

and

The '83 Heels:

Another super year!
Proud of you!

Thank you for
showing some real Class
to the rest of the world!

Skipper
Bowles

3-27-83

Hargrove "Skipper" Bowles was a close friend of the program who was also instrumental in raising the funds for the Smith Center.

"The first time I walked in, I couldn't believe it," said Bob Bennett. "You walked in and saw a sea of blue. It was new and clean and big, and the finish on the floor was brand new. The stands were permanent, not portable like at Woollen. The place would erupt when we came out for that first layup line. It was exhilarating to run out of the locker room into that beautiful place."

The noise in Carmichael became legendary. The Tar Heels went two full seasons without losing a home game. When Mitch Kupchak arrived on campus in the fall of 1972, George Karl issued a stern command to the freshman: "At Carolina, we don't lose home games."

"It was an incredible home-court advantage," Kupchak said. "Today, in the newer arenas, it takes two or three minutes to walk from the court to the locker room. From our locker room, we opened a door that was six and a half feet high, everybody ducked to get out, and after five or six steps you were on the court. We'd sit in the locker room and we could hear the crowd outside. To come rushing into that setting with people right on top of you sent chills up and down your spine."

The noise level was aided by the fact that Dean Smith was assembling some of the best teams in the country. Beginning with the famous 8-points-in-17-seconds game in 1974, those teams began to create remarkable comebacks on a regular basis. In 1982 Michael Jordan helped topple Tulane in triple overtime. In 1983 Jordan's steal and dunk against Virginia capped a 10-point comeback in 4 minutes, 12 seconds. In 1985, against regular foil Lefty Driesell, Dave Popson hit a 16-foot jumper to seal a last-second comeback.

"My first Blue-White game at Carmichael was astounding," Bill Chamberlain said. "It was the biggest crowd I'd ever played in front of, and they were all howling and screaming. It sounded like the roar of the sea when you put a big conch shell up to your ear, except louder by about 50 decibels. I went out on the court, went to lay the ball up, and I missed the layup completely because I had so much adrenaline I was jumping higher than I'd ever jumped. I was trying to make a layup but I was looking down at the rim, and I remember thinking, 'What am I doing up here?'"

"There were times at Carmichael when the crowd was so loud that a referee would call a foul or a violation and nobody would stop playing," said Tom LaGarde. "The ref would have to almost tackle the guy with the ball because it was so loud. It was nutty in there, and it was hot."

Oh yes, the temperature. Legends are rampant—fueled partly by Driesell and Virginia's

The Smith Center was paid for entirely with private funding. (Photo courtesy of UNC Athletic Communications)

Terry Holland, who both had little success in the building—that Smith doctored the Carmichael thermostat. Kupchak confirms that it was often warm in Carmichael for practice, because Smith wanted to replicate the feel of a crowded, stuffy gym. But Smith never copped to the ploy. On one occasion, a caller to his radio show asked him if he ever tinkered with the temperature.

"That's a good story," Smith said, "but totally ridiculous. I couldn't find the thermostat that controls the heat in Carmichael if my life depended on it. All I know is that it gets hot in there when you put a lot of people in the stands."

Longtime assistant Roy Williams agreed, independently, for almost exactly the same reason.

"People used to talk about Coach Smith turning up the heat in Carmichael," Williams said. "I guarantee you that for $1,000, Coach Smith couldn't have found the thermostat or the light switch in Carmichael Auditorium."

Despite Carolina's success in Carmichael, ticket scarcity—and the accompanying windfall associated with the prospective ability to sell more seats—prompted the university to look into a new facility in the mid-1970s, barely a decade after the program had moved into Carmichael. At the same time, however, UNC was deep into a broad fund-raising initiative known as the Carolina Challenge.

"Chancellor [Ferebee] Taylor and the board of trustees felt an arena campaign would be in conflict with the Carolina Challenge," said John Swofford, UNC's athletic director at the time. "When the Challenge ended in 1979, some serious groundwork began."

Serious groundwork, however, didn't equal dollars. A 25-person steering committee that was convened to shepherd the project included some members skeptical that a showplace of

the type that was being discussed could ever be funded privately. No state funds were to be used. Reaching the NCAA final in 1981 helped spur discussions, and the national title in 1982 may have been the tipping point. Contributions came in from thousands of Tar Heel fans, ranging from six-figure checks to coin-filled envelopes from schoolchildren.

One source that was not as generous was the student body. During the building process, students had the opportunity to approve a fee increase that would have preserved the seating arrangement they had at Carmichael Auditorium, including prime courtside seats. But college students rarely look very far into the future—that's what makes them college students, people who jump off fraternity balconies into pools or stay up all night studying for an exam—and the proposal was voted down, meaning that other sources of funding were needed. The Rams Club turned to its members, which contributed the then-unheard-of sum of $34 million for the project. At the time, no one had any idea that the students' vote would still be discussed 25 years later.

The Student Activities Center, as the building was originally conceived, was intended to be a showplace. Even the most-optimistic forecasters knew it would not be as loud as Carmichael, even with over 21,000 seats. The sheer immensity of the building would prevent the same roar. The trade-off would be the fact that Carolina would play in the nation's best arena. Carmichael was awe-inspiring during games but not particularly dazzling when it was empty. The new building was designed to be just as stunning on a typical June Sunday as it was on game day.

"On my recruiting visit, I walked in when they were still completing it," said Pete Chilcutt. "I played in a gym that held about 200 people if I was lucky. I was sold by the whole program. But that facility made it almost impossible not to walk in and be affected by it."

In many ways, designers had to be ahead of their time. Permanent seat licenses hadn't been invented yet, and the Smith Center was one of the earliest applications of that model. Donors had to be compensated for their funding; the solution was to give them rights to the seats they selected. Designers even beat the luxury-box rush by almost two decades. Twenty boxes at the top of the lower level were intended for top contributors. As it turned out, those contributors preferred to be closer to the court and the sightlines from the boxes weren't optimal. Many of the boxes were converted into normal lower-level seats years after the building opened.

Against Smith's wishes, the facility was named in his honor, although he continued to call it the Student Activities Center. After a raucous building-opening win over Duke—because of construction delays, there were actually two "last games" at Carmichael, one a win over Clemson at the close of the 1985 season and the other a midseason victory over NC State the next season—the building's crowds began to get contented. Perhaps a little too contented.

Carolina Basketball crowds had never been unruly, due largely to Smith's influence. He discouraged fans seated behind the basket from waving their arms during free throws, considering it unsportsmanlike. When opposing starting lineups were introduced, he stood at the end of the Carolina bench and applauded, and he expected his home crowd to, at minimum, show respect by remaining silent rather than booing.

By the early 1990s, what had once been respectful was turning into reserved, partly as a result of the cavernous dimensions of the Smith Center. But two transformative events happened, approximately a decade apart, that helped preserve the Smith Center's home-court advantage. The first was the assertion by Florida State's Sam Cassell after an 86–74 Seminole

Welcome to the GREATEST
rivalry in Sports!!!
NORTH
34
CAROLINA
NORTH
CAROLINA
DUKE
TM FLS
PLR FLS
CAROLINA
TAR HEELS

win during the 1991–92 season that UNC home crowds were "cheese and wine" crowds. He might have mixed up his phrase, but it still hit its intended target.

The next season, Cassell and the 19th-ranked Seminoles were the victims of one of the all-time-great Carolina comebacks—and a raucous fan response that rivaled anything from Carmichael. FSU head coach Pat Kennedy spent his pregame down time flipping through the pages of the Tar Heel media guide that were devoted to classic comebacks. He had no idea that he was about to be part of one.

Florida State led 45–28 at halftime, prompting Cassell and his teammates to dash off the court with broad smiles and hands waving in the air. In the FSU locker room, Cassell was vocal about his disdain for the Tar Heel defense. With under nine minutes left in the game, the Seminoles still held a 73–54 lead. But Carolina dashed off 15 straight points, helped by long-range marksmanship from Henrik Rödl. Smith also called a classic Tar Heel time-out—waiting until his team showed a little life but was still down by double digits—just to make Florida State realize a Carolina comeback was possible.

With under two minutes to play, George Lynch stole a crosscourt pass at midcourt. He slammed the ball home with two hands to give the Tar Heels the lead, prompting one of the loudest single-basket responses in Carolina history.

"Believe it or not, Sam is a great guy," Lynch said. "And he was right. Our crowd could get a little comfortable with expecting to win games and not giving opponents enough respect. When he said that, he changed some things. It changed the atmosphere of a Carolina basketball game."

Another turning point was an otherwise nondescript win over Maryland on January 27, 2000. A freak snowstorm had blanketed the Triangle, preventing thousands of ticket holders from reaching the Smith Center. Athletic department officials made a decision: tickets would still be honored, but just before tip-off, students would be allowed to claim any unoccupied seats. The result was a mad frenzy that included students climbing across the plush midcourt seats, creating a raucous home atmosphere.

When Matt Doherty was hired a few months later, he expressed a desire to be open with students. Addressing their seating concerns was an easy way to show his commitment. Working with the Rams Club and the student-run Carolina Athletic Association, administrators devised a plan that created several rows of student riser stands on one baseline.

The results have been impressive. In the Roy Williams era, the Tar Heels have recorded the third perfect home season in Smith Center history and won 89.5% of their home games.

Within the next five years, the Smith Center will pass Woollen Gym as the longest-tenured home court in Carolina history. Over that time, it has grown from a basketball showplace into a feared destination for opponents.

"I think I've never been in a building that was as loud as that building," Ohio State head coach Thad Matta said in the fall of 2005.

"This," Connecticut coach Jim Calhoun said, "is one heck of a home-court advantage."

(opposite)
UNC students moved closer to the action in the early 2000s when the Smith Center added risers in the end zone nearest the Tar Heel bench.
(Photo by Jeffrey A. Camarati)

15 : ENDINGS AND BEGINNINGS

n addition to housing numerous comeback wins and court-storming celebrations, the Smith Center was also the setting for two very important
press conferences that took place exactly 2,013 days apart. One was marked
by tears, the other by both tears and joy. Those 2,013 days represent the
only true transition era in the last nearly half century of Carolina Basketball. As is typical of the Tar Heels, by the end of the transition, the program had
indeed moved forward—but only by taking with it a sizable piece of its past.

The first press conference came on October 9, 1997, and it felt vaguely fune-
real. The previous night, word had begun to trickle out: Dean Smith was retiring.
There had been no hints that the news might be coming, no public statements
from Smith that retirement was even being considered. His closest associates
knew he took some time to recharge each summer, especially over the last six to
eight years, but by the time he returned in the fall, he was always eagerly antici-
pating a new season. This time, the anticipation was lessened.

Although it was only a little more than a decade ago, Smith's retirement came before the
Internet was widespread and before news was delivered on cell phones. Accessing the Internet at home was still a luxury. Rather than today's constant 24-hour barrage of information,
news cycles still existed. The six o'clock news was a big deal in most households. ESPN's
SportsCenter had already become an essential sports mainstay, and that was where many Tar
Heel fans received their first inkling of the breaking story. The next morning, when newspapers began hitting driveways across the state, banner headlines announced the stunning
news that Smith was stepping down.

It was a where-were-you-when moment, the Kennedy assassination or Challenger tragedy
of Carolina Basketball fandom. Yes, it was just a coach retiring. But it also felt like the end

Roy Williams, Dean Smith, Bill Guthridge, and Matt Doherty chat prior to the 1993 Final Four in New Orleans. (Photo by Hugh Morton; courtesy North Carolina Collection, UNC–Chapel Hill)

of an era that no one was prepared to see end, and it was stunning. It wasn't time for Smith to go. He had a powerhouse team returning, fresh off a Final Four appearance in 1997 and loaded with Antawn Jamison, Vince Carter, Shammond Williams, Ed Cota, and Ademola Okulaja. He had just broken Adolph Rupp's all-time wins record, getting the record-setting win in Winston-Salem in the NCAA Tournament in one of the toughest tickets in Carolina Basketball history (because of the slim NCAA allotments, even some former Tar Heel players had to buy tickets off the street).

It felt like Smith was still near the middle of a golden era, not approaching its end. In the few hours between the time the news leaked and Carolina held a press conference, numerous rumors spread, including speculation about the head coach's health.

The on-court celebration of Dean Smith's last regional final win was a family affair. Vince Carter and Mitchell Ford (son of Tar Heel assistant coach Phil Ford) enjoyed the festivities. (Photo by Robert Crawford; courtesy of UNC Athletic Communications)

"It's almost like [people feel] something has to be wrong," Smith said at the press conference. "I'm 66 years old."

Smith had known that his career was in its final chapter. When he went out recruiting in September, he told the prospects he visited that he would not be there for their senior years. His contract ran until 2001, and by that point he would retire, Smith told them.

When the fall of 1997 rolled around, he just couldn't muster the excitement necessary to coach another season. And the fact that the 1997–98 team would be so formidable was a factor, too; he had always intended to leave his successor with a quality team.

All the members of that team were present for Smith's announcement. The gathering, held in Bowles Hall, was a major event. In an era when live sports news-conference coverage was not common, ESPN2 carried the event in its entirety. Numerous former players came to Chapel Hill just to be there in person, and a significant portion of athletic-department staff were in attendance, along with every media outlet within driving range and a number of national media members who flew in on short notice. Fans stood upstairs on a walkway outside the building, trying to peer in to catch a glimpse of Smith. One fan held a homemade sign urging the coach not to retire.

Athletic director Dick Baddour called it "a very important day in the life of the University of North Carolina." Smith broke down only once, when he said, "What loyalty I've had . . . from my players. They're really special."

As Smith pushed away the microphone, there was rousing applause, including from members of the usually stonefaced media. The announcement that Bill Guthridge would be the new head coach followed, and the assembled group took a few questions.

When the press conference was over, Smith had one final duty. With the rest of the sports world knocked cockeyed by his announcement, he drove Georgetown head coach—and close friend—John Thompson to the airport.

NEARLY SIX YEARS LATER, the introduction of Roy Williams as Carolina's new head basketball coach took place in the same room in the same building. It was fitting, though, that the room could scarcely be recognized. It had been transformed from a pregame gathering spot to a practice gym. Windows had been blacked out. Where the stage was once set up to

Shammond Williams celebrated the first of two straight Final Four trips after Carolina's win over Louisville at the Carrier Dome in 1997.
(Photo courtesy of UNC Athletic Communications)

accommodate Smith at his final press conference as head coach, a backboard and rim hung over the floor.

There had been more than just cosmetic changes in Carolina Basketball during the previous six seasons. The switch from Smith to Guthridge had been smooth—perhaps even more smooth for those inside the program, who were familiar with the low-profile Guthridge's attributes and abilities, than for those outside the program. For example, players and ex-players already knew the value of Guthridge Time, which required being at least three minutes earlier than the actual time. Guthridge was the creator of the seemingly strange departure times for Carolina travel parties. The team bus never left at 2:00 P.M.; it left at 1:57 P.M.

"A Major Basketball-Related Press Conference"

It was Wednesday, October 8, 1997, seven days before the first practice of what was to be Dean Smith's 37th year as head coach. Coach Smith asked me to come to his office, whereupon I was met not only by him but also by director of athletics Dick Baddour and assistant coach Bill Guthridge, who had matching "you're not going to believe this" looks on their faces.

Dick said, "Coach Smith is going to step down and Coach Guthridge is going to be the head coach, effective immediately." I answered, "Okay."

Dick laughed and said it wasn't a joke. I didn't laugh and said I didn't think this was the kind of thing you would bring me in here and make jokes about, so I figure you're telling the truth.

For the next few minutes, the three of us politely but firmly spoke to Coach Smith about the need to have a press conference to make this rather historic pronouncement. Coach Smith wanted to wait a few hours to tell his team and call some prospects—namely Jason Capel and Kris Lang—then announce the news in a simple press release.

No, that was not going to do, we argued successfully. Well, somewhat successfully. Coach Smith agreed to conduct a press conference the next day, but he insisted that the team be allowed to play pickup while the press conference was being held, because he didn't want them to think they had to attend.

For the sake of moving on with what I knew would be about a thousand details to hammer out in the next few hours, we said we would discuss that with the players and agree to their wishes.

The team photo and annual mile run had previously been scheduled for that afternoon, and Coach Smith did not want his news to adversely affect the players' times. Thus he waited until after the team's return from the track at Fetzer Field before he told the players his intentions.

Meanwhile, sports information director Rick Brewer and I were allowed to call the media and inform them only that a "major basketball-related press conference" was going to take place the next day. I remember giving both local and national writers only two clues: Coach Smith's health was not in question and it was not related to any NCAA sanctions.

Despite our rather coy invitations, word leaked out, and it came pretty much straight from the source. The Philadelphia 76ers were holding part of their training camp at the Smith Center and former Carolina greats Eric Montross and Jerry Stackhouse were on the court when the current Tar Heels came pouring out of the locker room in tears. Antawn Jamison, Vince Carter, Shammond Williams, and the other Tar Heels were unable to hide their emotions or the news that had them in such a state. Word went from the Sixers to ESPN's David Aldridge, who was covering the team, and, voilà, the story went national.

Writers such as *Sports Illustrated*'s Alex Wolff, Dick Weiss of the *New York Daily News*, Tony Barnhart of the *Atlanta Journal-Constitution*, and others from Baltimore, Boston, Chicago, Dallas, Kansas City, Philadelphia, and all over the country quickly descended upon Chapel Hill for the next day's news conference. They did so in part to cover a major news event, but also as a measure of respect for Coach Smith.

The current team's players not only insisted upon attending—Jamison laughed when told of Coach Smith's concern—but did so wearing suits and ties to honor their departing coach. Georgetown coach John Thompson, an assistant to Coach Smith in the 1976 Olympics, also was among those who attended.

Coach Smith seemed tired and relieved when it was over. He hated the fuss and is probably still mad at us for insisting we have a press conference. But it was Coach Smith, it was the end of an era, and judging by the outpouring of love and respect people displayed that day for him, it was worth it. It was a day that changed college basketball forever—not just in Chapel Hill, but across the country. It was a part of history.—*Steve Kirschner*

His reasoning? People might misinterpret 2:00, thinking it really meant 2:15 or even 1:45. But 1:57 was 1:57.

Guthridge piloted the 1998 team to the Final Four and won consensus National Coach of the Year honors. He won more games in his first two years (58) than any coach in NCAA history and compiled an 80–28 three-year record. He also oversaw a remarkable turnaround from the 2000 team, which stood at 18–13 after the ACC Tournament—drawing some intense criticism for Guthridge—but advanced to the Final Four.

"I tell people that Coach Smith and Coach Guthridge are my light-skinned fathers," said Antawn Jamison, who was the National Player of the Year for the 1998 team. "Together, they taught us basketball is secondary. They made sure we knew it wasn't the most important thing in the world, but that we had been given a talent, and it was our job to use it."

The usually stoic Guthridge—whose veneer could be cracked by an occasional insolent referee—couldn't bear to tell his staff in person that he was retiring, so he passed out handwritten notes. It was an emotional moment for a man whose impact perhaps can be measured by his history with one player. The coach's relationship with guard Shammond Williams was sometimes tempestuous, including an incident at Virginia when Williams walked

Antawn Jamison was the consensus National Player of the Year in 1998, Bill Guthridge's first season as UNC head coach.
(Photo by Scott Sharpe; courtesy of UNC Athletic Communications)

(opposite)
This thunderous alley-oop dunk by Julius Peppers came in one of 18 consecutive wins in 2000–2001.
(Photo courtesy of UNC Athletic Communications)

off the court. Guthridge benched him for the remainder of the game. But when Guthridge announced his retirement on June 30, 2000, Williams—then with the Seattle SuperSonics—made the effort to take a commercial flight to North Carolina to attend the press conference, flying out again as soon as it was over.

As reporters caught wind of the impending announcement, Matt Doherty was preparing for an approach shot on the 15th hole at Warren Golf Course in South Bend, Indiana. His first thought: "Coach Williams will be the next Carolina coach, and maybe I'll get a call about replacing him at Kansas."

The next 11 days were painful for everyone connected to Carolina Basketball. The most startling thing about the events was the uncertainty cast over the program, which had been built on stability and confidence. Now, in a period that included a long Fourth of July weekend, everything was undecided.

Chief among those undecided participants was Roy Williams. The *Durham Herald-Sun* ran a story reporting he had accepted the job. He hadn't. After several days of soul-searching, Williams announced at a press conference that he was staying in Lawrence.

Members of the UNC media watched Williams's press conference in the Smith Center press room. When it was over, Carolina convened its own press conference at 10:30 P.M. and then began preparing to search for a new coach. Baddour left the press conference and immediately called Notre Dame's Doherty, who took the call in a South Bend Walmart.

Over the next few days, the national perception was that the Tar Heels were encountering some trouble finding a coach. The truth was that numerous candidates were indicating interest—John Calipari made known his availability, among others—but as Guthridge and Smith had indicated on June 30, a coach with Carolina ties was preferable.

On July 11, Doherty accepted the job. Even though he had only one year as a head coach on his résumé, he had virtually no choice. What 38-year-old who wants to make coaching his life's occupation would turn down the head-coaching job at North Carolina? The morning he made his decision to take the job, he received a 7:30 A.M. phone call from Michael Jordan.

"When our conversation was ending, Michael said that Carolina might go 'outside the family' for its next coach if I didn't get the job," Doherty said. "That settled things in my mind."

Matt Doherty earned National Coach of the Year honors in 2001. (Photo by Jeffrey A. Camarati)

(opposite)
At Duke in 2001, Joseph Forte had one of the most complete games ever by a UNC guard, scoring 24 points and grabbing 16 rebounds. (Photo by Robert Crawford; courtesy of UNC Athletic Communications)

Doherty's first season as head coach was alternately exhilarating and disappointing, thrilling and unsatisfactory. There was little doubt that the program looked different under his direction. Showing the type of loyalty that he'd been taught by Smith—and the same type of loyalty that Williams would show three years later—he brought his entire Notre Dame coaching staff to Chapel Hill. But that displaced the current UNC assistants, creating some confusion for a fan base that had grown accustomed to having Phil Ford and his fellow coaches as a part of the program.

Six minutes into his first game as the Tar Heel head coach, Doherty earned a technical foul against Winthrop. The outburst was applauded by the Smith Center crowd.

Doherty's signature win came three months later— a road victory at Duke. The win propelled Carolina to the nation's number-one ranking.

"We won a lot of games in a row there," said Michael Brooker (1998–2001). "We got to number one for a little while. That's when we started to get a little full of ourselves to a certain degree. That ultimately was our downfall. As a group, we started feeling a little too good about ourselves and stopped listening to the coaches a little bit, which was completely our fault."

After an ACC Tournament semifinal win over Georgia Tech, Doherty tried to regain his team's focus by blistering them for a perceived poor effort. The outburst had the opposite effect, and his team slumbered through a 26-point whipping to Duke in the next day's championship game. One week later, the season ended with a second-round NCAA loss to Penn State.

Since taking the job, Doherty had known his second season would be a struggle because of a talent gap and the need to rely on freshmen. It turned out even worse than he anticipated, as the Tar Heels limped to 8–20. In a sign of how far things had fallen, Carolina resorted to holding the ball against Duke—as much as the shot clock would allow—in the quarterfinals of the ACC Tournament to limit the damage. After clubbing the Tar Heels by 29 and 25 points in the previous two meetings, the Blue Devils won by just 12 in the tournament.

In the offseason, guards Brian Morrison and Adam Boone transferred, and Doherty— despite bringing in one of the nation's best recruiting classes in Raymond Felton, Sean May, and Rashad McCants—was again under an intense media spotlight.

"The scrutiny surprised me," Doherty said. "Even having played here and coached at Kansas and Notre Dame, I didn't realize the microscope this position was under. That may sound naïve, and you'd think that if anybody would have a handle on it, it would be me."

Injuries, blowout losses, and communication frustrations derailed Doherty's third year. Every big win seemed to be accompanied by a similarly large firestorm over coach-player issues. A victory over top-ranked Connecticut came on the same day a story was released questioning Doherty's relationship with freshman Raymond Felton. A win over Maryland in the ACC Tournament was followed by a local TV news story detailing unrest among parents of players. At some programs, the strife would have been a minor footnote. But Carolina fans and family members had grown accustomed to a certain standard. Part of the value of being a Tar Heel was the shared experience of every player from the 1960s to the present. As the 2003 season came to a conclusion, for the first time there was a sense that the players' experience had changed.

A torturous five days of meetings ensued. During the five days between Carolina's NIT loss to Georgetown and a press conference on April 1, Carolina Basketball was almost unrecognizable. Reporters camped out in the Smith Center parking lot, waiting to pounce on any player, coach, or administrator who happened by. Rumors and innuendo filled the Internet, talk radio, and even some newspapers. For the first time in 40 years, the program seemed rudderless.

At the press conference announcing Doherty's resignation, Baddour referred to Carolina Basketball as a "public trust." Chancellor James Moeser also referenced the importance of the program beyond wins and losses. "To be sure, we want good athletes and we want to win," Moeser said. "But on this campus coaches are also responsible for creating an environment for learning, for character development, for building a team of good leaders and good citizens. That's the Carolina standard."

Because of Smith's one-of-a-kind approach, expectations were different at Carolina than anywhere else. That was a source of pride in Chapel Hill, but it was also a daunting stan-

The résumé Roy Williams sent to Kansas in 1988 when applying for the head-coaching job included a very important reference: Dean Smith.

dard. Partially for that reason, Carolina Basketball was in the same position it had been three years earlier: looking for a coach.

And looking, again, toward Roy Williams. Several other big-name candidates made their interest known through intermediaries, but as Baddour acknowledged, Williams was the home-run hire. Carolina was in a position familiar to UCLA and Kentucky, two dynasties that had struggled to maintain their greatness. Within a decade of John Wooden's retirement in 1975, the Bruins had fallen into mediocrity, notching 10-plus losses in six out of seven seasons in the mid-1980s. Kentucky managed a national championship six years after Adolph Rupp's retirement in 1972, but the pressure to continue the success—in Lexington, unlike at UCLA or Carolina, the standard was largely set only by win-loss percentage—eventually landed the program on a three-year probation.

Other coaches, perhaps, could have assumed the reins and quickly returned the Tar Heels to NCAA prominence. But no one other than Williams had such a deep understanding of the on- and off-court expectations associated with being North Carolina's head basketball coach. Carolina didn't just need Williams to win; they needed him to smooth relationships with former players, restore the summer pickup games to the stuff of legend, and move Tar Heel basketball back to its centerpiece role in the Chapel Hill community.

This time, the Kansas coach's situation had changed in Lawrence. His relationship with the Jayhawks' athletic director had soured. Health issues in his family made a move to North Carolina make sense. And, quite simply, he couldn't turn down Smith again.

So, 2,013 days after Smith's press conference, the media reassembled in Bowles Hall. At Doherty's request, the facility had since been converted into a practice gym, but on this night it was a media center. Just like at Smith's event, a few members of the athletic department staff attended and broke out into applause when Williams was announced. That reception was nothing compared to what Williams had seen when he first arrived at the Smith Center. Fans who couldn't gain access to the building had lined up outside in the parking lot. Every time a car turned into the lot, the crowd murmured. When Williams finally did arrive, he was greeted by raucous cheers. Some fans ran alongside the car like paparazzi chasing a movie star.

Two weeks after his hiring—after he had handed out Krispy Kreme doughnuts at the Old Well and flown back to Lawrence to attend the KU basketball banquet—Williams met with the media again. His most important words would set the tone for the next era of Carolina Basketball.

"There is only one [information] source for Carolina Basketball," Williams said, "and that is me. That was one of the problems that made it so difficult here before. There were so many sources. It came out that Matt was doing this or Matt was doing that, and somebody forgot to ask Matt."

Roy Williams handed out Krispy Kreme doughnuts on campus with Chancellor James Moeser the morning after accepting the Carolina job in 2003.
(Photo by Dan Sears)

The first sign of his influence came in the summer counselors' basketball game, an annual feature of the Carolina Basketball Camp. The camp spanned three one-week sessions. In the second session, with a sparse turnout from the alumni—the annual parade back to Chapel Hill in the summer had slowed considerably—the veterans still beat the current players. NCAA rules prohibited Williams from watching the game, but word of the outcome quickly reached him.

That night, Williams made the rounds to the various gyms used by the camp, tracking down each of his players.

"I let them know individually that to me, it's not okay to lose," Williams said. "If you think it's okay to lose, that's how you lose 36 games in two years. Winning is important. It's not okay to just go through the motions, whether it's a pickup game, pool, or marbles. You should compete to the best of your ability and invest something in every competition we have."

The counselors' game in the third week of camp was much more intense. No layups were given. Trash was talked. No one knew it at the time, but the game bore much more of a resemblance to the pickup games later in Williams's tenure than the one the previous week.

"I had never played in a pickup game that intense," said Baltimore native Melvin Scott (2002–05). "Baltimore pickup games are tough. They are physically tougher. But there's not as much talent."

Coming Home

When Roy Williams became Carolina's head basketball coach on April 14, 2003, it was one of the most important and fortuitous hires the university had ever made.

Important because, amid much controversy, the Tar Heels had missed the NCAA Tournament for the previous two seasons, and the basketball program that Dean Smith had built into a nationally visible, much-envied, multimillion-dollar institution was tilting in the steady breeze created by Duke and the rest of the Atlantic Coast Conference.

Fortuitous because when, in 2000, Williams first turned down the UNC job, he'd meant what he said about ending his Hall of Fame career where it began: at Kansas. Luckily for Carolina, Williams had grown unhappy with several decisions made by the KU administration over the previous three years, and he was no longer resigned to staying there.

Williams also came home because "the family business needed me" and he needed to be closer to his remaining family in the mountains of North Carolina. His father, Babe, and older sister, Frances, would die within Williams's first four years back at Carolina, and he was happy to have had the time he spent with both.

As in 2000, Williams took a week to huddle with his wife, Wanda, his children, and his closest friends before making his decision. He knew he had let down millions of UNC alumni and fans three years earlier and wanted to be sure he was still welcome back in Chapel Hill. He also had to find the right words to tell his Kansas players that he was leaving to "go home."

He asked his mentor, Coach Smith, three questions.

"Do you think everyone there will be pleased with me coming back?"

"Would I be their first choice?"

"Are you sure you want me to take this job?"

The last question was important because of all those Tar Heels he had disappointed in 2000, Williams felt the worst about saying no to the man who gave him his start in college basketball.

When Smith answered "yes" to all three questions, Williams said he would meet with his Kansas players the next day and be ready to fly to Chapel Hill that evening.

"I couldn't turn Coach Smith down a second time," Williams said.

The special bond Williams had with his former players and coaching colleagues at both schools made leaving Kansas so painful and returning to Carolina so heartfelt. At his introductory press conference in Bowles Hall, Williams wore a tie bearing crimson and blue because he wanted everyone watching that night or on *SportsCenter* the next morning to know how much his 15 years as a Jayhawk meant to him.

But he had a going-forward message for his old and new Tar Heel family members. Turning to the players who had endured 36 losses over the preceding two seasons, Williams raised an open hand and then closed his fist. He promised them that if they played together and listened to him, they would be successful.

Within one year, the Tar Heels were back in the NCAA Tournament. Within two, they won the university's fifth—and Williams's first—national championship. Welcome home, indeed.—*Art Chansky*

Eventually, the current players prevailed by two points. That night, Williams again sought out his new players at gyms across campus. This time, they told him the day's outcome with broad smiles.

Without ever coaching a game or running a practice, Williams had set the tone for a new era of Carolina Basketball—one built on the foundation of the old era, but with perhaps even more triumphant results.

16 : 2005 TAKING BACK
THE NEIGHBORHOOD

Today, it's hard to comprehend the magnitude of Carolina's win over Duke on March 6, 2005. Most Carolina fans are too far removed from it. They've become too comfortable with the Tar Heels' recent success against the Blue Devils (Carolina has won six of the past nine meetings). They're used to an era when an entire class of Tar Heel seniors graduated without ever losing in Cameron Indoor Stadium.

But in March 2005, the Carolina seniors were about to depart having never won in Cameron Indoor Stadium. In March 2005, Duke was the Atlantic Coast Conference's dominant program. The Tar Heels hadn't finished in the top three of the ACC regular-season race since 2001 and hadn't been to an NCAA Tournament regional final since 2000.

But those league and national results were secondary to a cold, simple fact: Duke had won 15 of the previous 17 meetings between the two schools, and those 15 Tar Heel defeats had been by an average of 13.9 points. During that streak, the two programs met four times in the postseason. Duke prevailed in all four games, including a 23-point shellacking in 1999, a 26-point whipping in 2001, a 12-point win in 2002 (when Carolina stalled as much as they could with a 35-second shot clock), and then another 12-point win in 2003.

Duke wasn't just dominating the Carolina rivalry: they were actively seeking out new rivalries, including some drummed-up enmity with Maryland that at least one national media member claimed had surpassed the Carolina-Duke battles.

That was the reality of Carolina-Duke in 2005. The frustration had continued in Roy Williams's first year, as the Tar Heels looked bound for an upset of top-ranked Duke at the Smith Center until Chris Duhon dashed the length of the court to provide an 83–81 Blue Devil

Raymond Felton celebrates the comeback win over Duke that clinched the 2005 ACC regular-season championship. (Photo by Jeffrey A. Camarati)

win. Duke had won again at Cameron to end the 2004 regular season and then snapped a five-game Carolina winning streak in February 2005 with a frustrating 71–70 win.

In that game, Carolina had the ball with seconds remaining and a chance to win—and break the Blue Devils' hex. But Raymond Felton and Rashad McCants miscommunicated, and then the ball trickled out of bounds off the hands of David Noel. The game ended with the perfect snapshot of Carolina-Duke relations at that point, as Felton and McCants stood face-to-face, crushed, while jubilant Blue Devils celebrated all around them.

But one important observer saw a glimmer of hope in the loss.

"I was really disgusted about the way we performed on the last play," Roy Williams said. "But I told them in the locker room that we did not play very well. We weren't sharp. We weren't smooth. But we competed and had a chance to win at the end when we had been so sorry. I told them I was not trying to con them, that I was pleased about that part. We had a chance to win the dadgum game at Cameron Indoor Stadium against Duke University, and we had played poorly."

By the time the two teams met again on March 6, Carolina had again gone on a winning streak. A win three days earlier over Florida State had made it six in a row and guaranteed the Tar Heels a share of the regular-season championship for the first time since 2001. Mindful of the opportunity to celebrate a win with a group that hadn't had much practice winning titles, Williams offered his seniors the chance to cut down the Smith Center nets after the victory over the Seminoles.

"No way," Jackie Manuel said. "We don't want to just tie for the title. We want to win it outright."

A win over Duke would provide that outright championship. A loss would drop Carolina into a three-way tie for first with the Blue Devils and Wake Forest. Barring something very unexpected in the ACC Tournament, a win would virtually guarantee an NCAA Tournament top seed. If Carolina lost, the ACC Tournament in Washington, D.C., would become much more important. The first and second rounds of the NCAA Tournament were slated for Charlotte, so Carolina, Duke, and Wake were competing for the chance to play close to home. Defeating Duke and winning the regular-season title would place Carolina in prime position for getting one of the two Charlotte slots. A loss would make the picture cloudier.

And those were just the tangible stakes. The game marked Senior Day for the class of Jawad Williams, Melvin Scott, and Manuel. Roy Williams, whose formative years as a young assistant coach were spent watching some of Carolina's most memorable Senior Days, placed a premium on the final home game of the season. He'd never lost a home finale in his head-coaching career. The final game for the trio in Chapel Hill carried significant emotional weight for a group that started their Tar Heel career suffering through an 8–20 campaign.

"Some of the most emotional days I've ever had in my career are Senior Days," Coach Williams said. "With that group specifically, Jawad and Jackie and Melvin, what they had gone through was very emotional for me. They went through a lot as freshmen, but they didn't leave. They didn't transfer. They came back to try and make it better."

Here was the problem: Duke was very good, and they were in Carolina's head at least slightly. After a couple of uncharacteristic late-season road losses, the Blue Devils were coming off a 24-point shellacking of Miami. They had a potent inside-outside combination in Shelden Williams and J.J. Redick, with both of those players bound for first-team All-ACC honors. The Tar Heels were playing without Rashad McCants, who was sidelined with an intestinal disorder.

So it wasn't entirely unexpected that Duke built a 73–64 lead with three minutes remaining. After the Devils' Lee Melchionni banged in a three-pointer from in front of the Duke bench, Roy Williams called what would be a fateful time-out.

For Jawad Williams, it all felt very familiar. It was another big game against Duke—and of course Duke was going to win.

But over the next three minutes, Carolina Basketball would undergo a dramatic change.

"Get your head up," Roy Williams barked at Jawad, who was hanging his head in the team

Sean May had 26 points and 24 rebounds in his final game in the Smith Center.
(Photo by Robert Crawford)

huddle during a time-out. "If you'll do exactly what we say, and you'll give me a total commitment on every possession—not to do well, but to do the best—we're going to win this game."

Williams said later, "It was one of those things where as a coach, you're willing to try anything. But I really believed it."

There were definite echoes of Dean Smith in Williams's strategy. He laid out the final three minutes for his team, describing not only what he expected of his players but how Duke would respond to all of Carolina's maneuvers.

"We walked over to the huddle, and you could just look into everybody's eyes and see it," Sean May said. "The past couple years, you could see it in their eyes when we thought we were going to lose a game. But I looked around—looked at Marvin, looked at Jackie, looked at Ray—and you would have thought we were up by ten. Everybody was so calm, cool, and collected."

"Here's how we're going to win the game. First, we're going to get a great shot."

They did. Jackie Manuel missed a runner, but May corralled the rebound—one of 24 he'd grab on a day when he had an incredible 26 points and 24 rebounds. His follow shot missed, but Jawad Williams tipped it back in.

"Then we're going to get a stop."

Carolina's defense forced a turnover by Daniel Ewing with 2:23 remaining.

"Then we're going to get another great shot."

The Smith Center crowd, which had carried a sense of impending doom after Melchionni's three-pointer, began to rise as Felton brought the ball across the midcourt stripe. Something, it seemed, might be different. Felton missed on a drive, but Carolina retained possession. Marvin Williams was fouled and made a pair of free throws with 2:03 left. Duke, 73–68.

"Then we're going to get another stop."

This time the stop was a little more unconventional. Noel bumped Demarcus Nelson, but Nelson missed the ensuing free throw. May—of course—got the rebound.

"Then we're going to come down and get a great shot."

Leaving Home

To be honest, it was probably Coach Williams that really got me there to Chapel Hill. He worked so hard recruiting me and he spoke so highly of the university. It's funny, it was right after he'd left Kansas and he'd recruited me to go to Kansas, but I was really sold on Coach and I really liked the University of North Carolina. I grew up a Tar Heel fan, believe it or not. My dad is from Burgaw, down near Wilmington, so I learned about the Tar Heel tradition early. And playing on national TV as often as Carolina does, I knew my family would be able to watch most of my games.

Being so far from home was tough at first, absolutely. I was a homebody growing up and I'd never been away from my mother and brothers for any long period of time. It was definitely a transition for me, but it was something I needed to do. I needed to grow up and I knew it would be worthwhile in the end. It definitely paid off.

The main thing about Coach that really struck me was he really cared about Marvin Williams the person, not as much the basketball player, and that was what was really important to me. One thing he told me when he was recruiting me was that if anything was to happen to me while I was playing, he promised me I'd be able to get my degree from the University of North Carolina. Him saying that was so big because I always had the reassurance in the back of my mind that if basketball didn't work out, I'd have a degree from a great university and be able to get a job anywhere in the world. That's all my mom needed to hear.

Coach Williams's success was also important to me. I think every high school player knows how much he's won and been successful. We're talking Final Fours, so many NCAA Tournament appearances and Big 12 championships at Kansas, and that's continued at Carolina. I knew I was going to work hard, but I knew we were going to win.

I couldn't have made a better choice than to come to Carolina. I was 17 years old, and it would've been easy to stay closer to home and play on the West Coast, but I've never doubted that I made the right decision. Hindsight is always 20/20, but I couldn't have made a better decision.

Any free time I get, I love going back to Chapel Hill, and I spend a good part of my off-seasons there. It's such a great college town with a perfect atmosphere. I try to spend as much time as I possibly can there. Coach Williams gives me the opportunity to come back and work with the college guys and work out with Jonas Sahratian, the team's strength coach. A lot of guys don't go back to their college after they leave for the NBA, but it's such a blessing for me to be able to do that.

And working to finish my degree is part of my love for Carolina. I'm a junior now and will keep working until I graduate. My parents have always taught me that if you start something, you should finish it. I told Coach Williams I was going to come back and finish my degree. I know he's a man of his word, and he teaches his players to be the same. I'm definitely a man of mine and I've been working to finish it for me—not just for him or my family or anyone else. I know I can't play basketball forever, and with a degree from the University of North Carolina, you can get a job doing anything, anywhere. A degree from such a prestigious college carries a lot of pride for me.

—*Marvin Williams*

It *was* a great shot. Felton penetrated and dished to May, who missed his initial attempt but got his own rebound, put the ball back in the basket, and drew a foul. His free throw made it 73–71 with 1:44 remaining. Carolina had trimmed seven points off the deficit in just over a minute.

"Then we only need one more stop, and we'll be right there at the end."

After the two teams traded possessions—Duke's included a wide-open miss by Redick, who was struggling through a 5-for-13 day at the defensive hands of Manuel—Carolina got that stop in a most surprising way.

In the first half, Roy Williams had ordered Noel to stay in front of his man defensively.

(left)

Rashad McCants earned all-tournament honors at the Syracuse Regional and the Final Four. (Photo by Kevin Cox)

(right)

Marvin Williams's willingness to come off the bench was a key to the 2005 team's success. (Photo by Peyton Williams)

Noel had a tendency to let the dribbler go by and then try to swipe the ball from behind. "You can't do that against them," Williams told him. "They're too good."

But with 30 seconds left, Ewing went by Noel near midcourt. Noel swiped for the ball, and it came free. Felton picked up the loose ball and called a time-out.

In the previous installment of the rivalry, Felton had drawn some criticism for failing to assertively make a play on Carolina's final possession. Roy Williams responded to that criticism by compiling a list of a dozen plays. All of them contained an error by a Carolina player or coach. "This game is not on Raymond," Williams told his team after that game. "Look at these plays. Jawad screwed it up. Sean screwed it up. Marvin screwed it up. Roy screwed it up. We all screwed it up. Our team lost that game."

This time, Felton knew exactly what to do. Once again, he got penetration into the lane. Near the left block, he elevated for a shot and drew a shooting foul. With 19.4 seconds left, Felton had two free throws. Making them both would tie the game.

The first was perfect. The second was hard—much too hard. It bounced almost all the way back to the free-throw line. Felton was supposed to get back on defense and not follow

Despite ups and downs, David Noel's growth as a player during the 2005 season prepared him for a standout senior season in 2006. Roy Williams has called Noel "the best leader I have ever coached." (Photo by J.D. Lyon Jr.; courtesy of UNC Athletic Communications)

Getting Coach That Trophy

My dad, Scott, taught me not only to respect the game of basketball but also to appreciate the history of its great teams, players, and coaches. Growing up in Bloomington, Indiana, the home of the Hoosiers, I was pretty often reminded of the 1976 Indiana team that went undefeated and won the national championship. Of course, my dad was the National Player of the Year that season and was MVP of the Final Four.

So you can only imagine how I felt the day after we won the 2005 NCAA title and I walked into the locker room back at the Smith Center and found, waiting for our arrival on a table, an advance copy of the next *Sports Illustrated*. There was a photo of me on the cover, touting our national championship triumph. Father and son, 29 years apart, each winning a ring and earning MVP honors, too—how much better can it get?

When I came to Carolina, I certainly had a sense of the history that players like Michael Jordan and Phil Ford had created before me. In all honesty, I wanted to someday be mentioned by Tar Heel Nation in the same sentence with players like that. I will always appreciate Coach Matt Doherty for giving me the chance to be a Tar Heel; and Coach Williams made me a champion by teaching me to run hard every possession, grab every rebound like it would be my last, and have confidence that we could win it all.

The players knew we were national championship–caliber my junior year. Seniors Jackie Manuel, Melvin Scott, and Jawad Williams had been through the depths of 8–20 and became tougher, better players; my class had future pros like Raymond Felton, Rashad McCants, and David Noel; and we added a phenom in Marvin Williams.

We wanted to win the outright ACC regular-season title because no Tar Heel team had done that since the 1993 team that won a national title. We got that done by beating Duke in what proved to be my last home game. We were down nine with three minutes to go, but we came back to win. I saved my best for last at the Smith Center, scoring 26 points and ripping down 24 rebounds. I will always be proud of that performance because some of the people around the program said that game is among the best ever played against Duke by a Tar Heel. Knowing the history of those two programs and how much I liked to play (beat) them, that is something I will always remember. That and how loud it was in the Dome.

That game came in the late-season stretch when I had eight straight double-doubles. It gave me the confidence that I was one of the best players in the country and could play a big role in important games. I remember Melvin telling Coach Williams against Wisconsin in the Elite Eight not to draw up any plays, just get the ball to Sean. It's an amazing feeling to hear a teammate say that to Coach during a game, and it gave me the added confidence I needed.

But I really wanted to give Coach Williams his first national title. We already knew he was a Hall of Fame coach, but we wanted to be the first group to get him that trophy, cut those nets, and be on the stage with him when they played "One Shining Moment." So when we beat Illinois—whom every TV analyst said was the better team—the first person I wanted to celebrate with was Coach. That was one of the best feelings I've ever had.

I've said it many times: Carolina was the perfect choice for me, and no matter where I play or where I live, part of me will always be in Chapel Hill.—*Sean May*

the ball. But he hung around just long enough to get a hand on it. The ball trickled through the hands of several Tar Heels and Blue Devils before finding Marvin Williams near the right block. He scarcely paused. There was plenty of time remaining, but the freshman went right back to the hoop with the ball. The referee's whistle blew, but almost no one heard it. They were too busy watching Williams shot-put the ball off the glass and through the hoop, giving Carolina a one-point lead.

In that moment, half a decade's worth of frustration was released. The Carolina bench spilled onto the court, with Roy Williams frantically trying to push them back onto the

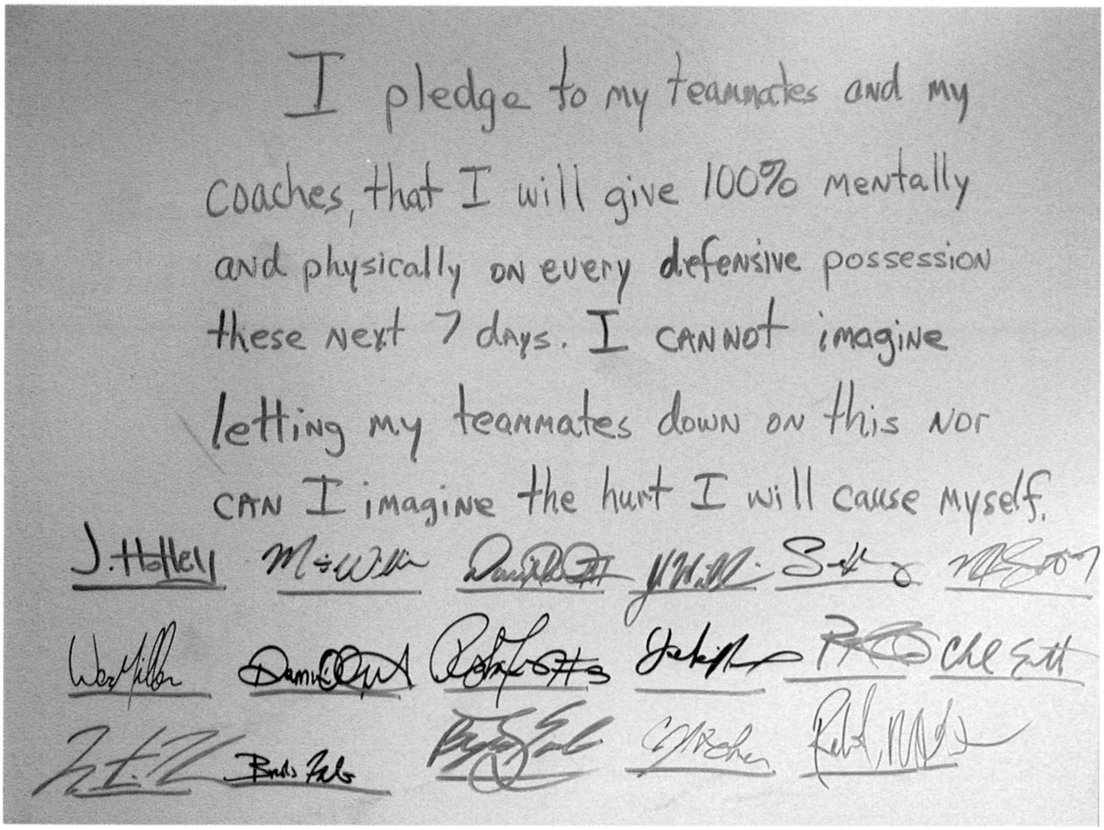

Tar Heel players committed to defense on the Monday before the Final Four. (Photo by Steve Kirschner)

The handwritten pledge reads:

> I pledge to my teammates and my coaches, that I will give 100% mentally and physically on every defensive possession these next 7 days. I cannot imagine letting my teammates down on this nor can I imagine the hurt I will cause myself.

sideline to avoid a technical foul. Noel hoisted the taller Marvin Williams into the air in a bear hug. Pandemonium engulfed the Smith Center, where many of the fans were too busy jumping around to even realize that Williams still had a free throw yet to come.

"That's the loudest I have ever heard the Smith Center, and it's not even close," Roy Williams said.

Marvin Williams, with the familiar free-throw routine of touching the tattoo honoring his mother on his left bicep, swished the shot for a 75–73 Carolina lead. It had been an 11–0 Tar Heel game-closing run. Carolina still had to survive a Redick missed three-pointer—over the outstretched arms of Noel and Manuel—and a missed Ewing 17-footer. But when May grabbed the final rebound, the magnitude of the win became obvious.

The Smith Center crowd swarmed the court. It wasn't one of the de rigueur court stormings where the crowd meanders onto the court out of a sense of obligation. This was a crowd that needed to be on the court, needed to be a part of what they had just seen. Within seconds of May's rebound and the final seconds elapsing, the court was almost completely covered with fans.

"It was probably the biggest moment of my life, as far as sports goes," Marvin Williams said.

It was also the biggest single shot of the Roy Williams era. If Marvin Williams's shot had

"Ties That Nobody Can Break"

The summer before my senior season, I had a vision that we were going to win the national championship. There was no question we had the talent to do it, even though we'd only made the second round of the NCAA Tournament the year before. A lot of people probably would've laughed if I'd told them.

It just seemed to make sense to me because it would be such a storybook ending for our senior class—Melvin Scott, Jackie Manuel, and me. We came in as freshmen and were part of one of the worst seasons in Carolina history and the worst season of our lives. Going 8–20 was definitely difficult, there's no denying that. I thought if it happened, there could be no topping a Hollywood story like ours: starting at the very bottom and ending with the national title four years later.

Melvin and Jackie were like my brothers while we were at Carolina, and they still are. Melvin is the one that plays all the time, and Jackie's the so-called quiet guy. Having those guys around all four years made life a lot easier as we got adjusted to life at UNC and college basketball in general. Melvin was always joking, keeping situations light, and Jackie—he's just always been there for me. We came in together, and we definitely helped each other through the hard times, especially during that 8–20 season. Sean May, Raymond Felton, David Noel, Rashad McCants, and those guys—when they came in the next year, we were like a big family.

Like I said, we had all the talent in the world, but we hadn't won anything. When we lost, we lost to better *teams*. I decided to take everything my senior year one moment at a time—not one day at a time, but one moment. Live for the moment and have fun with it. I enjoyed going to practice because I made myself have fun. The harder you work, the more fun you have.

That's what I tried to do all year long, and I was really relaxed that last night before the national championship game. I think that came from the visions I'd had of us winning. I knew it was only a matter of time before the clock ran out and we would be celebrating. All the things I'd imagined doing if we won—I did none of them. It didn't matter, because it was still one of the best feelings I've ever had in my life. Winning that championship with that group of guys, and the closeness we'd had through all we'd endured together, those feelings will always be with me.

I left Carolina with ties that nobody can break. I learned how to be a man. I definitely grew up a lot and left as a much more mature person than when I'd arrived in Chapel Hill in the summer of 2001. The tough times were all worth it because we were able to leave as national champions. A lot of guys I've come across in the NBA can't say that, and they tell me they're jealous and wish they'd won a national title.

I live near Chapel Hill in the offseason and always love coming back to the Smith Center to work out and play pickup games with the current team. I always try to remind them to stick with it during tough times because it's worth it. I also remind them that I'm a national champion and they have a big legacy to live up to—that's what we as former players try to do to help the current guys win another title.—*Jawad Williams*

Jawad Williams hoists the NCAA trophy, culminating a journey from 8–20 as a freshman to national champion as a senior. (Photo by Jeffrey A. Camarati)

not gone in, everything would have been different. It would have been different on that day: with the ball and a one-point lead, Duke would have simply fed the ball to Redick, who made 93.8% of his free throws that season.

It would have been different the rest of that year: rather than coast through the ACC Tournament, Carolina would have had to compete for a prime NCAA Tournament slot. Had they, for example, switched seedings with Duke, they would have been placed in the South Regional, meaning a trip to Austin, Texas, for the regionals. They would have faced a red-hot Michigan State team in the round of 16 and then played Kentucky in the regional final. And they could potentially have even faced Duke in a Final Four matchup.

But Williams's banked-in leaner took Carolina from they're-good-but-they-still-can't-beat-Duke to outright regular-season champions in one all-important play. It rendered the next weekend's ACC Tournament virtually meaningless—and Carolina played like it, slumbering through a quarterfinal win over Clemson before falling to Georgia Tech in the semifinals.

But they were still rewarded with the coveted top seed in the East Region. Williams memorably forced the team to practice without rims after a regional final victory over Wisconsin, and the defensive practice paid off with solid performances against Michigan State and Illinois in the Final Four.

May, who had completely reshaped his body over his UNC career thanks to long hours in the weight room with Jonas Sahratian and a dramatically changed diet, went on to have one of the best postseasons in Tar Heel basketball history, including winning Final Four Most Outstanding Player honors. Felton became Carolina's first winner of the Bob Cousy Award for the nation's best point guard. McCants rebounded from the illness and was a member of the Final Four All-Tournament team. Jawad Williams, Scott, and Manuel completed an improbable trip from the least successful Tar Heel team of all time to one of—at the time—just five national championship teams in 94 years of the school's basketball history. There was a time when the trio was worried they might be remembered as a blot on the storied history of Tar Heel basketball; now they were one of its crowning jewels.

Melvin Scott and Roy Williams cut down the nets after Williams's first NCAA title.

(Photo by Jeffrey A. Camarati)

David Noel and Roy Williams watch "One Shining Moment" after winning the national title in St. Louis.
(Photo by Getty Images)

(opposite)
Seniors Melvin Scott, Jawad Williams, and Jackie Manuel went old school in vintage Tar Heel uniforms for this 2004–05 team poster shot.
(Photo by Bob Donnan)

"We're the 2005 national champions," Jawad Williams said in the Carolina locker room after the 75–70 win over Illinois. "And that's something no one can ever take away from us."

Williams, Manuel, and Scott helped change the direction of Carolina Basketball—both locally and globally. Carolina would win six of its next eight meetings against Duke, the best Tar Heel stretch in the rivalry since the Jerry Stackhouse–Rasheed Wallace era. Finally, they owned the backyard again. And finally, they could move on to national goals.

Was beating Duke as big as winning the national championship? Of course not. But it's what made a national title—or anything, really—seem possible.

17 : 2009
THE LATEST GOLDEN ERA

On the road to a national championship, there's always one unexpected challenge.

The 1957 Tar Heels had to endure back-to-back triple-overtime games in the national semifinals and national championship game—and that was only after surviving a two-point win over Wake Forest in the ACC Tournament semifinals, when a loss would have disqualified Carolina from the NCAA Tournament.

Even though they were loaded with James Worthy, Sam Perkins, and Michael Jordan, the 1982 squad had to survive James Madison in the round of 32. Carolina struggled from the free-throw line (12–23) and three late misses allowed the hot-shooting Dukes (56.2% from the floor) to get within 52–50 at the buzzer.

In 1993 Carolina had back-to-back scares in the East Regional. First, Dean Smith designed a beautiful backdoor play to Donald Williams to seal an 80–74 win over Arkansas in the round of 16. Then, with a Final Four berth on the line, Derrick Phelps's second-half defense on Nick Van Exel allowed Carolina to survive a fluky Brian Reese missed dunk at the close of regulation to win 75–68 in overtime.

The 2005 team had to essentially play a pair of road games in the Final Four, beating Michigan State and Illinois to claim Roy Williams's first national title. But the closest call had come in Syracuse in the East Regional against Villanova. The Wildcats' four-guard offense, coupled with foul trouble for Raymond Felton (the junior point guard fouled out with 2:11 remaining), gave Carolina fits. Senior Melvin Scott stepped in to play point guard and nailed two key free throws with 28.9 seconds left to clinch the win.

Even though they had the most dominant NCAA Tournament of any Carolina team in history, the 2009 squad still had one close call. It didn't come in the regional semifinal against a well-coached Gonzaga squad. It didn't even come in the regional final against Oklahoma and National Player of the Year Blake Griffin. Instead, it came in one of the most Tar Heel–friendly NCAA venues of all time: the Greensboro Coliseum, where Carolina had never lost in NCAA play.

Eighth-seeded LSU was the opponent. The Tigers were a formidable eight seed, having won the SEC regular-season title, but the game wasn't expected to be especially close.

Assuming, that is, that Ty Lawson's big toe cooperated.

Leading up to the LSU game, most of the sports chatter revolved around the uncertain status of the most famous Carolina Basketball body part since Kenny Smith's broken wrist in 1984. (If that other speedy Tar Heel point guard hadn't been hammered by LSU's John Tudor, breaking the momentum of an unbeaten Carolina team, Dean Smith probably would've won his second NCAA title in three years). Injuries had played a key role in Carolina's post-season fortunes before. The 1977 Final Four team played through a knee injury to Tom LaGarde, an elbow injury to Phil Ford, and a broken thumb for Walter Davis. Derrick Phelps was wiped out of the 1994 NCAA Tournament with a concussion after a hard foul against Boston College. Ford's sprained ankle in 1976 limited him in NCAA play, and James Worthy missed the second half of his freshman season with a broken ankle. Carolina missed a chance to repeat in 1958 when Joe Quigg broke his leg.

So Tar Heel fans could be forgiven for being skittish about Lawson's health. On the Friday before the regular-season finale against Duke, the second-ranked Tar Heels were going through typical practice drills. They were about to find out just how delicate that ranking could be. In the course of sprinting back on defense, Lawson took a nudge from Mike Copeland. The contact sent Lawson across the baseline, where he banged his toe on the basket support. He would leave the arena on crutches after practice.

Thus began two weeks of breathless toe coverage. Lawson's teammates found the extensive reporting humorous, and at one point Wayne Ellington jokingly fanned the flames by opining that he didn't believe Lawson was really hurt. It did seem a little unusual that something as simple as a big toe injury could potentially derail a quest for a national championship. But this was Lawson's toe, and in early March 2009, no one was entirely sure about Lawson's toughness level.

Wayne Ellington bit seven second-half three-pointers against Miami on January 17, 2009. (Photo by Jeffrey A. Camarati)

(left)

Marcus Ginyard sat out all but three games in 2008–09 with a stress fracture in his foot. (Photo by Getty Images)

(right)

Bobby Frasor forced a tie-up to seal the victory over Duke at home. (Photo by Jeffrey A. Camarati)

As a sophomore, Lawson had missed seven full games and parts of two others due to two separate ankle injuries. One of those missed contests was a game against Duke. Normally, to justify a player missing one of those battles requires bone sticking out of skin; Lawson had only a simple brace. Doubters chirped. The player also had the reputation of being a bit of a goofball. Lawson watched cartoons and sometimes neglected to tie his shoelaces. Roy Williams had jokingly called him "Dennis the Menace" on multiple occasions.

But earlier in his junior year, Lawson had quietly played through flulike symptoms at Miami, scoring 17 of his team-high 21 points in the second half—including Carolina's final 11 points. Just two days after injuring his toe, he took a painkilling shot to suit up against the Blue Devils and responded with 13 points and 9 assists, a performance that helped him seal ACC Player of the Year honors.

The toe swelled up after the game, forcing him to miss Carolina's two ACC Tournament

games and the NCAA-opening win over Radford. The day before the LSU game, Lawson was termed a "game-time decision." Williams indicated that he would not allow his point guard to take another painkilling shot, even if that was the only way for him to play—sparking even more frenzied toe coverage.

"It was crazy," Lawson said. "I saw it all over ESPN, the news, everywhere. I thought it was just my toe and it would not be that big a deal. I think my teammates got tired of hearing it."

"Ty has had some injuries in the past that have taken him a while to come back from," Ellington said. "We needed him against LSU, there was no question about that."

The Tigers were virtually ignored in all the toe talk. The first half was fairly nondescript, with Lawson playing ineffectively and scoring only two points but Carolina building a 38–29 halftime lead. The story line seemed obvious: the Tar Heels would coast to an easy win in front of the partisan Greensboro crowd.

Williams knew otherwise. As his team prepared to go back on the court for the beginning of the second half, the head coach grabbed his point guard. "Remember the Duke game at home on Senior Day," Williams said. "You didn't play as well in the first half, but you were great in the second half. You're going to be great right now."

The results were not immediately obvious. LSU began the second half with a 13–3 run, prompting Williams to call a very rare time-out. During the break, he looked at seniors Bobby Frasor, Tyler Hansbrough, and Danny Green.

A Very Special Class

The first time I called Tyler Hansbrough, I had already committed to Carolina; two months went by, and he never called me back. On our second day rooming together in Chapel Hill, he told me he'd played quarterback in high school and pulled up a photo on the Internet of some guy wearing a helmet that he claimed was him—which was so incredibly not true. But that's the kind of character I lived with for four years.

It worked out well, though. I guess we are both a little wacko, and we might have clashed with anyone else. Add Marcus Ginyard and Danny Green, and the chemistry and fun we had were major reasons we won the national championship as seniors. There is no doubt about it.

I never thought we would be together for four years, because that's so rare today, especially after Tyler played so well as a freshman. He could have left for the NBA after any of those first three years. We all thought maybe he would stay one more year, but for him to stay four with Danny, Marcus, Mike Copeland, and me—it just so happened that we had a great class stay in place.

It was really cool because we did everything with those guys. We went to study hall together, ate together, and got a comfort level so that once we were out on the court, we could trust each other to know what was going to happen and not worry about guys missing their assignments.

It truly was a storybook ending to win the national championship in our last opportunity. Had we won it earlier, guys would have left, Tyler included. It was much sweeter to have an extra couple of years of memories that no one thought we would have.

The losses to Georgetown in the Elite 8 in 2007 and to Kansas in the 2008 Final Four were hard because we wanted it so bad, and all of a sudden it's over. I thought, "Okay, there goes our chance" after the Kansas game because I felt Tyler, Ty Lawson, and Wayne Ellington were going to the NBA. But they came back, and by my senior year, we had grown closer and matured so much that we were the best team in the country. I wish every player could experience growing together and maturing over four years and fully enjoying college basketball. Not many people can say that; we were so lucky to be a part of it.

The university, Carolina Basketball, and the guys on the team were the perfect blend. We all loved Chapel Hill, loved Coach Williams and our teammates, and loved playing college basketball. When those guys decided to return, it wasn't like, "Oh, no, we have to go back to school for another year." It was, "I get another year at Carolina," and they were excited about it. People say being in college is the best time of your life. We realized that, had a blast together, and have memories that will last forever.

I've actually been asked if I regretted going to Carolina because Ty came along and started ahead of me the last two-plus years. People who think that are crazy. I could have gone to another school, where I would have started for four years and averaged maybe 15 points a game. But I wouldn't trade my torn knee, my broken foot, or coming off the bench for the people I met at Carolina, the relationships I formed, the experiences I will never forget—and, ultimately, the chance to win a national championship, wear that ring, and point to that banner and say I won one.
—Bobby Frasor

"Hey," Williams said, "if you guys want to end your careers tonight, keep playing the way you're playing."

"I was surprised when Coach called the time-out," Frasor said. "That's not typically his style. But I think he had the memory of that huge run Kansas had against us the year before. And then he jumped on us in the time-out. That really lit a fire under us, and we got going from there."

The Tar Heels got going because of a remarkable second half from Lawson. His signature play came with Carolina holding a 64–63 lead. After picking up a loose ball at the top of the LSU key, Lawson began to sprint down the court with Green and Ellington on the wings and Deon Thompson trailing the play. Only two Tiger defenders were back. It was a situation where a hobbled point guard could be forgiven for kicking the ball to the wing and letting one of his teammates make the play.

Lawson decided otherwise. Upon reaching Carolina's three-point line, he put his head down and split the two Tigers. The decision seemed to take the defense by surprise. As he had done so effectively throughout his career—"I used to practice those when I was little," Lawson said—the suddenly very healthy-looking Lawson spun the ball off the top of the backboard while drawing a foul from Marcus Thornton. It bounced off the backboard, hung on the rim for just a second, then dropped through the net.

Later in the game, Lawson would cap his evening with an ankle-breaking crossover and layup against LSU's Bo Spencer that gave the Tar Heels a 72–63 advantage. He finished with 23 points, 21 of them after halftime. After the game, Jim Nantz of CBS Sports would call the performance one of the best he had ever seen.

"After I hit my first two shots, my toe stopped hurting," Lawson said. "I was so intense, and the crowd was yelling, and I just forgot about the pain. I really did not think about my foot. . . . Every time I made one play, I got more confident. It's part of overcoming an injury. You learn how far you can push it after each shot. And after every shot I made, I got more confident and was feeling no pain."

Tyler Hansbrough's Smith Center salute on Senior Day. (Photo by Jeffrey A. Camarati)

"I think that was the best half Ty has ever played," Hansbrough said. "It showed how this team has matured, because we realized they couldn't guard Ty."

"That performance was about as good as it gets," assistant coach Steve Robinson said. "For one guy, knowing what he has come off of in terms of missing games and still fighting the injury, he showed a burning desire that he didn't want to lose that game and he was going to do everything he could to help our team be successful. You talk about trying to get all you can out of a guy? We got all we could get out of him in that game."

There were actually two moments when it looked as if the Tar Heels might not get anything out of Lawson against LSU. The first came before the game, of course, when it was unsure whether he would be healthy enough to play at all. But the other, more ominous moment came midway through the first half. While making a move with the ball, Lawson grimaced. Later, he would say he heard a pop in his foot. He left the game almost immediately and sat on the bench next to trainer Chris Hirth.

Danny Green played against Villanova despite injury. (Photo by Jeffrey A. Camarati)

"I went over to the bench and I thought I was going to be done for the game," Lawson said. "I really could not walk. It was so painful."

Hirth provided some treatment. After Lawson had been on the bench for a couple of minutes, assistant coach Joe Holladay went to check on the point guard.

"What do you think?" Holladay asked him.

"It hurts more than anything I've ever had in my life," Lawson told him.

"A lot of people would've been down on the end of the bench with their shoe off talking to the trainer," Holladay said later. "But he had made up his mind after the Kansas game that nothing was going to keep him out of those NCAA games. Nothing."

It might not be entirely accurate to say that Lawson had made up his mind immediately after the Kansas loss that he'd make amends the next season. Before he returned for his junior season, he applied for the NBA Draft, taking advantage of an NCAA rule that allowed underclassmen to go through individual workouts and assess their draft stock. While Lawson appreciated being a Tar Heel and enjoyed Chapel Hill, he'd grown up with NBA dreams, not college dreams. He had several friends already in the pros, including Kevin Durant and Michael Beasley, who had occasionally told Lawson they thought the point guard's play in college had been too restrained. In the pros, perhaps, Lawson would have more freedom on the court.

But with just eight days until the deadline to choose between staying in the draft or removing his name from consideration and returning to school, the point guard may have unwittingly made his decision. On June 8, he was ticketed for a traffic and alcohol violation. The incident appeared to scare off some teams that might have otherwise been interested.

"I think it hurt me with the Pacers," Lawson said. "Coach Williams talked to Larry Bird, and he said they had had some problems with incidents like that."

Lawson always maintained that his decision to return to school was a function of failing to be assured a draft spot by any interested teams. He thought he would be chosen in the top 20, but no one ever firmly committed to selecting him there. Without a guarantee, he returned to school. So, too, did teammates Ellington and Green, who also went through the draft process.

Without Lawson for the entire season, the complete dynamics of the 2008–09 team would

Wayne Ellington scored 17 first-half points against Michigan State. (Photo by Bob Donnan)

have changed. They got a glimpse of the team they would have been during his absence from the toe injury. Frasor moved back into the starting lineup, where he spent the three games during Toegate doing a credible job running the Carolina attack.

After the ACC Tournament semifinal loss, Williams reminded Frasor that even without Lawson, the head coach still expected a breakneck tempo. The Frasor-ignited offense responded with 101 points in the first-round win over Radford. The senior quietly had a tremendous NCAA Tournament, including key plays on the offensive backboard in the Final Four win over Villanova. Lawson's backcourt partner, Ellington, also blossomed in the second half of the season, eventually earning Most Outstanding Player honors during the Final Four. And, as always, there was Hansbrough, the 2008 National Player of the Year who came back to school to win a national title and even learned to subvert his game to Lawson on occasion in order to give Carolina the best chance to win.

Since Lawson was mostly ineffective in the first half against LSU, it's possible that the Tar Heels still could have built the nine-point halftime lead. But responding to the Tigers'

Ty Lawson and Roy Williams embrace at the close of the national title game. (Photo by Jeffrey A. Camarati)

(opposite)
Tyler Hansbrough ended his career as a national champion.
(Photo by Getty Images)

second-half run would have been much more challenging without the momentum-stealing point guard. Frasor—and, to a lesser extent, freshman Larry Drew II, who was serving a point-guard apprenticeship under Lawson—moved the ball upcourt rapidly with passes. Lawson could do it with his dribble.

The final 20 minutes against LSU proved to be a perfect illustration of the fragility of a national championship run. Without Lawson—if either he had chosen to sit out one more game because of the toe injury or the pop in his foot during the game had been more serious—the 2009 team might have been remembered much differently and achieved much less.

"When you have Tywon out there, you're a lot more comfortable and I think guys play a little different type of role," Ellington said. "When Tywon's out there, he orchestrates things. Bobby and Larry did a great job for us, but when you play with somebody all year long at the point guard position and suddenly it switches, it's tough for a team to adjust. When we got Tywon back, things got back to normal and I think we started rolling from there."

Indeed, with Lawson, the Tar Heels' roll was almost unstoppable. The toe practically became a nonstory the next weekend at the regionals in Memphis, where Carolina cruised past Gonzaga and Oklahoma. The regional wins showed just how successfully the entire Carolina team had locked its focus on the singular goal of a national title. Both the 'Zags and Sooners were quality, Final Four–caliber teams. But against a Tar Heel squad that coupled a stingy team defense with a blitzkrieg offense (three different players led the team in scoring in the first four NCAA games), both opponents looked average.

Carolina would eventually become the first team to win six games by at least a dozen points in the same NCAA Tournament. During the entire tournament, the Tar Heels trailed for just 9 minutes and 50 seconds—7 minutes and 15 seconds of which came against LSU.

Lawson would go on to win the Bob Cousy Award, which is given to the nation's best point guard. Less than a month earlier, he'd been in danger of suffering an unhappy end to his Carolina career. Now, as a national champion and national award winner, he had the chance to write his own career summary.

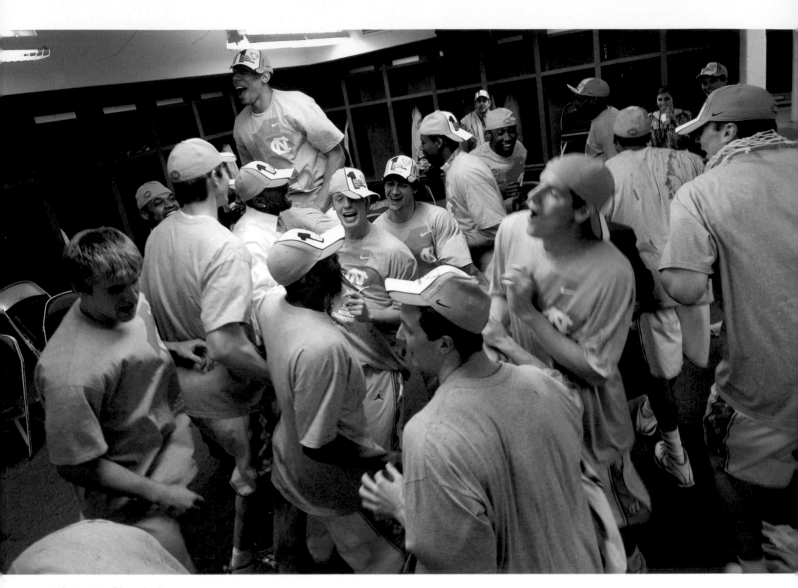

The Tar Heels' mosh-pit celebration in the Ford Field locker room after beating Michigan State. (Photo by Jeffrey A. Camarati)

"I hope people say I'm one of the top point guards to play here," Lawson said. "I'd want them to say I played hard and was one of the fastest players to play here. They can say I was a goofy player off the court and loved to have fun, but on the court I was a serious player. And I would do anything to help my team win."

The win over Michigan State in the championship game capped the greatest five-year stretch in Carolina Basketball history. It marked the first time the Tar Heels had ever won two national titles in the same decade. One of the best players in school history, Hansbrough, had set an all-time scoring record unlikely to ever be broken in the current incarnation of college basketball. The head coach had been inducted into the Basketball Hall of Fame. Standing on the White House lawn in the spring of 2009, the president of the United States had praised Carolina for the program's achievement on the court and in the classroom.

The decade began with the uncertainty of a coaching change. It ended with the program once again the unquestioned standard-bearer for college basketball.

18 · LIFE LESSONS

Three months after leading his team to a title, Ty Lawson would become one of Carolina's 40 NBA first-round picks. The Tar Heels have also produced nine Hall of Famers. And yet it's unlikely that any of the guardians of the program over the last half century would use those figures as an acceptable measure of success.

That's not to say that professional success doesn't matter. Almost every recruit making a college choice envisions himself playing pro basketball one day. First, it was Dean Smith who was well-known for preparing players for the NBA. Former Orlando Magic vice president of basketball operations John Gabriel once called Carolina a "plus-four school," meaning the fundamentals learned in Chapel Hill boosted a Tar Heel four places on the draft board over where he might otherwise have been selected. "If I rate a player as the 10th-best player in the NBA Draft, being a Tar Heel automatically jumps him to number six," Gabriel said. "The plus-four rating is based upon the success of former Tar Heels in the NBA."

Under all four head coaches in the past 50 years, Carolina has consistently been one of the highest-scoring teams in the country. But players like Michael Jordan don't just enter the NBA as proficient scorers. After all, Jordan was also a record nine-time all-defense selection. Every time he pulled on those trademark Carolina shorts under his Chicago Bulls uniform, he became a walking advertisement for the all-around basketball education received in Chapel Hill.

Smith made a habit of getting the best high school players. But once those players arrived on campus, they developed into something more, transitioning from raw athletes to versatile, team-oriented basketball players. Other than the ill-fated Cunningham experiment in 1964, no Tar Heel team since then has ever been built around one person.

Growing up in Every Way

Moving from life as an NBA player to "real" life was difficult from the standpoint of not playing competitive basketball anymore, which was something I'd done my whole life. The NBA wasn't just a job for me. I love basketball. I can play it, watch it, or talk about it all day long. So it was tough to end my career, but there was also a lot of joy in looking back at the things I'd been able to experience as a player.

The great thing about it is, out of all the things I learned at North Carolina, the *last* thing I learned was basketball. Coach Smith, Coach Guthridge, and the coaching staff gave me examples and tools for life off the court. That helped me make a transition at the end of my career to broadcasting, helped me be a good father and a good husband. Basketball was very important at Carolina, but Coach Smith and Coach Guthridge made it so basketball wasn't everything. I can never thank them enough for how much that helped me. In that aspect, moving to broadcasting wasn't that tough of a transition at all.

It's funny how things work out. I never thought about broadcasting and wasn't interested in it at all while I was a player. I was sitting on the bench in 2004 during my last year in the NBA with the New Jersey Nets. I wasn't playing much that season, and we had a game against the New Orleans Hornets. Coach Lawrence Frank put me in the game. I ended up being the player of the game and getting interviewed on the radio and on television.

It was the only game that I played significant minutes for the Nets, but a broadcasting agent from New York City was at home and happened to see my interview on the local news. He called my agent and got my number, and then he called me. He asked if I'd be interested in broadcasting, and I said, "No way." I told him I'd been in speech-therapy class since I was in elementary school and had problems with pronunciation. A lot of those problems came from speaking in front of people, so the last thing I wanted was to be talking on national television.

He was persistent and tried to get me just to try out, and still I said it just wasn't my thing. He kept bugging me throughout the year and finally got me to try out for ESPN a year later. To get him off my back, I went up there and did it. I had to call a mock game with Rece Davis—Texas versus Wake Forest—and I ended up getting a job while I was up there. Five years later, my number-one thing still is that I don't like talking in front of people, but I absolutely love my job.

You can ask the secretaries in the basketball office who knew me when I was at Carolina. I was so shy coming in as a freshman. But by the time I was a senior, they couldn't shut me up. I grew so much in my time at Carolina, and that's why I just love college. It's a shame sometimes to see so many guys go early to the NBA because they don't know what they're missing in college. The four years are great for basketball, but they also help you mature as a person. I needed those years, and Carolina sure was the right place for me to grow up and feel more confident in myself.—*Hubert Davis*

right; Carolina brought back the '57 uniforms during the 100-year festivities as a retro tribute.) Players wore blazers on the road and were expected to be "Carolina gentlemen" at all times. For a core of players accustomed to zoot suits in New York City, McGuire's standards required some adjustments.

"Before I came to Carolina, I wore pink shirts and I was a zoot-suiter," Harvey Salz said. "Then I came to Carolina, and Coach McGuire expected us to wear a blue blazer, white shirt, and gray slacks with penny loafers. It was a preppy kind of thing, but I loved dressing up. By the time I left, I was wearing Lacoste shirts and plaid Bermuda shorts. Coach McGuire laid the groundwork for that classy image we have of Carolina basketball."

On December 21, 1958, West Virginia snapped a 37-game Carolina winning streak with a 75–64 win at the University of Kentucky Invitational. A few days later, McGuire received a letter from a West Virginia fan.

"You and your boys are real gentlemen, real champions, and are heavily endowed with that intangible thing called 'class,'" the letter read. "I had the great pleasure to talk with and observe several of your boys Saturday night, and without exception they were the most clean-cut, wholesome group of young Americans I have ever seen."

Smith maintained that philosophy. Suits and ties were requirements on road trips, a rule that was in place from the earliest days of the Smith era. During the 1960s, freshmen were still ineligible for varsity competition. Teams fielded freshman squads that were essentially glorified junior varsity teams, and Smith coached the Carolina freshman squad during his tenure as an assistant coach under McGuire. The year before Smith assumed the head-coaching position for the 1961–62 season, he left an indelible impression on one of the members of his freshman squad.

"The last Dixie Classic was my freshman year," remembers Mike Cooke, who earned three letters as a Tar Heel point guard. "It was a big event, and I had gotten a brand new sweater for Christmas, and that was a big deal. The freshman team had tickets to sit in the stands for the Dixie Classic, and I was all decked out in my new sweater. When we came back to school, Coach Smith passed me at the gym and said, 'I saw you at the Dixie Classic. You didn't have a coat and tie on. Don't let me ever see you without a coat and tie on.'"

That rule remained in place as the importance of television grew during the 1980s. At many schools, players would do their postgame interviews moments after stepping out of the shower, usually while still wrapped in a towel. At Carolina, however, players were required to get dressed before appearing on television. Skeptics of the Tar Heel basketball program often referred to them, sometimes not in a complimentary fashion, as the "IBM of college basketball." It was intended to be a jab at the buttoned-down image the Tar Heels projected, but it illustrated just how refined the public concept of Carolina Basketball had become.

While Williams has somewhat relaxed the dress code—he doesn't wear a jacket in the office every day, and players

(top)
Jerry Stackhouse and Antawn Jamison both returned to graduate after leaving early for the NBA. (Photo by Dan Sears)

(bottom)
Vince Carter returned to Chapel Hill for graduation ceremonies on the same day that he played in a play-off game for the Toronto Raptors. (Photo by Dan Sears)

The 2009 senior class all
graduated after winning
the national championship.
(Photo by Jeffrey A. Camarati)

occasionally catch a break on the road dress requirements—standards remain. Players take
out any earrings before television interviews. Preseason media-education sessions ensure
that even the rawest freshman is comfortable holding a conversation with a writer. In today's world, though, dealing with the public doesn't always mean talking to someone with
a media credential.

Today, a Tar Heel basketball player receives more national attention than ever; all but one
game during the 2009–10 season was televised. The way the world relates to those players
has changed. Carolina basketball players no longer belong to the small town of Chapel Hill.
They still live in dormitories with other students and still grab lunch on Franklin Street,
but the way fans interact with them has changed. Some diehards still wait outside the Smith
Center after games to score an autograph. But thousands more follow the Twitter feeds of
individual players, enabling them to communicate directly with the same players they'll
watch on television 35 times per year.

A fan in China is just as likely to exchange a few tweets with Dexter Strickland as a UNC
student is to see Strickland at the campus bookstore. The quest for information has changed.
Once, we gathered to talk about it with our friends. Now, we can discuss Carolina Basketball
any time of the day, and sometimes we can even interact with the players themselves. Our
high-speed Internet connection is our broadband Franklin Street, where we might bump
into a Tar Heel at any time.

While some relationships have changed, however, others are virtually identical. Smith
tried to make sure that his players learned more off the court than on the court, placing

(opposite)
Pearce Landry attended
Carolina on a Morehead
Scholarship and contributed
on the court from 1993 to
1995. (Photo courtesy of UNC
Athletic Communications)

(top)

Roy Williams and the Tar Heels host a clinic for Special Olympians each year. (Photo by N.C. Special Olympics)

(bottom)

Danny Green at the 2008 Special Olympics clinic.

(Photo by N.C. Special Olympics)

a priority on school and nonbasketball life. As soon as it was financially possible, Carolina traveled via charter plane. The intent was simple: no matter what time the previous night's game ended, Smith could be sure his players were back in class the next morning. An 8:00 A.M. class after a 9:00 P.M. game the previous night in Atlanta was not considered an excused absence.

An incredible 17 of Smith's first 27 lettermen went on to graduate school. Included in that group are lawyers, bankers, and doctors. At the 1991 Final Four in Indianapolis, Tar Heel fans wore team stickers—not with the squad's latest Associated Press poll ranking, but with the current graduation rate under Smith (97.4%) proudly displayed in Carolina blue.

"I don't think Coach Smith ever wanted being a Carolina basketball player to define us," said Steve Hale (1983–86), who went on to become a pediatrician. "I wouldn't want to be a pediatrician and have people come see me because I played basketball. I would want them to come see me because I was a good pediatrician."

Williams continues that philosophy today. He half-jokingly maintained for his first six seasons at Carolina that the most important member of his coaching staff was academic advisor Wayne Walden. In December 2009, rather than go on a walk-through of the palatial Cowboys Stadium—a facility that was the marvel of the modern sporting world—before a game against Texas, the Tar Heels stayed in Chapel Hill so two players could finish exams. They were on the ground in Dallas for less than 24 hours for a game between two top-ten teams.

No matter how long ago they played, most Tar Heel lettermen can still recite at least one of the Thoughts for the Day that remain fixtures at the top of a UNC practice plan. Sometimes those nuggets are basketball related (Box Out!). Many times, however, they are not.

"The biggest thing I took from Carolina Basketball was that you're only successful at the moment you're succeeding," said Dick Grubar. "That prepares you for the fact that you're not always going to be in the limelight. Things aren't going to always go your way, and you have to be ready to be successful every day."

"One Thought for the Day I remember the most is, 'When you've done all you can, sit back and await the results,'" said Pearce Landry. "I have this image of Coach Smith during a game. You'd look over and he would be sitting there, watching the game while the other coach was running around sweating and yelling at the players. Coach Smith prepared so much that he did everything he could do before the game started. He was faithful with what he was given, with the traits and gifts he had. But he also realized the result wasn't up to him. As I've walked through life, I've realized people are not in the results business. We're in the being-faithful business. I have to use where I am to the best of my ability. The results aren't up to me. There's a contentment Coach Smith helped bring to my life."

Even as a young coach, Smith remained resolute about teaching his players lessons that would go beyond 94 feet of hardwood and a leather ball.

"Coach Smith would talk about fairness and equality and social responsibility," Bill Harrison said. "That was part of his values. It never felt like we were being lectured, but you knew it was part of who he was as a human being."

Smith often acted on those beliefs, whether he was breaking the UNC athletic color barrier, pushing for equality in Chapel Hill, speaking out in favor of a nuclear freeze, or decrying the cultural bias of standardized tests. Today, social activism remains a part of the Carolina program. Williams helped start a breakfast benefiting cancer research on the first day of the season and helped to raise over $1 million for cancer research in his first six seasons as Carolina's head coach.

Williams also imported several community activities from Kansas, many of which have become highly anticipated parts of the basketball calendar. Each season, his team holds a clinic for Special Olympians from across the state. Special Olympics coaches have been known to drive for five or six hours, rousting their team from bed at 3:00 or 4:00 A.M., just to be a part of the clinic.

Each holiday season, the entire Tar Heel team shops for underprivileged families at a local store. The shopping is completely player driven, as each team member is given a general "wish list" and then asked to find the items that best fit the list. With a spending limit in place, the afternoon usually turns into a highly competitive, *The Price Is Right*–style battle to see which player can come closest to the limit without going over.

Those are the activities that tend to stay with players long after they've graduated. Community-relations staffers with the Timberwolves and Cavaliers noted two early-season standouts in the fall of 2009 who were consistently willing to make appearances: Wayne Ellington and Danny Green.

"It's a feeling of satisfaction knowing there are people out there who are going to have a good Christmas," Green said of Carolina's shopping excursion. "I know what it's like as a kid to open a present on Christmas morning and get something you really want, and hopefully some of these kids will have that same experience."

That's a part of the Carolina experience that has ideally stretched from McGuire to Smith

The Tar Heels annually shop for Christmas gifts for families in the Chapel Hill area. (Photo by Jeffrey A. Camarati)

to Williams and beyond. It would be a nice footnotc if Tar Heels were only using the lessons learned to make an impact in basketball. As it turns out, however, the recipients of the principles taught within the program have spread them well beyond basketball.

Some lettermen are doctors. Some are lawyers. Some own their own businesses. When Harrison was named CEO of JP Morgan Chase, he organized leadership sessions for his new staff.

"I was one of the least talented lettermen in Coach Smith's 35 years," Harrison said. "But there's an unbelievable brand for having been associated with Coach Smith and Carolina. And when I became CEO, I made sure to talk about the values of the UNC program. I really do believe that a lot of it is transferrable from basketball to business. The discipline, values, teamwork, work ethic, and organization are things we can take into the business world very easily from what we learned at Carolina."

19 : BEYOND THE FIRST CENTURY

For most members of the Carolina Family, the future of Tar Heel basketball began on April 14, 2003. That's the day Roy Williams officially accepted the job as UNC's head coach.

Williams came equipped with all the requirements of a winning head coach. He'd won conference championships at Kansas and taken the Jayhawks to multiple Final Fours. When he took the job, he was fresh off an appearance in the national championship game. He had the added credibility of having served an apprenticeship under Dean Smith.

Carolina's on-court results under Williams have been stunning—perhaps even surpassing the record book of achievements amassed by Smith. After winning two NCAA titles in the previous 45 years, the Tar Heels won two national championships in a span of five seasons under Williams's direction. At the conclusion of the 2008–09 season, he had directed three straight 30-win seasons, the first time in Tar Heel history that milestone was reached. Taken in sum—two national titles, three Final Fours, four ACC regular-season titles, five top-10 final Associated Press rankings, eight NBA first-round draft picks—it was the most decorated five-year stretch in 99 years of highly decorated Carolina Basketball.

"Coach Williams has done an excellent job," Antawn Jamison said. "He's brought Carolina back to what it was and taken it even beyond that. But what I like is that he has the same philosophy Coach Smith has. It's not about basketball. It's about life and doing what's expected of you. He expects you to live your life to the fullest. It couldn't have happened to a better, more deserving person than Coach Williams."

"As long as Roy is here, we're going to have continued success," Phil Ford said. "Kids want to play for him. He has the perfect personality to run a big-time program like ours. He's fiery and confident enough to keep kicking the pig. But he's also confident and humble enough to know it's about the players. The way we play is so appealing to young guys. In the future, we're going to continue to get the student-athletes who give us opportunities to win

Jackie Manuel and Mitch Kupchak pose at the Carolina Basketball reunion in 2004. (Photo by Robert Crawford)

national titles. And Roy is going to continue to do a great job of coaching them."

Based on the way Williams recruits—constantly, intensely, and successfully—there's no reason to believe the on-court results will change. But it was another element of Williams's résumé that ensured the future was secure. As a former Smith assistant, he'd watched his mentor cultivate a relationship with former lettermen. He understood the difference between simply winning games and winning games as a family. When he was hired, the quantity of alumni making the annual summer pilgrimage back to Chapel Hill had noticeably decreased. At his introductory press conference, he announced plans to hold a reunion in the spring.

Williams had long understood the importance of alumni contributions. Letterman Bob Bennett sent his two sons to Carolina basketball camp during Williams's tenure as an assistant coach. Bennett knew Williams was struggling on a third assistant's salary and would usually include a check with his sons' luggage to give to the underpaid young assistant. But his sons would always return with the check and the news that Williams had rejected it once again.

Finally, Bennett mailed the check along with a note directly to Williams. "I know how much of your income this check represents," Bennett wrote. "I'm not rich, but I can afford this."

A few days later, Bennett received a handwritten note from Chapel Hill. Folded inside the envelope was his check, still uncashed. The note, signed by Williams, read as follows: "Bob—if you understand my economic circumstances you know how difficult it is for me to pay for stamps. Please don't make me send this back to you again."

Just as Williams predicted, his first UNC reunion was a resounding success—the perfect example of connecting with the past to solidify the future. A total of 220 lettermen returned to Chapel Hill. The weekend included an invitation to practice on the day before a home game against Florida State, tickets to the game, a halftime introduction of all attendees, and a private banquet after the game. It was the first formal gathering for lettermen since the Smith Center was dedicated in 1986.

The banquet turned into the weekend highlight, as some players shed tears when explaining their past experiences—and their commitment to the future.

"Everyone in this room loves you," King Rice said during his speech as he addressed the current team. "When I was here, the former guys came back and got on me when I did the wrong thing. I'm sorry I haven't done that for you. I'm sorry we haven't been together like

Sam Perkins, James Worthy, and Michael Jordan smile at the 2007 reunion of the 1957 and 1982 NCAA champions. (Photo by Jeffrey A. Camarati)

this. I'm ashamed of myself because everyone in this room has to come together to support you guys."

It was a remarkable statement regarding where the program had been, the stumbles in recent years, and a blueprint for upcoming seasons. It was also an accurate prediction of what would happen in the years to come. With Williams in charge, reunions became a semi-regular occurrence. The program honored the 50th anniversary of the 1957 team and 25th anniversary of the 1982 team in 2007. Over 250 lettermen returned for Celebration of a Century weekend in February 2010.

"This is our family," Williams said as he opened the banquet that accompanied the 1957/1982 banquet. "And we always want our family to feel good about coming back."

Today's lettermen are tomorrow's reunion attendees. When they're welcomed back to

*Tar Heel lettermen
George Karl and Doug Moe
take in the 2005 Final Four.
(Photo by Robert Crawford)*

Chapel Hill, alums inevitably depart with warm feelings for their alma mater. It's enough to make you wonder why other schools don't simply copy the format. After all, if the fraternity of Tar Heel basketball is what has Carolina on solid footing for 2011 and beyond, why wouldn't other schools simply throw together a reunion or two and reap the benefits?

"The reason it's hard to replicate is because not many people are willing to put the time into making it happen," said Eddie Fogler, who has head-coaching experience at three other major programs. "It takes a long time to make it work. Unfortunately, coaches don't stay in one place for any length of time anymore. It will be very hard for anyone else to stay in one place and build the type of family bond we have at Carolina.

"Coach Smith spent so much time putting the pieces together into building the greatest family of all time. It has sustained itself over a long period of time and I don't see it stopping anytime soon. Coach Guthridge continued it and Roy continues it today."

Of course, Smith had the benefit of forging those bonds when most players stayed in school for four years. In today's era, the basketball world is different. If Williams is recruiting the very best players, and if the very best players are unlikely to stay in school for the full four years, then it seems reasonable to be concerned that the family could fray under the weight of early departures.

So far, though, that hasn't been the case. Ty Lawson, who left after his junior season, requested special permission from the Denver Nuggets to spend a day in Chapel Hill after the Nuggets played a game in Charlotte during his rookie season. The team traveled on to the next destination; Lawson hung out with his former Tar Heel teammates. Sometimes, the players in the NBA spend more time savoring their Tar Heel experiences than they ever did when they were undergraduates.

"Carolina gets in your blood," said Vince Carter. "You see all the former guys coming back, and you want to be part of that. It just seems like something you're supposed to do as a Carolina guy, and no matter how long you stay in school, you always look forward to coming back. In the NBA, Carolina guys look after each other. We're part of each other's lives."

As Williams himself acknowledges, the basketball program in Chapel Hill is bigger than one person, even if that one person is the head coach. He's said he would like to coach six to ten more years. Smith probably retired a couple of years earlier than he would have liked because of the outside commitments associated with being the UNC head coach. Williams has done a credible job of limiting those commitments. But he's a new grandfather who values family time, and at some point in the next decade, he'll decide he's coached enough basketball games. Some coaches hang on because they don't have anything to do when they

Danny Green's "Jump Around" dance routine in 2008. (Photo by Grant Halverson)

retire. Williams has two loves—family and golf—that will make him content when he no longer has game film to watch at 9:00 P.M.

When that happens, one of the most intriguing coaching searches in college basketball will take place. Williams was the obvious candidate in both 2000 and 2003. Right now, there's no Williams equivalent waiting for the coronation.

Lettermen—those who best understand the role that family has played in the Carolina experience—are confident that no matter what direction that search takes, Tar Heel basketball will endure.

"There's so much tradition," Dick Grubar said. "You're talking about a great university in a great state and a great place to go to school. That will always give Carolina the opportunity to recruit the top players. You can't be a great coach without great players. With the right hire, things will continue into the future because Carolina will always have ex-players in the pros, and kids growing up will always want to be like those pros."

"It starts at the top," said Mitch Kupchak. "It starts with the university and their com-

Connections

The first time I met Roy Williams was when he was recruiting me. He was from North Carolina and he had that southern accent, and the fact that he was able to build a great bond with my father appealed to me. I felt like Coach Williams had the background that helped him understand where I was coming from. You could sit down and talk to him and he wasn't intimidating.

What I came to learn about him is that he is a fierce competitor. He beat me in pool once, although I don't think he could beat me now. I didn't handle it very well, but I had to accept it because he was my elder. Even today, when we play golf together, his attitude toward winning is very similar to mine. I may not get as angry as he does, and I may channel my energy a little differently than he does, but we hate losing in the same way.

On the court, what makes him successful is his willingness to understand the athlete and get the best out of the athlete—his patience, his knowledge of the game, his effort and diligence to understand the game and understand the player and how they can coexist. To me, that's a Hall of Fame–type guy, someone who makes adjustments according to the personnel rather than forcing his way of thinking on a team or a player.

Coach Williams learned a lot from Coach Smith. He utilizes many of the same instructional principles. But his temperament is a little bit different. He has created his own identity, which is important for people to understand. He's put in a lot of work to get where he is today. It's not just a case of copying someone. On the way up, he did every job you can do below head coaching. He's a little more forgiving to the personality of players than Coach Smith. But their teachings are very similar.

Coach Williams has done a great job of coming back and connecting to the former players again. He knew why that was important, because he went to Carolina and he coached at Carolina. He felt the need to come back and connect the dots a little more than they were at the time. He calls us constantly to keep us updated on what's happening with the program. It's a very special feeling that we have at Carolina, because we're all connected to everyone, even though we may not see each other regularly. He's helped ensure that that feeling continues.—*Michael Jordan*

mitment to the program. Coaches who take the job at Carolina understand what they're in for. They're people who enjoy that type of challenge. It's like playing baseball for the Yankees or playing basketball for the Celtics or Lakers. Carolina Basketball is right there with those types of programs."

Other than speculation about the length of Williams's tenure, the most uncertain part of Carolina's basketball future might be the long-term viability of the Smith Center. The building just barely predated the luxury-suite craze that has created revenue streams in other buildings. Six other Atlantic Coast Conference schools have opened new buildings since the Smith Center debuted in 1986.

Physically, for a 25-year-old building, it remains in reasonable condition. The least impressive part of the physical structure has long been the actual basketball offices. At the conclusion of the 2009–10 season, the athletic department began an $8 million renovation project. The new offices will completely change the look and feel of that side of the Smith Center, with high ceilings and lots of light replacing the existing somewhat dark confines.

As a companion to the renovation project, a fund-raising drive also sought to raise an additional $17 million to ensure the long-term viability of the program. The money from that endowment can be used for the occasional necessary Smith Center upgrades. In recent years, the facility has received new video boards, new LED signage, upgraded strength-and-conditioning and training facilities, and a renovated locker room. Most significant, a healthy chunk of that new money was donated by former players. It was the first time in program history that former players had ever been asked to give back to the program, and their response was overwhelming.

There's one element of the Smith Center that not even donations can alter. When it was built, the arena was a reaction to the overwhelming ticket demand at

ENTRY TOWER
View of the new entry to Men's Basketball Suite

LETTERMEN'S LANE
The walkway between the Smith Center and
Koury Natatorium honoring past players

CAROLINA BASKETBALL FAMILY FUND

Carmichael Auditorium. The purpose was simply to ensure that practically every Carolina fan could get a ticket to watch the Tar Heels. Arenas were getting bigger, and UNC more than doubled its capacity.

Twenty-five years later, however, the program has new competitors—not in the expanded ACC, but in the homes of fans. As ticket prices climb and high-definition televisions become ubiquitous, staying home to watch games is no longer the inferior option that it once was. No home theater can replicate the emotion and intensity of a key ACC game, but that still may leave a dozen less-desirable home games on the schedule. The average attendance at the first seven home games of the 2009–10 season—most of the nonconference games—was 17,432 per game. The average attendance at the first seven games of the 2008–09 season— which did include some more attractive games, including a matchup against Kentucky— was 20,754.

It's not an exact comparison, but a dropoff of over 3,000 fans per game is enough to spark some serious conversation about the future. There's annual debate about the best way to

The basketball offices in the Smith Center underwent renovations after the 2009–10 season.

The 2009–10 team posed for a Tar Heel "team photo" prior to the pro alumni game in September 2009. (Photo by J.D. Lyon Jr.)

encourage students to attend games, and the student ticketing policy has changed on an almost yearly basis. Over the last two seasons, students have picked up their full allotment for only the two Duke games and the Evansville game in December 2008 (during which Tyler Hansbrough broke Phil Ford's scoring record and students had a reduced allotment due to Christmas break).

In a building where 6,000 tickets are allotted to students—almost double the total of any other ACC school, and a percentage of capacity that ranks in the top third of the league—changes in their attendance patterns are noticeable. One of Williams's annual selling points to recruits is his program's nationwide rank in attendance. When that fluctuates, the head coach notices.

For most of the first 100 years of the program, Carolina put very little effort into the marketing of its home basketball games. It simply wasn't necessary. Demand was great enough that merely releasing the schedule was good enough for a near sellout.

Especially in the Williams era, however, more thought has been given to the home-game experience. Long a tradition-dominated arena, the Smith Center has arguably been the most understated of any of the nonhistoric venues. No roaring motorcycle like at Wake Forest's Lawrence Joel Coliseum. No DJ spinning pregame tunes like at Miami's BankUnited Center. No elaborate pro-style introductions and in-game theatrics like at NC State's RBC Center.

Over time, though, the Carolina Basketball home-game experience has been updated. It began with the upgrading of the arena's video boards. Then, limited use of PA music to supplement the band was introduced, which led to the very popular pregame rendition of "Jump Around" that now seems like a longtime Tar Heel tradition. Before the 2009–10 season, the sound and lighting systems were upgraded, which allowed the lights to be turned off for pregame introductions—something Williams had wanted since he took his team to Lexington to face Kentucky in his first season at Carolina and saw the way the Wildcats were introduced.

Those introductions are a good example of the goal for the atmosphere at the Smith Center. At many other arenas, the player intros are accompanied by fireworks, lasers, or loud music. Carolina staffers chose a more traditional route, with a drum line from the Tar Heel pep band taking the floor and creating a subtle yet stirring background to the announcer's voice.

That's the balance that Tar Heel basketball is trying to strike as the program moves into its second century. The history of the team's great success is appealing. But in a world of short attention spans, relying too much on that history risks allowing it to become musty and less meaningful to new generations of Carolina fans. Instead, the aim is to embrace the program's history while adding a modern element that preserves the vibrancy that has defined Carolina Basketball during its first 100 years.

The members of the Tar Heel family that helped create and sustain the nation's best program are rightfully proud of Carolina's on-court achievements. But especially after they graduate and move into their adult lives, they develop a deeper appreciation for the way the program is perceived outside the narrow world of sports.

"What you get with Carolina is that it's not as much about basketball," said Jim Delany, who, in addition to his status as a letterman, gets a wider view of collegiate sports as the commissioner of the Big Ten Conference. "From a program standpoint, for a long time, Carolina has represented the notion that you can win big . . . with kids who graduate and do it within the rules. In many ways, Carolina Basketball has reflected well not only on the program, but on the sport. It's a model program. It shows that big-time sports can work."

AFTERWORD

Being the head coach of Carolina Basketball is a special privilege. I work every day in a building named for the man whom I believe to be the greatest coach in college basketball history. I work with the best staff in the country and have a chance to make a difference in the lives of some outstanding young players. And I get to do this at a university that prides itself on integrity and winning the right way.

I know it's not like that everywhere else. Being part of Carolina Basketball also brings with it some responsibility. We're not just doing this for us. We're part of something bigger, and I always want to make sure our players understand that. The "100 Years of Basketball" celebration was important because our current team was able to see that the former players they've heard about or seen in photos and videos are real people who still care very much about their Tar Heels.

When we played the NIT game in Carmichael this year, I spoke to our players about the past. They've heard about Carmichael and maybe even played a pickup game there, but I wanted them to understand that many of the moments that made Carolina Basketball what it is today happened right there. So at our shootaround, I showed them spots on the court where certain plays were made— "there's where Walter Davis made the shot against Duke in 1974, and that's where Michael Jordan stole the ball from Rick Carlisle in 1983." Those moments are a fundamental part of our rich history.

National championships, ACC championships, National Players of the Year, Hall of Fame coaches, great wins, epic battles, even the heartbreaking defeats— these define us and matter to so many people. Watch opposing teams playing in

232

the Smith Center for the first time: when they're stretching, you'll see them looking up in the rafters. Sometimes their eyes grow large when they recognize the great names on the retired and honored jerseys and see the championship banners. We see them every day, and sometimes it starts to seem normal. But it's not. It's extraordinary.

The basketball tradition and the history at the University of North Carolina mean a great deal to many people. The former players never stop being Tar Heels. Our great fans share their excitement with their loved ones, and it becomes part of their family. That passion goes from generation to generation. It is a phenomenal experience.

It's a blessing for me to be a part of Carolina Basketball. It's something I take very seriously. Every single day, everything I do is based on one principle: how can I make Carolina Basketball—the program, not an individual team—better today? That's how Coach Smith did it, that's how I do it, and that's how we'll do it together as we start these next 100 years.

—ROY WILLIAMS

CAROLINA IN THE SOUTHERN CONFERENCE

Year	Overall	Southern Conf.	SC Tournament Finish	Postseason	Coach
1910–11	7–4				Nat Cartmell
1911–12	4–5				Nat Cartmell
1912–13	4–7				Nat Cartmell
1913–14	10–8				Nat Cartmell
1914–15	6–10				Charles Doak
1915–16	12–6				Charles Doak
1916–17	5–4				Howell Peacock
1917–18	9–3				Howell Peacock
1918–19	9–7				Howell Peacock
1919–20	7–9				Fred Boye
1920–21	12–8				Fred Boye
1921–22	15–6	3–3, 7th (T)	Champion		No coach
1922–23	15–1	5–0, 1st (T)	Second round		No coach
1923–24	26–0	7–0, 1st (T)	Champion		Norman Shepard
1924–25	20–5	8–0, 1st	Champion		Monk McDonald
1925–26	20–5	7–0, 1st (T)	Champion		Harlan Sanborn
1926–27	17–7	7–3, 8th	Semifinalist		James Ashmore
1927–28	17–2	8–1, 3rd (T)	Round of 16		James Ashmore
1928–29	17–8	12–2, 2nd (T)	Quarterfinalist		James Ashmore
1929–30	14–11	4–7, 16th	Round of 16		James Ashmore
1930–31	15–9	6–6, 9th (T)	Quarterfinalist		James Ashmore
1931–32	16–5	6–3, 5th (T)	Finalist		George Shepard
1932–33	12–5	5–3, 5th (T)	Semifinalist		George Shepard
1933–34	18–4	12–2, 2nd (T)	Semifinalist		George Shepard
1934–35	23–2	12–1, 1st	Champion		George Shepard
1935–36	21–4	13–3, 2nd	Champion		Walter Skidmore
1936–37	18–5	14–3, 2nd	Finalist		Walter Skidmore
1937–38	16–5	13–3, 1st	Quarterfinalist		Walter Skidmore
1938–39	10–11	8–7, 7th	First round		Walter Skidmore
1939–40	23–3	11–2, 2nd	Champion		Bill Lange
1940–41	19–9	14–1, 1st	Quarterfinalist	NCAA Final 8	Bill Lange
1941–42	14–9	9–5, 7th	Quarterfinalist		Bill Lange
1942–43	12–10	8–9, 11th	Did not compete		Bill Lange
1943–44	17–10	9–1, 1st	Finalist		Bill Lange
1944–45	22–6	11–3, 4th	Champion		Ben Carnevale
1945–46	30–5	13–1, 1st	Semifinalist	NCAA Finalist	Ben Carnevale
1946–47	19–8	10–2, 2nd	Finalist		Tom Scott

Year	Overall	Southern Conf.	SC Tournament Finish	Postseason	Coach
1947–48	20–7	11–4, 3rd	Semifinalist		Tom Scott
1948–49	20–8	13–5, 3rd	Semifinalist		Tom Scott
1949–50	17–12	13–6, 5th	Quarterfinalist		Tom Scott
1950–51	12–15	9–8, 9th	Did not compete		Tom Scott
1951–52	12–15	8–11, 11th	Did not compete		Tom Scott
1952–53	17–10	15–6, 8th	Quarterfinalist		Frank McGuire

Southern Conference Totals:

43 seasons	304–111 (.733)	9 Regular-season titles, 8 Tournament titles

CAROLINA IN THE ATLANTIC COAST CONFERENCE

Year	Overall	ACC	ACC Tournament Finish	Postseason	Coach
1953–54	11–10	5–6, 5th	Quarterfinalist		Frank McGuire
1954–55	10–11	8–6, 4th (T)	Quarterfinalist		Frank McGuire
1955–56	18–5	11–3, 1st (T)	Semifinalist		Frank McGuire
1956–57	32–0	14–0, 1st	Champion	NCAA Champs	Frank McGuire
1957–58	19–7	10–4, 2nd (T)	Finalist		Frank McGuire
1958–59	20–5	12–2, 1st (T)	Champion	NCAA 1st Rd.	Frank McGuire
1959–60	18–6	12–2, 1st (T)	Semifinalist		Frank McGuire
1960–61	19–4	12–2, 1st	Did not compete		Frank McGuire
1961–62	8–9	7–7, 4th (T)	Quarterfinalist		Dean Smith
1962–63	15–6	10–4, 3rd	Semifinalist		Dean Smith
1963–64	12–12	6–8, 5th	Semifinalist		Dean Smith
1964–65	15–9	10–4, 2nd (T)	Quarterfinalist		Dean Smith
1965–66	16–11	8–6, 3rd (T)	Semifinalist		Dean Smith
1966–67	26–6	12–2, 1st	Champion	NCAA 4th place	Dean Smith
1967–68	28–4	12–2, 1st	Champion	NCAA Finalist	Dean Smith
1968–69	27–5	12–2, 1st	Champion	NCAA 4th place	Dean Smith
1969–70	18–9	9–5, 2nd (T)	Quarterfinalist	NIT First round	Dean Smith
1970–71	26–6	11–3, 1st	Finalist	NIT Champs	Dean Smith
1971–72	26–5	9–3, 1st	Champion	NCAA 3rd place	Dean Smith
1972–73	25–8	8–4, 2nd	First round	NIT 3rd place	Dean Smith
1973–74	22–6	9–3, 2nd (T)	Semifinalist	NIT First round	Dean Smith

CAROLINA IN THE ATLANTIC COAST CONFERENCE *(continued)*

Year	Overall	ACC	ACC Tournament Finish	Postseason	Coach
1974–75	23–8	8–4, 2nd (T)	Champion	NCAA Final 16	Dean Smith
1975–76	25–4	11–1, 1st	Finalist	NCAA 1st Rd.	Dean Smith
1976–77	28–5	9–3, 1st	Champion	NCAA Finalist	Dean Smith
1977–78	23–8	9–3, 1st	Semifinalist	NCAA 1st Rd.	Dean Smith
1978–79	23–6	9–3, 1st (T)	Champion	NCAA 2nd Rd.	Dean Smith
1979–80	21–8	9–5, 2nd (T)	Semifinalist	NCAA 2nd Rd.	Dean Smith
1980–81	29–8	10–4, 2nd	Champion	NCAA Finalist	Dean Smith
1981–82	32–2	12–2, 1st (T)	Champion	NCAA Champs	Dean Smith
1982–83	28–8	12–2, 1st (T)	Semifinalist	NCAA Final 8	Dean Smith
1983–84	28–3	14–0, 1st	Semifinalist	NCAA Final 16	Dean Smith
1984–85	27–9	9–5, 1st (T)	Finalist	NCAA Final 8	Dean Smith
1985–86	28–6	10–4, 3rd	Quarterfinalist	NCAA Final 16	Dean Smith
1986–87	32–4	14–0, 1st	Finalist	NCAA Final 8	Dean Smith
1987–88	27–7	11–3, 1st	Finalist	NCAA Final 8	Dean Smith
1988–89	29–8	9–5, 2nd (T)	Champion	NCAA Final 16	Dean Smith
1989–90	21–13	8–6, 3rd (T)	Quarterfinalist	NCAA Final 16	Dean Smith
1990–91	29–6	10–4, 2nd	Champion	NCAA Final 4	Dean Smith
1991–92	23–10	9–7, 3rd	Finalist	NCAA Final 16	Dean Smith
1992–93	34–4	14–2, 1st	Finalist	NCAA Champs	Dean Smith
1993–94	28–7	11–5, 2nd	Champion	NCAA 2nd Rd.	Dean Smith
1994–95	28–6	12–4, 1st	Finalist	NCAA Final 4	Dean Smith
1995–96	21–11	10–6, 3rd	Quarterfinalist	NCAA 2nd Rd.	Dean Smith
1996–97	28–7	11–5, 2nd	Champion	NCAA Final 4	Dean Smith
1997–98	34–4	13–3, 2nd	Champion	NCAA Final 4	Bill Guthridge
1998–99	24–10	10–6, 3rd	Finalist	NCAA 1st Rd.	Bill Guthridge
1999–2000	22–14	9–7, 3rd	Quarterfinalist	NCAA Final 4	Bill Guthridge
2000–01	26–7	13–3, 1st (T)	Finalist	NCAA 2nd Rd.	Matt Doherty
2001–02	8–20	4–12, 7th (T)	Quarterfinalist		Matt Doherty
2002–03	19–16	6–10, 6th (T)	Semifinalist	NIT Quarterfinal	Matt Doherty
2003–04	19–11	8–8, 5th	Quarterfinalist	NCAA 2nd Rd.	Roy Williams
2004–05	33–4	14–2, 1st	Semifinalist	NCAA Champs	Roy Williams
2005–06	23–8	12–4, 2nd	Semifinalist	NCAA 2nd Rd.	Roy Williams
2006–07	31–7	11–5, 1st (T)	Champion	NCAA Final 8	Roy Williams
2007–08	36–3	14–2, 1st	Champion	NCAA Final 4	Roy Williams
2008–09	34–4	13–3, 1st	Semifinalist	NCAA Champs	Roy Williams
2009–10	20–17	5–11, 9th (T)	First Round	NIT Finalist	Roy Williams

ALL-TIME CAROLINA BASKETBALL RECORDS

TEAM SINGLE-SEASON RECORDS

Most games played
39 in 2007–08 (36–3)
38 in 1992–93 (34–4)
38 in 1997–98 (34–4)
38 in 2006–07 (31–7)
38 in 2008–09 (34–4)

Most wins
36 in 2007–08 (36–3)
34 in 1992–93 (34–4)
34 in 1997–98 (34–4)
34 in 2008–09 (34–4)

Most consecutive wins
37 (1956–1957)
34 (1923–25)
21 (1983–84)
21 (1985–86)

Most losses
20 in 2001–02 (8–20)
17 in 2009–10 (20–17)
16 in 2002–03 (19–16)

Highest scoring average per game
91.3 in 1986–87
90.0 in 1988–89
89.9 in 2008–09

Highest average scoring margin
17.8 points in 2008–09
17.8 points in 1992–93
17.7 points in 1971–72
17.7 points in 2004–05

Highest scoring average per game allowed
79.7 in 1988–89
78.9 in 2001–02
78.8 in 1969–70

Highest field-goal percentage
55.9 in 1985–86
54.3 in 1983–84
54.0 in 1984–85

Highest free-throw percentage
78.3 in 1983–84
76.1 in 1984–85
75.8 in 1959–60

Highest three-point field-goal percentage
43.7 in 1982–83
43.6 in 1986–87
43.0 in 1987–88

Highest rebounding average per game
49.9 in 1960–61
48.8 in 1963–64
48.1 in 1955–56

Highest assist average per game
25.9 in 1972–73
24.2 in 1973–74
23.5 in 1985–86

Most blocked shots
219 in 1993–94
196 in 2008–09
188 in 1997–98

Most steals
362 in 2004–05
357 in 1992–93
356 in 1976–77

TEAM SINGLE-GAME RECORDS

Most points
129 vs. VMI, 12/17/94
129 vs. Manhattan, 12/27/85
128 vs. Dartmouth, 12/5/72

Fewest points
8 at NC State, 2/18/26
13 at Roanoke, 2/9/16
14 at Virginia Tech, 2/19/19

Largest margin of victory
84 vs. Manhattan, 12/27/85
69 vs. Davidson, 2/7/45
68 vs. The Citadel, 2/18/91

Largest margin of defeat
43 at Lynchburg Elks, 2/20/15
42 at Kentucky, 1/9/50
40 vs. NC State, 2/19/49

INDIVIDUAL SINGLE-GAME RECORDS

Most points
49 Bob Lewis vs. FSU, 12/16/65
48 Billy Cunningham vs. Tulane, 12/10/64
47 Lennie Rosenbluth vs. Furman, 12/3/56

Most three-pointers
8 Hubert Davis at FSU, 2/27/92
8 Dante Calabria vs. FSU, 1/25/95
8 Jeff McInnis at Clemson, 2/14/96
8 Shammond Williams at Georgia Tech, 2/8/98 (2 OT)
8 Raymond Felton at NC State, 1/26/2003
8 Rashad McCants vs. Clemson, 3/2/2004

Most rebounds
30 Rusty Clark vs. Maryland, 2/21/68
28 Billy Cunningham vs. Maryland, 1/13/64
27 Billy Cunningham vs. Clemson, 2/16/63

Most assists
18 Raymond Felton vs. George Mason, 12/7/2003
17 Jeff Lebo vs. UT Chattanooga, 11/18/88
17 Ed Cota vs. UNLV, 12/4/99

Most steals
9 Derrick Phelps at Georgia Tech, 2/2/92
8 Derrick Phelps vs. Central Florida, 12/7/91
8 Dudley Bradley vs. Oregon State, 11/30/77
8 Tyler Hansbrough vs. UNC Asheville, 12/28/2005
8 Ty Lawson vs. Michigan State, 4/6/2009

Most blocked shots
10 Brendan Haywood vs. Miami, 12/4/2000
9 Warren Martin vs. Stanford, 12/20/85

ALL-TIME CAROLINA BASKETBALL RECORDS *(continued)*

INDIVIDUAL SEASON RECORDS

Highest scoring average
28.0 Lennie Rosenbluth 1956–57
27.4 Bob Lewis 1965–66
27.1 Charles Scott 1969–70

Highest field-goal percentage
69.7 Brendan Haywood 1999–2000
66.8 Bobby Jones 1971–72
65.4 Rasheed Wallace 1994–95

Highest three-point field-goal percentage
49.6 Dante Calabria 1994–95
48.9 Hubert Davis 1990–91
47.2 Ty Lawson 2008–09

Highest rebounding average
16.1 Billy Cunningham 1962–63
15.8 Billy Cunningham 1963–64
14.3 Billy Cunningham 1964–65

Highest assist average
8.1 Ed Cota 1999–2000
7.44 Ed Cota 1998–99
7.41 Ed Cota 1997–98

CAREER RECORDS

Most points
2,872 Tyler Hansbrough 2005–09
2,290 Phil Ford 1974–78
2,145 Sam Perkins 1980–84

Highest scoring average
26.9 Lennie Rosenbluth 1954–57
24.8 Billy Cunningham 1962–65
22.1 Bobby Lewis 1964–67

Highest field-goal percentage
63.7 Brendan Haywood 1997–2001
63.5 Rasheed Wallace 1993–95
62.0 Brad Daugherty 1982–86

Highest three-point field-goal percentage
43.5 Hubert Davis 1988–92
42.8 Jeff Lebo 1985–89
41.9 Reyshawn Terry 2003–07

Most three-pointers
233 Shammond Williams 1994–98
229 Wayne Ellington 2006–09
221 Donald Williams 1991–95

Highest free-throw percentage
84.9 Shammond Williams 1994–98
84.7 Marvin Williams 2004–05
84.5 Danny Green 2005–09

Most rebounds
1,219 Tyler Hansbrough 2005–09
1,167 Sam Perkins 1980–84
1,097 George Lynch 1989–93

Highest rebounding average
15.4 Billy Cunningham 1962–65
10.6 Doug Moe 1958–61
10.5 Pete Brennan 1955–58

Most assists
1,030 Ed Cota 1996–2000
768 Kenny Smith 1983–87
753 Phil Ford 1974–78

Highest assist average
7.5 Ed Cota 1996–2000
6.9 Raymond Felton 2002–05
6.1 Phil Ford 1974–78

Most steals
247 Derrick Phelps 1990–94
241 George Lynch 1989–93
197 Rick Fox 1987–91

Most blocked shots
304 Brendan Haywood 1997–2001
245 Sam Perkins 1980–84
190 Warren Martin 1981–86

Most games played
152 Deon Thompson 2006–10
145 Danny Green 2005–09
142 Tyler Hansbrough 2005–09

PLAYERS BY JERSEY NUMBER
(* denotes honored jersey; ** denotes retired jersey)

0
Jesse Holley

00
Eric Montross,* Brendan Haywood,* Jesse Holley

1
Melvin Scott, Marcus Ginyard

2
Raymond Felton,* Wayne Ellington, Marc Campbell

3
Jimmy Howard, Herbert Porter, Clive Thompson, Taylor Thorne, Charlie Thorne, Irving Turk, Jeff Denny, Pat Sullivan, Shammond Williams, Vasco Evtimov, Brian Morrison, Reyshawn Terry

4
Wray Lewis, Lewis Hayworth, Vic Seixas, Bob Paxton, William White, Lynwood Robinson, James Daye, Kenny Harris, Larry Davis, David Neal, Makhtar Ndiaye, Scott Williams, Brooks Foster, Bobby Frasor

5
Ed Antolini, George Paine, Larry James, Ira Norfolk, Vic Seixas, Dan Nyimicz, Marion Godwin, Richard Patterson, Henrik Rödl, Jeff McInnis, Ed Cota, Jackie Manuel, Ty Lawson,* Dexter Strickland

6
Julian Smith, Dick Hartley, Walter Markin, E. B. Stevenson, Mark Nathan

7
Bobby Gersten, P. A. Lee, Jim White, Don Anderson, Mervin Cole, Simon Terrell

8
Bob Rose, Jim Jordan,* James Hamilton, Fred Ryan

9
Chuck Harnden, Ellis Freedman, Jim Hayworth, Fred Bauer, Norman Mitchell

10 (retired)
George Paine, Bobby Gersten, Cam Rodman, Roger Scholbe, Darius Wells, Lennie Rosenbluth**

11
Paul Severin, James White, Harvey Weinstein, John Tsantes, Richard Patterson, Wayne Harpold, Charles Ellenwood, Ken Rosemond, John Crotty, Larry Brown,* Ray Hassell, Gerald Tuttle, John Austin, Tony Shaver, Keith Valentine, Mike Pepper, Rodney Hyatt, Scott Cherry, Michael Brooker, Quentin Thomas, Larry Drew II

12 (retired)
George McCachren, Vincent DiLorenzo, Coy Carson, Hal Ferraro, Al Lifson, Lee Shaffer,* Harry Jones, Ray Respess, Jim Frye, Richard Tuttle, Ray Hite, Phil Ford**

13
Ed Shytle, Ellis Freedman, John Dillon,* Benton Bennett, William White, Vince Grimaldi, Ian Morrison, Dick Grubar, Steve Previs, Brad Hoffman, Ademola Okulaja, Neil Fingleton, Will Graves

14
Hugo Kappler, Simon Terrell, Skippy Winstead, Dave Hanners, Derek McAllister, Jeff Lebo, Derrick Phelps, Ryan Sullivan, Jonathan Holmes, Danny Green, Terrence Petree

15
Hank Feimster, Reid Suggs, Bob Altemose, Bill Voris, Jack Fitch, Hank Lebed, Hugo Kappler, Bill Smith, Vince Grimaldi, Willis Henderson, John Kuester, Brian Ellerby, Courtney Dupree, Jason Burgess, Shammond Williams, Vince Carter,* Kenny White, Damien Price, Charlie Everett, Dewey Burke, J. B. Tanner, Leslie McDonald

16
Reid Suggs, Ed Shytle, Dan Marks, Michael Fisher, Norman Kohler

17
Joe Nelson, Don Wilson, Manuel Alvarez, Miles Hall, Ed Wagner, Irving Turk

18
Bob Rose, Bill Wood, Harold Spurlock, Sherman Nearman

19
Hank Pessar, Cam Rodman, Bob Shuford, W. G. Allen, Mark Nathan, Norman Kohler, Fred Swartzberg

20 (retired)
George Glamack,** Dan Marks, Frank Wideman, Lester Hughes, Dan Nyimicz, Hal Ferraro, Ike Neeley, Cooper Taylor, Paul Anisko, Gene Glancy, Bob Young, Wallace Graham, Don Walsh, Peppy Callahan, John Yokley, Eddie Fogler, Bill Chambers, Ray Harrison, David Colescott, Cliff Morris, Steve Bucknall

21
Bill Locke, Wray Lewis, John Fields, Fred Ryan, Bill Miller, Howard Deasy, Jerry Vayda, Al Lifson, Mitch Kupchak,* Jimmy Black, Michael Norwood, King Rice, Donald Williams,* Terrence Newby, Jawad Williams, Deon Thompson

22
Junie Bailey, Benton Bennett, Paul Likins, Edward Sutton, Roy Searcy, York Larese,* Mike Cooke, Bob Lewis,* Jim Delany, George Karl, Dudley Bradley, Buzz Peterson, Kevin Madden, Pearce Landry, Webb Tyndall, Scott Williams, Ronald Curry, Justin Bohlander, Wes Miller, Wayne Ellington*

23 (retired)
John Tsantes, Bud Maddie, Skippy Winstead, Buddy Clarke, Jimmy Guill, Ged Doughton, Michael Jordan**

24
Ernie Schwartz, Walter Davis,* Jim Braddock, Joe Wolf, Doug Elstun, Dante Calabria, Max Owens, Jesse Holley, Marvin Williams, Surry Wood, Justin Watts

PLAYERS BY JERSEY NUMBER *(continued)*

25

Jippy Carter, Albert Long, James Smith, Donnie Smith, Randy Wiel, Steve Hale, Jason Capel, Damion Grant

30

Darius Wells, Jack Wallace, Cliff Walker, Bill Hathaway, Ray Stanley, Dieter Krause, Jim Moore, Mike Iannarella, Greg Campbell, Al Armour, Dale Gipple, John O'Donnell, Woody Coley, Al Wood,* Kenny Smith,* Rasheed Wallace,* Phillip McLamb, Will Robinson, Jack Wooten, Thomas Thornton

31

Charlie Thorne, Tom Gaines, Al Lifson, Gerry McCabe, Gehrmann Holland, Ken McComb, Bruce Bowers, Bill Taylor, Charlie Burns, Bob Bennett, Bill Bunting, Bill Chamberlain,* Mickey Bell, Loren Lutz, Mike O'Koren,* Matthew Brust, David May, Brian Reese, Adam Boone, Jonathan Miller, Thomas Wilkins, John Henson

32

Leonard Guyes, Frank Redding, Bob Phillips, Gerry McCabe, Bob Cunningham, Lou Brown, Peppy Callahan, Billy Cunningham,* Mark Mirken, Dave Chadwick, Darrell Elston, Tom Zaliagiris, Eric Kenny, John Brownlee, Pete Chilcutt, Orlando Melendez, Rashad McCants,* Alex Stepheson, Ed Davis

33 (retired)

Sherman Nearman, Bob Phillips, Gerry McCabe, Danny Lotz, Jim Hudock, Bill Brown, Charles Scott,* Roger Jamison, Ranzino Smith, Kevin Salvadori, Antawn Jamison**

34

Frank Redding, Bill Ellington, Francis Goodwin, Dick Kepley, Richard Vinroot, Bruce Bowers, Charles Hassell, Terry Ronner, Jim Moore, Jim Bostick, Don Eggleston, Bobby Jones,* Pete Budko, J. R. Reid,* George Lynch,* Charlie McNairy, David Noel, Brandan Wright, David Wear

35

Cooper Taylor, Pete Brennan,* Doug Moe,* Charlie Burns, Bill Galanti, Ralph Fletcher, Lee Dedmon, Bob McAdoo,* Charles Waddell, Dave Popson, Joe Jenkins, Travis Stephenson, Brad Frederick, Jim Everett, C. J. Hooker, Patrick Moody, James Gallagher

40

Dick Kocornik, Tommy Kearns,* Yogi Poteet, Bill Harrison, Earl Johnson, Donnie Moe, Ricky Webb, Bill Chambers, Donn Johnston, Bruce Buckley, Gary Roper, Hubert Davis, Ed Geth, Joseph Forte,* Mike Copeland

41

Paul Likins, Joe Quigg, Hugh Donahue, Terry Ronner, Jim Smithwick, Joe Brown, Mike Earey, Joe Cox, Geoff Crompton, Sam Perkins,* Byron Sanders

42

Bud Maddie, Walter Green, Hilliard Greene, Harvey Salz, Charlie Shaffer, Tom Gauntlett, Gra Whitehead, Kim Huband, Bill Chambers, Jeff Wolf, Brad Daugherty,* Scott Williams, Jerry Stackhouse,* Kris Lang, Sean May*

43

Jerry Vayda, Grey Poole, Art Katz, Mike Smith, Rusty Clark, Craig Corson, Ed Stahl, John Virgil, Jeb Barlow, Curtis Hunter, Matt Laczkowski, Travis Wear

44

Tony Radovich, Mike Steppe, Brian McSweeney, Mark Mirken, Larry Miller,* Dennis Wuycik,* Donald Washington, Eric Harry, Matt Doherty, Rick Fox, Clyde Lynn, Will Johnson, Tyler Zeller

45

Tommy LaGarde,* Chris Brust, Marty Hensley, Clifford Rozier, Serge Zwikker, Julius Peppers, Jesse Holley, Greg Little

50 (retired)

Rich Yonaker, Cecil Exum, Bill Akins, Octavus Barnes, Brian Bersticker, Tyler Hansbrough**

51

Timo Makkonen

52 (retired)

James Worthy**

54

Steve Krafcisin, Warren Martin, John Greene, Vasco Evtimov

55

Matt Wenstrom

The following University of North Carolina student-athletes have earned varsity letters in men's basketball, according to Athletic Department and university records.

Name	Years Lettered	Hometown (if available)
Aitken, Stewart "Snooks"	1933–35	Charlotte, N.C.
Alexander, Tom	1930–32	Raleigh, N.C.
Allen, Bill	1945	Tulsa, Okla.
Altemose, Bob	1943–44	Stroudsburg, Pa.
Alvarez, Manny	1945	Clarksburg, W.Va.
Anderson, Don	1944–46	Ottawa, Ill.
Andrews, Ezra	1914–16	
Austin, John	1971	Charlotte, N.C.
Barber, Howard	1925	
Barlow, Jeb	1981–82	Fuquay Varina, N.C.
Barnes, Octavus	1995	Wilson, N.C.
Barrett, Jon	1971–72	Charlotte, N.C.
Beale, William	1933–34	
Bell, Mickey	1973–75	Goldsboro, N.C.
Bennett, Benton	1949–50	Norwood, N.C.
Bennett, Bob	1964–66	Mt. Lebanon, Pa.
Bershak, Andy	1936–38	
Bersticker, Brian	1998–99, 2001–02	Virginia Beach, Va.
Black, Jimmy	1979–82	The Bronx, N.Y.
Blood, Ernest	1934–35	Burlington, Vt.
Bohlander, Justin	2004	Winston-Salem, N.C.
Boone, Adam	2001–02	Minneapolis, Minn.
Boone, Pete	1938	
Bostick, Jim	1967	Atlanta, Ga.
Bowers, Bruce	1962	Wellesley Hills, Mass.
Bowman, Dave	1940	Palm Harbor, Fla.
Box, Boyce	1944	
Braddock, Jim	1980–83	Chattanooga, Tenn.
Bradley, Dudley	1976–79	Edgewood, Md.
Brandt, George	1932–33	Charlotte, N.C.
Branson, Les	1939	Raleigh, N.C.
Brennan, Pete	1956–58	Brooklyn, N.Y.
Brooker, Michael	1998–2001	Sandersville, Ga.
Brown, Bill	1963–65	Charlotte, N.C.
Brown, Joe	1967–69	Valdese, N.C.
Brown, Larry	1961–63	Long Beach, N.Y.
Brown, Lou	1959–60	Jersey City, N.J.
Brown, William	1929–30	
Brownlee, John	1982–83	Fort Worth, Texas
Brust, Chris	1979–82	Babylon, N.Y.
Buckley, Bruce	1974–77	Bladensburg, Md.
Bucknall, Steve	1986–89	London, England
Budko, Pete	1978–81	Lutherville, Md.
Bunting, Bill	1967–69	New Bern, N.C.

Name	Years Lettered	Hometown (if available)
Burgess, Jason	1992	Charlotte, N.C.
Burke, Dewey	2006–07	Philadelphia, Pa.
Burns, Charlie	1962–63	Wadesboro, N.C.
Calabria, Dante	1993–96	Beaver Falls, Pa.
Callahan, Peppy	1962–63	Smithtown, N.Y.
Campbell, Greg	1966	Bayonne, N.J.
Campbell, Marc	2008–10	Raleigh, N.C.
Capel, Jason	1999–2002	Fayetteville, N.C.
Carmichael, Billy	1920–22	
Carmichael, Cartwright	1922–24	
Carrington, George	1911–13	
Carson, Coy	1948–49	Asheville, N.C.
Carter, Jippy	1951, 1953	Charlotte, N.C.
Carter, Vince	1996–98	Daytona Beach, Fla.
Cathey, George	1928–29	Candler, N.C.
Chadwick, Dave	1969–71	Orlando, Fla.
Chamberlain, Bill	1970–72	New York, N.Y.
Chambers, Bill B.	1973–76	Greensboro, N.C.
Chambers, Bill L.	1970–72	Durham, N.C.
Chambers, Lenoir	1912–14	
Chandler, Stuart	1931–33	
Cherry, Scott	1990–93	Ballston Spa, N.Y.
Chilcutt, Pete	1988–91	Eutaw, Ala.
Choate, Page	1930–31	
Clark, Buddy	1955	Louisville, Ky.
Clark, Franklin "Rusty"	1967–69	Fayetteville, N.C.
Cleland, Thomas	1930–31	
Cobb, Jack	1924–26	
Cole, Mervin	1948	
Colescott, Dave	1977–80	Marion, Ind.
Coley, Woody	1975–77	Lumberton, N.C.
Conlon, Martin	1961	
Cooke, Mike	1962–64	Mount Airy, N.C.
Copeland, Mike	2006–09	Winston-Salem, N.C.
Corson, Craig	1970–72	Contoocook, N.H.
Cota, Ed	1997–2000	Brooklyn, N.Y.
Cox, Joe	1971	Sanford, N.C.
Creticos, Soc	1944	Philadelphia, Pa.
Crompton, Geff	1974, 1978	Burlington, N.C.
Crotty, John	1958–60	Bayonne, N.J.
Cuneo, Frank	1940	
Cunningham, Billy	1963–65	Brooklyn, N.Y.
Cunningham, Bob	1956–58	New York, N.Y.
Curry, Ronald	1999, 2001	Hampton, Va.
Cuthbertson, Reynolds	1917–19	

Name	Years Lettered	Hometown (if available)	Name	Years Lettered	Hometown (if available)
Dameron, Emerson	1930–31	Marion, N.C.	Frederick, Brad	1997–99	Lawrence, Kan.
Daugherty, Brad	1983–86	Black Mountain, N.C.	Freedman, Ellis	1943	Harrisburg, Pa.
Davis, Ed	2009–10	Richmond, Va.	Frye, Jim	1966–68	Homewood, Ill.
Davis, Hubert	1989–92	Burke, Va.	Fuller, Walter	1915	
Davis, Larry	1993–94	Denmark, S.C.			
Davis, Robert	1914–16		Galanti, Bill	1963–64	Brooklyn, N.Y.
Davis, Walter	1974–77	Pineville, N.C.	Garvin, Dick	1945	
Daye, James	1985–86	Burlington, N.C.	Gauntlett, Tom	1965–67	Dallas, Pa.
Deasy, Howard	1949–52	The Bronx, N.Y.	Gersten, Bobby	1940–42	Long Beach, N.Y.
Dedmon, Lee	1969–71	Baltimore, Md.	Geth, Ed	1993, 1995–96	Norfolk, Va.
Delany, Jim	1968–70	South Orange, N.J.	Ginyard, Marcus	2006–08, 2010	Alexandria, Va.
Denny, Jeff	1987–90	Rural Hall, N.C.	Gipple, Dale	1969–71	Burlington, N.C.
Devin, Billy	1924–25		Glace, Ivan "Jack"	1933–35	
Dewell, John	1944		Glamack, George	1939–41	Johnston, Pa.
Dillon, John "Hook"	1945–48	Savannah, Ga.	Glancy, Gene	1953	Belleville, N.J.
Dilworth, Ben	1938–40		Goodwin, Frank	1955	Belleville, N.J.
Dodderer, Bill	1924–26	Atlanta, Ga.	Graham, Tom	1923	
Doherty, Matt	1981–84	East Meadow, N.J.	Grandin, Elliott	1916	
Donnan, Dick	1944		Grant, Damion	2003–05	Kingston, Jamaica
Donohue, Hugh	1959–60, 1962	Yonkers, N.Y.	Graves, Will	2008–10	Greensboro, N.C.
Donohue, Jim	1960–62	Yonkers, N.Y.	Green, Danny	2006–09	North Babylon, N.Y.
Doughton, Ged	1976–79	Winston-Salem, N.C.	Green, John	1930	Seattle, Wash.
Dowd, William	1914, 1919		Green, Winton	1922–23	
Drew, Larry II	2009–10	Encino, Calif.	Greene, Hilliard	1955–56	Zebulon, N.C.
Duls, Ferdinand	1911		Greene, John	1989–90	Raleigh, N.C.
			Gribble, Dickson	1966	Raleigh, N.C.
Earey, Mike	1970	Chapel Hill, N.C.	Griffith, James	1919–20	
Edwards, Ben	1913–14		Grimaldi, Vince	1951–53	Philadelphia, Pa.
Edwards, Jesse	1930–32		Grubar, Dick	1967–69	Schenectady, N.Y.
Eggleston, Don	1969–71	Charlotte, N.C.	Grubb, Foy	1937–38	Durham, N.C.
Ellington, Wayne	2007–09	Wynnewood, Pa.			
Elston, Darrell	1972–74	Tipton, Ind.	Hackney, Bunn	1925–27	High Point, N.C.
Elstun, Doug	1988	Overland Park, Kan.	Hackney, Rufus	1927–29	
Erwin, Roy	1912		Hale, Steve	1983–86	Jenks, Okla.
Erwin, Jesse	1920	Durham, N.C.	Hamilton, Jim	1947	Weir, Kan.
Everett, Charlie	2005	Charlotte, N.C.	Hanby, Howard	1921	
Everett, Jim	2000–01	Charlotte, N.C.	Hanners, Dave	1974–76	Columbus, Ohio
Everett, Joe	2002	Charlotte, N.C.	Hansbrough, Tyler	2006–09	Poplar Bluff, Mo.
Evtimov, Vasco	1997, 1999	Sofia, Bulgaria	Harper, Puny	1929–30	
Exum, Cecil	1981–84	Dudley, N.C.	Harris, Kenny	1990–91	Petersburg, Va.
			Harris, William	1935	
Felton, Raymond	2003–05	Latta, S.C.	Harrison, Ray	1973–74	Greensboro, N.C.
Ferraro, Hal	1949–51	Arcadia, Kan.	Harrison, William	1935	
Fingleton, Neil	2002	Durham, England	Harrison, William Jr.	1964	Durham, N.C.
Fitch, Jack	1944	Etna, Pa.	Harry, Eric	1975–76	Durham, N.C.
Fletcher, Ralph	1966–68	Arlington, Va.	Hartley, Dick	1943, 1947	High Point, N.C.
Floyd, John	1911		Harvel, William	1926	
Fogler, Eddie	1968–70	Flushing, N.Y.	Hassell, Pud	1964–65	Beaufort, N.C.
Ford, Phil	1975–78	Rocky Mount, N.C.	Hassell, Ray	1964–66	Beaufort, N.C.
Forte, Joseph	2000–01	Greenbelt, Md.	Haywood, Brendan	1998–2001	Greensboro, N.C.
Foster, Brooks	2005	Boiling Springs, S.C.	Hayworth, Jim	1946–47	High Point, N.C.
Fox, Rick	1988–91	Nassau, The Bahamas	Hayworth, Lewis	1942–44	High Point, N.C.
Frasor, Bobby	2006–09	Blue Island, Ill.	Henderson, Willis	1955	Charlotte, N.C.

Name	Years Lettered	Hometown (if available)	Name	Years Lettered	Hometown (if available)
Henry, David	1932–33		Lebo, Jeff	1986–89	Carlisle, Pa.
Hensley, Marty	1987, 1989–90	Marion, Ind.	Lewis, Bob	1965–67	Washington, D.C.
Henson, John	2010	Tampa, Fla.	Lifson, Al	1952–55	Elizabeth, N.J.
Hines, Wilmer	1931–33		Likins, Paul	1952–55	Elkhart, Ind.
Hite, Ray	1972–74	Hyattsville, Md.	Lineberger, Henry	1924, 1926	
Hoffman, Brad	1973–75	Columbus, Ohio	Lipfert, Benjamin	1918–21	
Holland, Gehrmann	1957, 1959	Beaufort, N.C.	Little, Greg	2008	Durham, N.C.
Holley, Jesse	2004–05	Roselle, N.J.	Lobin, Ben	1955	
Holmes, Jonathan	2000–03	Bloomington, Ind.	Long, Albert	1954	Durham, N.C.
Homewood, Roy	1913–15		Long, Henry	1911–14	
Hooker, C. J.	2004–05	Palmer, Alaska	Long, Meb	1913–16	
Howard, Jimmy	1939–41	Norfolk, Va.	Long, Morris	1933–34	
Huband, Kim	1970–72	Wilmington, N.C.	Lotz, Danny	1957–59	Northport, N.Y.
Hudock, Jim	1960–62	Tunkhannock, Pa.	Lougee, Edgar	1943	
Hughes, Red	1946	Atlanta, Ga.	Lutz, Loren	1976	Alamosa, Colo.
Hunter, Curtis	1983, 1985–87	Durham, N.C.	Lynch, George	1990–93	Roanoke, Va.
Hutchinson, Joel	1930		Lynch, Percy	1918–19	
Hyatt, Rodney	1987–88	Wadesboro, N.C.	Lynn, Clyde	1995–96	Greensboro, N.C.
Jamison, Antawn	1996–98	Charlotte, N.C.	Madden, Kevin	1986, 1988–90	Staunton, Va.
Jamison, Roger	1972		Maddie, Bud	1951, 1953–54	The Bronx, N.Y.
Jenkins, Joe	1988	Elizabeth City, N.C.	Mahler, Carl	1922–23	
Johnson, Earl	1964		Makkonen, Timo	1981–84	Lahti, Finland
Johnson, John	1916		Manuel, Jackie	2002–05	West Palm Beach, Fla.
Johnson, Will	2000–03	Hickory, N.C.	Markham, William	1932	Greensboro, N.C.
Johnston, Donn	1971–73	Jamestown, N.Y.	Markin, Walter	1945	Hartford City, Ind.
Jones, Bobby	1972–74	Charlotte, N.C.	Marks, Dan	1943	Chapel Hill, N.C.
Jones, Charles	1932		Marpet, Artie	1929–31	
Jones, Harry	1961–62	Charlotte, N.C.	Martin, Warren	1982–83, 1985–86	Axton, Va.
Jordan, Jim	1945–46	Chester, Pa.	Mathes, Albert	1940	Tampa, Fla.
Jordan, Michael	1982–84	Wilmington, N.C.	May, David	1988–89	Greensboro, N.C.
			May, Sean	2003–05	Bloomington, Ind.
Kappler, Hugo	1949–51	Brooklyn, N.Y.	McAdoo, Robert	1972	Greensboro, N.C.
Karl, George	1971–73	Penn Hills, Pa.	McCabe, Gerry	1954–56	The Bronx, N.Y.
Katz, Art	1962–64	Williston Park, N.Y.	McCachren, Dave	1932–34	Knoxville, Tenn.
Kaveny, Paul	1935–36	Montclair, N.J.	McCachren, George	1943	Charlotte, N.C.
Kearns, Tommy	1956–58	Bergenfield, N.J.	McCachren, Jim	1934–36	
Kenny, Eric	1979–81	Asheville, N.C.	McCachren, William	1937, 1939	Raleigh, N.C.
Kepley, Dick	1958–59, 1961	Roanoke, Va.	McCants, Rashad	2003–05	Asheville, N.C.
Kocornik, Dick	1954	West Orange, N.J.	McComb, Ken	1961	White Plains, N.Y.
Kohler, Norm	1947–48	New York, N.Y.	McDonald, Leslie	2010	Memphis, Tenn.
Koonce, Donald	1924		McDonald, Monk	1921–24	
Krafcisin, Steve	1977	Chicago Ridge, Ill.	McDonald, Sam	1923–26	
Krause, Dieter	1961–63	Norfolk, Va.	McDuffie, Lewis	1917	
Kuester, John	1974–77	Richmond, Va.	McInnis, Jeff	1994–96	Charlotte, N.C.
Kupchak, Mitch	1973–76	Brentwood, N.Y.	McKinney, Bones	1946	Durham, N.C.
			McKnight, Roy	1911–12	Chapel Hill, N.C.
Laczkowski, Matt	2000	Westminster, Md.	McLamb, Phillip	2002–04	Charlotte, N.C.
LaGarde, Tommy	1974–77	Detroit, Mich.	McNairy, Charlie	1995–97	Kinston, N.C.
Landry, Pearce	1994–95	Greensboro, N.C.	McSweeney, Bryan	1962–64	Hewlett, N.Y.
Lang, Kris	1999–2002	Gastonia, N.C.	Melendez, Orlando	1999–2002	Juana Diaz, Puerto Rico
Larese, York	1959–61	New York, N.Y.			
Lawson, Ty	2007–09	Clinton, Md.	Meroney, David	1937	

Name	Years Lettered	Hometown *(if available)*	Name	Years Lettered	Hometown *(if available)*
Miller, Jonathan	2003–04	Burlington, N.C.	Poole, Jimmy	1923–25	
Miller, Larry	1966–68	Catasauqua, Pa.	Popson, David	1984–87	Ashley, Pa.
Miller, Wes	2005–07	Charlotte, N.C.	Poteet, Yogi	1960–61, 1963	Hendersonville, N.C.
Minor, William	1935	Charlotte, N.C.	Potts, Ramsay	1936–37	Washington, D.C.
Mirken, Mark	1965–67	Brooklyn, N.Y.	Previs, Steve	1970–72	Bethel Park, Pa.
Mock, Bernie	1944	Waynesville, N.C.	Price, Damien	2002–04	Greensboro, N.C.
Moe, Donnie	1966–67	Brooklyn, N.Y.	Price, James	1927–29	
Moe, Doug	1959–61	Brooklyn, N.Y.	Purser, Carr	1927–28	
Montross, Eric	1991–94	Indianapolis, Ind.	Purser, John	1922–23, 1925	Lumberton, N.C.
Moody, Patrick	2008–09	Asheville, N.C.			
Moore, James	1931	Trenton, N.C.	Quigg, Joe	1956–57	Brooklyn, N.Y.
Moore, Jim	1966	Wilmington, N.C.			
Morris, Billy	1926–28		Radovich, Tony	1953–57	Hoboken, N.J.
Morris, Cliff	1984–85	Durham, N.C.	Ranson, Lucius	1913	
Morris, John	1919–21		Redding, Frank	1952	Asheboro, N.C.
Morrison, Brian	2001–02	Redmond, Wash.	Redmon, Herman	1913	
Morrison, Ian	1965	St. Petersburg, Fla.	Reese, Brian	1991–94	The Bronx, N.Y.
Mullis, Pete	1936–38		Reid, J. R.	1987–89	Virginia Beach, Va.
			Respess, Ray	1963–65	Pantego, N.C.
Nagy, Fritz	1943	Cuyahoga Falls, Ohio	Rice, King	1988–91	Binghamton, N.Y.
Nathan, Mark	1948		Ritch, Marvin	1911	
Ndiaye, Makhtar	1997–98	Dakar, Senegal	Roberson, Foy	1939–40	
Neal, David	1995–96	Raleigh, N.C.	Robinson, Lynwood	1982	Mt. Olive, N.C.
Nearman, Sherman	1947–50	Charleston, W.Va.	Robinson, Will	2006	Chapel Hill, N.C.
"Nemo"			Rödl, Henrik	1990–93	Heusenstamm,
Neiman, Abe	1922				Germany
Neiman, David	1930	Hallandale, Fa.	Roper, Gary	1985	Andrews, N.C.
Nelson, Melvin	1934–36		Rose, Bob	1940–42	Smithfield, N.C.
Newby, Terrence	1997–2000	Siler City, N.C.	Rosemond, Ken	1956–57	Hillsborough, N.C.
Newcombe, Arthur	1926		Rosenbluth, Lennie	1955–57	The Bronx, N.Y.
Noel, David	2003–06	Durham, N.C.	Rourk, William	1920	
Norfolk, Ira	1945	Baltimore, Md.	Rozier, Clifford	1991	Bradenton, Fla.
Norwood, Michael	1986–87	Henderson, N.C.	Ruth, Earl	1936–38	Salisbury, N.C.
Nyimicz, Dan	1948–49	Rahway, N.J.	Ryan, Fred	1949	Trenton, N.J.
O'Donnell, John	1972–74	New York, N.Y.	Salvadori, Kevin	1991–94	Pittsburgh, Pa.
O'Koren, Mike	1977–80	Jersey City, N.J.	Salz, Harvey	1958–60	Brooklyn, N.Y.
Okulaja, Ademola	1996–99	Berlin, Germany	Sanders, Byron	2003–06	Gulfport, Miss.
Owens, Max	1998–2001	Macon, Ga.	Satterfield, Henry	1928–29	Chattanooga, Tenn.
			Scholbe, Roger	1946–48	Milwaukee, Wisc.
Paine, George	1941–42	Wynnewood, Pa.	Schwartz, Ernie	1951–53	Philadelphia, Pa.
Patterson, Richard	1950–51	Pilot Mountain, N.C.	Scott, Charles	1968–70	New York, N.Y.
Paxton, Bob	1945–48	Spokane, Wash.	Scott, Melvin	2002–05	Baltimore, Md.
Pepper, Mike	1978–81	Vienna, Va.	Scruggs, Boyce	1916	
Peppers, Julius	2000–01	Bailey, N.C.	Searcy, Roy	1956–58	Draper, N.C.
Perkins, Sam	1981–84	Latham, N.Y.	Severin, Paul	1939–41	Tarentum, Pa.
Perry, Henry	1917–18		Shaffer, Charlie	1962–64	Chapel Hill, N.C.
Perry, Sidney	1922		Shaffer, Dean	1981–82	Durham, N.C.
Pessar, Hank	1940–41	New York, N.Y.	Shaffer, Lee	1958–60	Pittsburgh, Pa.
Peterson, Buzz	1982–85	Asheville, N.C.	Shaver, Tony	1974	High Point, N.C.
Phelps, Derrick	1991–94	Pleasantville, N.Y.	Shepard, Carlyle	1917, 1920–21	
Phillips, Bob	1951–53	Chapel Hill, N.C.	Shytle, Ed	1941–42	Hendersonville, N.C.
Poole, Grey	1958–60	Raleigh, N.C.	Sides, Robert	1927	

Name	Years Lettered	Hometown (if available)	Name	Years Lettered	Hometown (if available)
Smith, James	1974	Lantana, Fla.	Washington, Donald	1973	Washington, D.C.
Smith, Julian	1941–42	Farmville, N.C.	Watson, Bill	1939	
Smith, Junius	1911–13		Watts, Justin	2009–10	Durham, N.C.
Smith, Kenny	1984–87	Queens, N.Y.	Wear, David	2010	Huntington Beach, Calif.
Smith, Larry	1992	Smithfield, N.C.			
Smith, Mike	1966	Indianapolis, Ind.	Wear, Travis	2010	Huntington Beach, Calif.
Smith, Ranzino	1985–88	Chapel Hill, N.C.			
Smith, Winslow	1931		Weathers, Virgil	1932–34	Shelby, N.C.
Smithwick, Jim	1965–66		Webb, Ricky	1968–69	Greenville, N.C.
Stackhouse, Jerry	1994–95	Kinston, N.C.	Webster, Bernie	1935–36	Greensboro, N.C.
Stahl, Ed	1973–75	Columbus, Ohio	Wells, Darius	1950–51	Roseboro, N.C.
Stanley, Ray	1958–60	Brooklyn, N.Y.	Wenstrom, Matt	1990–93	Katy, Texas
Stephenson, Travis	1992–93	Angier, N.C.	White, Jim	1943, 1946–47	Kannapolis, N.C.
Stepheson, Alex	2007–08	Los Angeles, Calif.	White, Kenny	2000	Chattanooga, Tenn.
Stevenson, Buster	1944		White, William	1949–51	Brooklyn, N.Y.
Strickland, Dexter	2010	Rahway, N.J.	Whitehead, Gra	1968	Scotland Neck, N.C.
Strong, George	1913		Wiel, Randy	1976–79	Curaçao, N.A.
Suggs, Reid	1941–42	Thomasville, N.C.	Wiley, John	1930	
Sullivan, Pat	1991–93, 1995	Bogota, N.J.	Wilkins, Thomas	2006	Cary, N.C.
Sullivan, Ryan	1996–97	Bogota, N.J.	Williams, Donald	1992–95	Garner, N.C.
Sutton, Ed	1955	Cullowhee, N.C.	Williams, Jawad	2002–05	Cleveland, Ohio
Swartzberg, Fred	1948	High Point, N.C.	Williams, Marvin	2005	Bremerton, Wash.
			Williams, Scott Christopher	1987–90	Hacienda Heights, Calif.
Tandy, George	1914, 1916				
Tanner, J. B.	2008–09	Hendersonville, N.C.	Williams, Scott Carmichael	1998–99	Lawrence, Kan.
Taylor, Cooper	1952, 1954	Raleigh, N.C.			
Tennent, Charles	1914–15		Williams, Shammond	1995–98	Greenville, S.C.
Tennent, George	1916–18		Wilson, Don	1942	Northbrook, Ill.
Terrell, Simon	1950	Warrenton, N.C.	Winstead, Skippy	1953–54	Roxboro, N.C.
Terry, Reyshawn	2004–07	Winston-Salem, N.C.	Wolf, Jeff	1977–80	Kohler, Wisc.
Thomas, Quentin	2005–08	Oakland, Calif.	Wolf, Joe	1984–87	Kohler, Wisc.
Thompson, Clive	1945	Washington, D.C.	Wood, Al	1978–81	Gray, Ga.
Thompson, Deon	2007–10	Torrance, Calif.	Wood, Surry	2006–08	Raleigh, N.C.
Thorne, Charlie	1949–51	Camp Hill, Pa.	Woodall, Junius	1921	
Thorne, Taylor	1946–48	Rocky Mount, N.C.	Wooten, Jack	2008–09	Burlington, N.C.
Tillett, William	1911–13		Worley, Dick	1938–39	Asheville, N.C.
Tsantes, John	1949–50	Wilmington, N.C.	Worthy, James	1980–82	Gastonia, N.C.
Turk, Irving	1950	Rocky Mount, N.C.	Wright, Brandan	2007	Nashville, Tenn.
Tuttle, Gerald	1967–69	London, Ky.	Wright, Henry	1937	Andrews, S.C.
Tuttle, Richard	1969–71	London, Ky.	Wright, Robert	1913	
Tyndall, Webb	1996–97	Kinston, N.C.	Wuycik, Dennis	1970–72	Ambridge, Pa.
Valentine, Keith	1976	Richmond, Va.	Yokley, John	1964–66	Mount Airy, N.C.
Vanstory, William	1927–28		Yonakor, Rich	1977–80	Euclid, Ohio
Vayda, Jerry	1953–56	Bayonnne, N.J.	Young, Bob	1955–57	New York, N.Y.
Vinroot, Richard	1962	Charlotte, N.C.			
Virgil, John	1977–80	Elm City, N.C.	Zaliagiris, Tom	1975–78	Livonia, Mich.
			Zeller, Tyler	2009–10	Washington, Ind.
Waddell, Charles	1973–74	Southern Pines, N.C.	Zwikker, Serge	1994–97	Maassluis, The Netherlands
Wakeley, William	1911				
Wallace, Jack	1951–53	Elkins, W.Va.			
Wallace, Rasheed	1994–95	Philadelphia, Pa.			
Walsh, Donnie	1960–62	Riverdale, N.Y.			

ACKNOWLEDGMENTS

THE ACKNOWLEDGMENTS SECTION is the hardest part of a book to write—especially for a book like this, when there are so many people involved that the chances of leaving someone out are great. A standard rule of writing a book: no matter how much you ponder the acknowledgments, you will instantly remember someone essential the day after the book goes to the printer. Let's give it a try anyway.

Steve Kirschner and Dick Baddour gave me the opportunity to write this book when there were many other qualified choices. I grew up a Carolina Basketball fan, never dreaming I'd have the chance to do a project like this. It's silly to even call this a "job." Both Steve and Matt Bowers were a big part of the first-person sidebars you see here and, along with Jeffrey Camarati, were a primary part of the photo-selection process.

This is my second partnership with UNC Press in the last 18 months. Once again, it was a positive experience. Mark Simpson-Vos was patient when deadlines were upcoming (and missed), and Jay Mazzocchi and Tema Larter provided important tweaks.

On almost every page of this book, you can see the work of Lauren Brownlow. Her endless hours doing research in the library and conducting interviews are reflected here; without Lauren, this book might have been released on the 105th anniversary of Carolina Basketball. Jason Tomberlin at UNC's North Carolina Collection was a constant help. Other research materials included three books by Dean Smith—*A Coach's Life*, *Basketball: Multiple Offense and Defense*, and *The Carolina Way*; Scott Fowler's *North Carolina Tar Heels: Where Have You Gone?* and *Tales from the Tar Heels*; and Ken Rappoport's *Tales from the Tar Heel Locker Room*. Over 100 Tar Heel players and coaches were interviewed for this book, and their insights were invaluable.

Lauren is part of a *Tar Heel Monthly* crew—Turner Walston, Ryan Zurawel, Grant Halverson, and Kathryn Young—that was understanding when book craziness prevented me from handling some aspect of my day job. John Montgomery at the Rams Club enables us to put together that publication, which in turn led to this opportunity.

In every book I've been a part of, I've tried to mention the three teachers who taught me how to write: Jill Whitaker, Sandy Umstead, and Jeff Jeske. Without them, I'm not sure I would have known that writing was a possibility—or a pleasure. They should take all of the credit, but none of the blame, for the final product.

The basketball traveling party might not have had the most enjoyable 2009–10 season, but it was never dull. Ben Alexander, Jones Angell, Ken Cleary, Woody Durham, Ray Gaskins, John Lyon, Eric Montross, and Billy Puryear all helped make it a more entertaining season.

David Culp provided proofreading and should be thanked in any Carolina Basketball book just because he's the type of fan the rest of us want to be. At many of the games described here, Clint Gwaltney and Karlton Creech helped get me in the door.

As part of my job, I get to communicate with Carolina Basketball fans all over the world. My constant goal through the writing of this book was to try and make sure there was something here for every one of those fans. Without them, there are no crazy e-mails about time-outs or free-throw shooting; but also without them, there's no book. Most important, without them, I'd have to get a real job, and the U.S. workforce probably isn't ready for that.

My parents, Jim and Dubba Lucas, helped introduce me to Carolina Basketball (a move they probably slightly regret at times) and have supported me from the time when most of my stories were about middle school volleyball to today.

This is the world's best job, but as many of the above people will tell you, the only negative is the travel that takes you away from can't-miss events like ballet recitals and T-ball games. Going to Carolina Basketball games is fun. But I want three very important people—Stephanie, McKay, and Asher—to know I've never been to a game, anywhere, anytime, when I wouldn't have rather been with them.

Approximately two weeks before this book was due, I spoke at my daughter's elementary school. (She's in the first grade, which is about my level of communication, so it worked out well.) It came on the heels of many late nights working on the book, when I would rather have been reading a good-night story, and many missed afternoons of shooting baskets in the driveway with McKay and Asher.

I was starting to resent the book and sometimes described it in less-flattering ways than simply "the book." But when I showed the last collaboration with UNC Press, *One Fantastic Ride*, to the class, they asked to see the page where McKay and Asher's names were mentioned. Their reaction—as if McKay had just handed out free popsicles to the entire school—made it worth it. I hope one day McKay and Asher will get the same thrill out of seeing their names in these pages, because that will be the ultimate author's reward.